Streetwise Parents,
Foolproof Kids

FOOLPROOF KIDS

DAN KOREM

NAVPRESS

BRINGING TRUTH TO LIFE
NavPress Publishing Group
P.O. Box 35001, Colorado Springs, Colorado 80935

The Navigators is an international Christian
organization. Jesus Christ gave His followers
the Great Commission to go and make disciples
(Matthew 28:19). The aim of The Navigators
is to help fulfill that commission by multiplying
laborers for Christ in every nation.

NavPress is the publishing ministry of The Navigators. NavPress publications are tools to help
Christians grow. Although publications alone cannot make disciples or change lives, they can help
believers learn biblical discipleship, and apply
what they learn to their lives and ministries.

Cover photograph: Jim Whitmer

Some of the anecdotal illustrations in this
book are true to life and are included with the
permission of the persons involved. All other
illustrations are composites of real situations,
and any resemblance to people living or dead is
coincidental.

Unless otherwise noted, all Scripture in this pub-
lication is from the *Holy Bible: New International
Version* (NIV). Copyright © 1973, 1978, 1984,
International Bible Society. Used by permission
of Zondervan Bible Publishers. Other versions
used include: the *International Children's Bible,
New Century Version* (ICB), copyright © 1983,
1986, 1988 by Word Publishing, Dallas, Texas
75039, used by permission; and the *King James
Version* (KJV).

Printed in the United States of America

FOR A FREE CATALOG OF
NAVPRESS BOOKS & BIBLE STUDIES,
CALL TOLL FREE 1-800-366-7788 (USA)
or 1-416-499-4615 (CANADA)

Contents

*Dedicated to the unrelenting effort
of the Joe White and Kanakuk family
who have given thousands of kids
a new vision for their lives
at K-5,
an extraordinary one-of-a-kind
inner-city summer camp*

(See page 326 for this story.)

CHAPTER ONE

The Challenge to Meet Unexpected Threats

◆

We want to believe that our neighborhoods are safe for our kids, but sometimes they aren't. . . . In the fall of 1988, our two youngest children—sons, ages six and eight—brought home an alarming note. Their school had been alerted that drug dealers were lacing LSD in the glue that goes on the back of stickers that kids put on their notebooks, walls, and school papers. These stickers featured everything from smiley faces to Mickey Mouse to the Space Shuttle. The dealers were giving out the stamps to covertly introduce *grammar school* kids to drugs.

Later in the year, our youngest son, who was in kindergarten at that time, came home with bizarre stories of how the father of one of his classmates encouraged his son to watch skin-flick cable movies and look at the nudies in *Playboy*. This kindergartner tried touching our son where he shouldn't have and encouraging him to do the same. Our son knew better: he fended him off and promptly told us about it.

In the spring of 1989, the teachers from the junior high my daughter would attend that fall called me. They were scared. They had confiscated hate literature distributed to students by older teen members of a neo-Nazi hate group called "skinheads." This particular skinhead group, the Confederate Hammerskins, was recruiting junior high students to join their gang.

Similar skinhead groups have sprung up all across the United States and Europe. Most are noted for their random violence, as were the Hammerskins. Several members of the Hammerskins were sent to prison in 1990 for beating a black man and for threatening to gas a local suburban synagogue—mimicking the gassing of millions of Jews during the Holocaust. None of the teachers had ever seen this kind of suburban gang/cult activity before. Dallasites had been used to hearing of gangs recruiting in the inner city, but not in the suburbs. However, in recent years hate gangs such as the skinheads have become more prevalent in neighborhoods across the U.S. with higher socioeconomic and educational levels.

As if all of the above weren't enough to cause alarm, in the fall of 1989, neighborhood kids were terrified when grisly looking characters, driving up in shiny new Cadillacs and wearing black-hooded robes, entered the home of a middle-aged couple in our neighborhood who were known to be occultists. (The husband works for a local high-tech firm.) Worshiping Satan or pagan deities is not against the law, but no one was comfortable with these folks living in a neighborhood loaded with youngsters. One man, not known to be associated with the same group, was arrested and convicted in our community for raping his daughter during a self-styled occult ritual only a few miles from our house.

If you're a real estate broker, you're probably thinking, "This isn't a neighborhood where I would want to sell homes. I sure wouldn't want to live there." Think again. Our school district consistently ranks as one of the best in the country; the mean income is over $40,000; homes cost from $100,000 to $250,000; our North Dallas suburb is often referenced in news stories as representative of mainstream America; and the corporate headquarters of J.C. Penney, Frito Lay, and Texas Instruments are located just minutes from our home.

Even after covering stories revealing negative youth trends, I was still shocked when some of those same trends personally confronted my own family. What we've seen and experienced makes it clear that today a "good" neighborhood is no longer a guarantee of protection from grim realities that can harm kids. This means that the ability to make good choices must be a high priority for families. This isn't paranoia. It's just the facts.

CONFRONTING DECEPTION

It's with good reason that most parents fine-tune their antennae when two words are used together: *deception* and *kids*. The deceptive and threatening trends confronting kids today are proliferating and becoming more complex.

As a concerned parent, the reason I wrote this book was to help parents understand *some of the important principles that allow deception to work in our minds, how these principles of deception are operative in the destructive trends that are affecting kids, and how parents can become streetwise in order to help their kids become nearly foolproof.*

As an investigative journalist I am a specialist. I select stories for my books and television specials that reveal the *principles* by which our minds can be deceived. As each story is told, the focus is placed on the mind games that allow a harmful activity to become widespread, rather than on the mechanical aspects of how people were deceived and harmed.

For example, in my first investigative television special, *Psychic Confession* (1983), I exposed the sleight-of-hand trickery used by an alleged psychic, James Hydrick. Hydrick, who was considered criminally dangerous, convinced a cult-like following that he had telekinesis—the purported ability to move objects via mind powers. While television viewers were helped by seeing the sleight-of-hand trickery—the mechanics—that Hydrick used to deceive, more people were inoculated against harmful cult activity when Hydrick explained on camera *why* peoples' *beliefs* are vulnerable and *how* he *manipulated* those beliefs.

Just as there are principles for being morally and ethically sound, there are also principles that allow deception to operate in and on our minds—little of which is commonly understood and rarely explained. I developed an interest in these psychological principles of deception due to my former career as a professional magician, which I pursued until 1981 (when I transitioned to journalism).

Unknown to most laymen, when magicians perform their tricks, usually two kinds of deceptions are used. The first kind is the mechanical or sleight-of-hand deception, which is used to fool the five senses. The second kind of deception, which fools the mind, is the psychology used in the presentation of a trick.

For example, the words and timing a magician uses to convince the *mind* that a coin has been placed in his hand (but has really been placed somewhere else) is often more important than the sleight-of-hand maneuver he employed to fool the *eye*. For me, studying why people were psychologically fooled became an invaluable asset when I later observed how people were deceived by harmful activities, lies, etc., in the stories I investigated. I have included some of these important ideas throughout this book.

(I want to make it clear that I never presented my tricks as powers. Also some have asked me if magic tricks are the same as occult practices, and the answer is a simple no. In fact, most magicians are the hardest persons to convince of the supernatural because they know how to do tricks that can look like powers. Interestingly, sleight-of-hand performers used to be called "jugglers" instead of magicians because of their clever physical dexterity. In the Old Testament, one word used for *occult* magic is *hartom,* which means one who draws circles—referring to astrologers. The New Testament Greek word from which our modern word *magic* is derived is *magos,* an Oriental scientist or "wise man." This gives us *Magi,* the wise men who traveled to worship the newborn Savior. [For further discussion of magic and the occult, see *Powers: Testing the Psychic and Supernatural,* listed in the appendix.])

KIDS IN A HOSTILE CULTURE

Some of the threats confronting kids are hard to detect, but others are not. In 1991, the National Commission on Children released a national survey on parenting—the first of its kind since 1975—revealing that nearly half of all parents felt that there wasn't a place outdoors anywhere in their neighborhood that was safe for their kids.

Some of these problems present in most communities are: drug and alcohol abuse . . . one million out-of-wedlock teen pregnancies a year . . . date rape . . . manipulation by an unmindful media . . . criminally active gangs in the suburbs as well as the inner city . . . teen satanic and occultic groups . . . rising numbers of cases of sexual and physical abuse in the home. Some of these trends affect kids in the mainstream, while others affect those who have been damaged the most by our culture. Faced with these entrapments, dealing with peer pressure, hormone changes, and the natural teenage temptation to rebel seems almost tame.

Increasingly, parents I interview whose kids have fallen into deceptive trends will say, "I had no idea that my child was into something like this. I didn't even know it was out there." As they stare off into their memories, they often comment, "Why didn't I know? *If only I had known,* maybe I could have done something."

Some of these parents are in denial, but many are not. In some cases a child just rebels, and nothing a parent can do will alter a collision course. But more often than not, a parent *could* have done something. A parent *could* have noticed the telltale signs that something was wrong.

Most parents want to know how to prepare their kids to make good choices—to help them resist the bad and turn to the good. But many parents feel so overwhelmed by the number of potentially harmful influences that they don't know where to begin.

But there's hope. *Parents can prepare their kids to think on their own so they won't be taken in by the pressures of our hostile culture.* But achieving this goal begins with understanding the basic principles of how the mind is deceived.

A HUNGER FOR THE TRUTH

Kids are receiving an overload of conflicting messages. Public service announcements decry teen pregnancy on the very same stations that blare sexually titillating messages directed at young audiences. School programs tell kids to say "no" to drugs while moms and dads get high on another drug that's just as lethal—alcohol. Many kids go to church with their families and hear the message "love your neighbor as yourself," then return home and watch their parents divorce at about the same rate as those outside the church.

Why should it surprise anyone that many kids will listen to a gang's seductive message: "We will take care of you"?

Even in the best homes, friends at school and in the neighborhood can lead vulnerable youths astray. Parents can't always be there when their kids have to make a choice. This is why kids must be taught not only to question, but more importantly, *how to ask the right kinds of questions when they have to make a choice.* To ward off deceptive options, *kids need fundamental skills in distinguishing between illusion and reality and between truth and deception in all areas of life.*

Activities don't usually deceive kids; rather, *it's the lies behind the activities that seduce young people.* Consider these typical examples:

◆ *Sex.* Premarital sex is fun. It can't hurt you. You'll never get AIDS.

◆ *Drugs.* Just try a little. You'll like it. It can't control you. You can stop anytime.
◆ *Destructive music, movies, TV shows.* Come on. You don't believe that something you hear or see can actually influence how you think?
◆ *Gangs.* Your parents don't understand you, but we do. We'll take care of you.
◆ *Powers.* If you can just imagine it in your mind, you can have anything you want.

Once kids understand the principles of how their thinking can be short-circuited, they'll be able to recognize the lie behind something that can harm them.

What are some of the concerns you have about your child's behavior or weak spots? Getting sucked into the wrong group of friends? Drugs? Music? Seeking acceptance through premarital sex? Cults? Discerning illusion from reality—which can be anything from watching movies and television news to knowing when a friend is telling the truth?

For some parents, just thinking about their offspring's potential vulnerabilities is enough to make them want to nail the doors shut and not let their kids out until they're grown. But paralytic fear—the kind that shuts down our ability to think and act—doesn't deter deception. In fact, it aids it.

Instead, we can draw on a powerful resource that our kids come by naturally: *their desire to know the truth.* Most kids want to know how to think—how not to be deceived.

On the level at which a child feels safe and can dialogue without fear, we must talk to them unapologetically about their need to think and what they must resist and avoid. Soft-pedaling what's coming at them—and therefore ignoring their need to be discerning—is setting up youngsters for a fall. The world has become too hostile a place.

UNMASKING LIES AND ILLUSIONS

To build up kids' immune systems for warding off deception, they need the following basic skills and knowledge:

◆ Discerning what is and isn't deception.
◆ The ability to distinguish between illusion and reality—what

is real and what isn't.

◆ The core concepts that can reveal if deception is at work.

◆ Awareness of current trends that can harm them.

◆ The importance of the family factor when defending against deceptive activities.

◆ How to find and cling to the good.

I know this sounds like a lot, but it can be learned. In fact, if we are to protect our kids it *must* be learned.

The purpose of this book is to help you teach your child these important skills. But opening your child's eyes to deception is not enough: With even greater intensity, you must teach him or her about the good—how to find it, how to remain in it, and how to encourage other kids to do the same. I'm convinced that many youths are just waiting for sound direction.

Recently, I spoke to a group of over fifteen hundred junior high school students. Although kids this age are often a bit awkward, they're also starved for direction—*for truth that will help them.*

Drawing on my experience as a professional magician, I did some tricks that appeared to be demonstrations of real mind powers. I created the illusion that I could read their minds at will and tell them what they were thinking. When I explained that each demonstration was a trick, they reeled in disbelief. Most had never seen a trick that appeared to be a real power—something more than just pulling a coin out of an ear. After being shown the secrets behind some of these "power" demonstrations, they were better armed to ask the question, "Is this real?" the next time they heard or saw someone who fraudulently claimed to have powers.

Switching gears, I explained how anyone can be deceived when that person doesn't know how to ask the right questions.

"For example," I said, "what do you do when someone comes up to you and says, 'What's the matter, you don't do drugs?' as if you're the dumb one?

"Listen," I encouraged them, "don't be deceived into thinking that *you* have to be on the defensive. Tell them, 'Hey, you've got the wrong question. The right question is: Why do *you* have to do drugs to have a good time?'"

The kids erupted into wild cheering. For many of them, it was the first time they realized that they didn't have to put up with a deceiving taunt—one that implied something was wrong with them.

Kids are under enormous pressure, but they're also hungry for the truth. When they cling to the truth, their thought armor goes up when confronted, and their hearts and characters are strengthened during the battle. And the family is the first line of defense.

You and your family are your child's greatest assets. In fact, landmark statistical studies show that the family is one of *the two most important factors* in deterring youths from becoming involved in a destructive trend. Together, we're going to work to make your kids "foolproof."

HOW THIS BOOK IS ORGANIZED

This book is the culmination of hundreds of interviews related to stories that I have investigated, produced, and written about during the past nine years. Additional research has been derived from over one thousand articles and studies specifically related to youths. I have cited a number of cases from the Dallas-Fort Worth Metroplex (DFW) because I have been able to observe them firsthand and because the DFW area represents a broad cross-section of the United States, including: rural towns and cosmopolitan cities; ethnic diversity; a varied economic base—high-tech to blue collar. Most trends that will affect the majority of youths in Western culture tend to surface in Dallas after first originating on the West Coast or in New York. With this pool of information to work from, I've organized the structure of this book to be as informative and easy-to-use as possible.

In the first section, "Deception and Your Kids," you'll find foundational information about deception: the difference between good and bad deceptions; handling lies and secrets; the difference between illusion and reality; when fantasy is acceptable and when it isn't; the difference between tricks and powers. When appropriate, I have also included demonstrations and suggestions for discussions, broken down by age groups: four to six; seven to twelve; thirteen to seventeen. Since these age groupings are generalizations, please adjust for individual kids based on their level of development. With a firm understanding of these concepts, kids will be equipped to ask good questions and make sound decisions in all areas of life.

The second section, "The Family Factor," addresses these key issues: why a stable family reduces a youth's chances of participating in a negative trend; the special needs of a single-parent home; and some practical guidelines for teaching young people how to make critical decisions.

The third section, "Know the Streets," zeroes in on specific problems such as harmful media, the entertainment industry, sexuality trends, drugs, gangs and cults, and educational trends. You'll learn the factors driving each trend, how each trend has shown itself, the profile of youths who are vulnerable to each trend, and proven and effective deterrents. Easily, a book could be written on each trend. Because of the limitation of space, I have selected those trends that affect the largest numbers of youths and the most important related issues. Of unique importance in this section is one of the first detailed profiles of those involved in skinhead activity, what these youths are seeking, and the eight specific reasons why they disengage, along with one of the first comprehensive comparison charts of cults and the occult.

The fourth section, "Know the Good," assumes that the best defense is a good offense. Here you'll find ideas for developing a strategy for helping youths in trouble, catalyzing effective community action, and building on the importance of the spiritual life.

The appendix, "Streetwise Resources," is a topical listing of print materials, visual media, and organizations that can provide helpful references especially in particular areas of concern to youth and their parents. A word of caution here: Since organizations and people can change with time, evaluate these resources on their own merit at the time you come into contact with them. Also, I have liberally used both "he" and "she" to be respectful of the fact that parents have sons and daughters, but in many cases the conventional "he" is used to avoid cumbersome wording.

FOR THOSE IN NEED OF IMMEDIATE HELP

If you are currently dealing with a problem and need immediate help, read the first and second sections of the book, then skip to the chapter in the third section that addresses the specific problem you're struggling with. Then read the last section of the book that details how to develop a strategic plan of action and work toward positive alternatives.

And be patient. If a youth is in trouble, immediate direction from a parent may help to correct a problem temporarily. Molding a youth's character, though, requires a parent's perseverance over a sustained period of time coupled with the youth making the right choices. For ultimately it is youths who must decide how they will think.

Dr. Lawrence W. Green, director of the Center for Health Promotion Research and Development at the University of Texas Health Science

Center, says that studies show that people who decide for themselves to change how they think fare better than those who are carried along by a group.[1]

Scientific studies, as well as common sense, make it clear that *those who make their own choices do the best over the long haul.* If youths are going to turn away from a harmful activity, *they* must make the decision to change—otherwise, when supports are removed they face a greater chance of failing. While we teach kids discernment, we must also encourage them to make their own good choices. Many parents have done this, and so can you.

THERE'S PLENTY OF REASON FOR HOPE

I have personally used what is in this text in our own family and have taught these concepts to thousands of youths and parents over the years. At our suburban church alone, where we have over 2,300 youths (that's not a typo), I regularly teach these concepts each year. Even more significant, I have taught these ideas to a unique group of at-risk kids who come to our church from an inner-city environment in the Dallas area. To my knowledge, not one of these kids—over *four hundred* in the last four years—has joined a gang, even though their environment remained the same: an area in which gangs are burgeoning, and violence is commonplace.

I had some hunches about the reasons for the success of this unique ministry, but I couldn't find objective validation for them until I came across a series of studies by social scientists which sought to determine the most significant deterrents to drug abuse and teen sexual activity. These studies, which I will refer to throughout the book, revealed that students who consider spiritual values important are less likely to take drugs or engage in sex than those who don't have any spiritual values. One of these studies involved over seventy thousand students over a period of five years.

These studies confirmed what I had believed to be true: that the spiritual and moral direction we gave our at-risk kids was the most significant factor in their lives, helping them become more stable, earn better grades, and increase their self-respect. This is why I've included a specifically Judeo-Christian perspective when appropriate in this book. However, even if you don't embrace the Christian faith and you find that my spiritual views conflict with your own, I'm confident that you will find much throughout this book that will benefit you and your family.

Let's take hold of the perspective King Solomon penned: *Preserve sound judgment and discernment, do not let them out of your sight; they will be life for you* (Proverbs 3:21-22).

Maintaining a sense of balance is important in educating kids about deception. Our families should remain optimistic about life, while not pretending that everything's okay when it's not. We must be cautious and have a healthy understanding of evil without becoming paralyzed with fear. We must instruct without smothering and love our kids without forcing them to lead a sheltered life. I know this is possible, because our family and many others have done it. Now let's get started.

SECTION I
DECEPTION AND YOUR KIDS

Foolproof kids know *when* to ask questions and *what kinds* of questions to ask in order to protect themselves from harm. These are skills that parents can teach to their kids with just a small investment of time. Chapters 2 through 6 will help you accomplish this goal.

The foundational concepts covered in this section include: deception; resisting lies and discerning between good and bad secrets; the importance of loving the truth more than fearing our pain; illusion versus reality; distinguishing between what's acceptable and unacceptable in stimulating kids' imagination; investigating today's power claims regarding the psychic and the supernatural.

Concrete guidelines will bring these abstract ideas down to earth, showing how they apply in everyday life. Adults will find that although the presentation is geared for teaching to youths, the concepts are equally applicable to all ages.

For maximum benefit, the insights in this first section should be reviewed periodically with the whole family as a safety check, and as new issues crop up. Later chapters, which focus on specific issues, will build on the foundational concepts presented here.

CHAPTER TWO

Deception:
A Misleading Word

◆───────

Jerry Andrus, a wiry sixty-year-old magician, carefully removed a deck of cards from its case. All eyes in the room were riveted on his hands and the cards as he playfully asked, "When a magician removes a deck of cards from its case, what is the first thing that you expect him to do?"

This little drama was taking place in a classroom at the University of Oregon. Jerry, the inventor of hundreds of professional tricks, had been invited to perform for the graduate psychology students of Dr. Ray Hyman, one of the world's leading experts on the psychology of deception—and known among students for his creative teaching methods.

"Shuffle it!" called back one of the students.

"Why?" Jerry asked.

"Because the deck may be stacked," the student glibly replied.

In response, Jerry shuffled the deck with an audible, carefree flurry. "Now as I shuffle the deck," he announced, "the last thing you would expect is that I'm really holding a *single* card and a solid block of plastic." To everyone's amazement, Jerry separated his hands and displayed just a single card in one hand and a clear block of plastic—the same size as a deck of cards—in the other.

"You simply assumed that I held a deck of cards as I created the illusion that I was shuffling a full deck. Just like many of you assume that I'm standing behind this podium. Or am I?"

With a slight push, Jerry rolled the podium on wheels to his left, revealing that he was actually kneeling on a stool.

"Now many of you think that I'm kneeling on a stool. Or am I?"

As all eyes and minds focused on his legs, bent at right angles at the knees, Jerry reached down, unhooked his two legs, and tossed them aside. The discarded legs were simply mannequin legs dressed in matching pants material and men's shoes. When he removed the cloth that covered the legs of the stool, everyone could see that he was actually standing through two holes in the wooden stool.

Laughter rippled through the class.

"Aha!" Jerry remarked. "So you're graduate students in psychology. Well, my message to you is: Don't ever trust that your thinking can escape deception."

———————◆———————

What is deception? Why is it possible for people to be deceived? Is there such a thing as a good deception? If the answer is yes, how can we tell the difference between good and bad deceptions? What is the difference between lying and just tricking someone?

These can be provocative questions, however, it's easy to teach kids about deception without being threatening. In this chapter you'll learn how you can explain these ideas to your child using some simple demonstrations.

WHY ANYONE CAN BE FOOLED

The graduate psychology students in Dr. Hyman's class learned the simple lesson that anyone can be fooled. People don't like to admit that they can be fooled, yet everyone likes a good trick. Jerry Andrus' demonstration evoked laughter because at each turn in his presentation, the students were surprised that they were taken in so easily.

That's one good thing about magic, the art of legerdemain. It reminds us in a non-threatening way—and we occasionally need to be reminded—that we can all be fooled. No one is exempt. Why? Because we're vulnerable: our mind and our senses can be tricked. Most of us aren't fooled because we're gullible, although that's true of some. Usually, we're fooled because our five senses and our mind never have, and never will, work perfectly. No one's perfect.

This is one reason why sleight-of-hand tricks have an even more universal appeal than music. Not everyone likes the same kind of music, but people everywhere share a common, cross-cultural appreciation—even without an interpreter—for the merriment that goes along with being fooled by a clever trick. It's a playful way to be reminded, "Yes, I can be fooled."

This provides the first non-threatening and important lesson for kids about deception: *Anyone can be tricked because our senses and mind don't work perfectly.*

The following two tricks will help you show your kids that they can be fooled easily. The first trick demonstrates that our senses can be tricked; the second emphasizes that our mind can be tricked. Although these illustrations are intended for younger kids, teens are also amused by them.

TWO SIMPLE TRICKS ILLUSTRATING THAT ANYONE CAN BE FOOLED

Fooling the Senses: The Apple Trick

Materials needed: One red apple, one yellow apple, and one piece of water chestnut. (If you don't have any water chestnuts, substitute a piece of raw potato.)

Preparation: Cut some small slivers from each apple and remove the peel. Now cut a piece from the water chestnut that is about the same size as the pieces of apple, but keep it hidden—for example, if you're seated at a table, hide it in your lap.

The trick: Explain to your youngster that our sense of smell helps our tongue taste food. Give her a piece from each apple, and then tell her to eat each one and see if she can taste the difference.

Now tell her to close her eyes and hold her nose so she can't smell—just like kids do when they have to take some awful-tasting medicine.

While her eyes are closed, explain that you're going to give her a piece of one of the apples, and that she has to guess which color apple it is. Instead, secretly give her the piece of water chestnut, which crunches and has the same texture as an apple.

After she guesses which apple slice she just ate, show her that you really gave her the water chestnut. Explain that she was tricked because her sense of taste was tricked.

The lesson: Explain that she was fooled because: (1) her sense of taste was fooled when she couldn't smell; (2) the water chestnut crunches just like an apple, fooling the mouth's sense of touch; and (3) you switched the apple for the water chestnut.

The point here is that anyone's senses can be tricked. The next demonstration makes the point that anyone's mind can also be tricked.

Fooling the Mind: A Simple Coin Trick

Materials needed: A handful of coins.

Preparation: Have your youngster put the coins in his pocket.

The trick: Say to your child, "I'll bet that if you take any coin out of your pocket and hold it in your fist, I will be able to tell you the exact date without looking at the coin."

Ask him to take a coin out of his pocket and hold it in his fist. Now call out today's date—such as, "It's October 10, 1993." You didn't say you would tell him the date on the coin, just the exact date! (With a small child you might have to explain before you do the trick that a date is stamped on each coin.)

The lesson: Explain that the coin trick shows us that our mind can be tricked. We think we hear one thing, but we actually hear something else. This doesn't mean that we're foolish or dumb, but rather that our senses and our mind don't work perfectly.

THE ILLUSION OF INVULNERABILITY

One of Dr. Hyman's favorite talks is on the illusion of invulnerability, the "not-me" syndrome: The other guy can be fooled, but not me.

Generally, once kids hit seven, they play this out to the hilt; they all think they can't be fooled. When I was in my early twenties, performing tricks for nine- and ten-year-olds drove me crazy. Some kid would always yell out, "Oh, I know that trick. My dad does it"—even if it was a trick I had just invented.

Preschoolers don't think this way. To them, everything is a wonder. When they see a trick for the first time, they're often disoriented. It doesn't compute. Or they simply absorb it and say, "Oh yeah, that's what's supposed to happen." They don't know any better. They really think that snapping my fingers causes a coin to appear. So they start snapping their fingers and become frustrated when the money doesn't materialize.

One of the world's great magicians, Ed Marlo, recounts the time when he was a youngster that he tried to make a cake in a hat, just as he saw a magician do in a show. Ed said that he broke an egg in his father's straw hat and then waved his hand over the hat. A cake didn't appear, but his father's ire did!

Young kids are impressionable. That's why I reinforce with small children that what they're seeing isn't real magic, but just a trick. I reinforce this until I'm certain that they've learned this important lesson. Although I can't reveal my professional secrets, I often explain the secret of a simple trick to be sure that this important point is plainly understood.

Thank goodness that as kids get older and reach their mid-to-late teens they start coming to grips with the fact that they can be fooled. Usually by the time they graduate, teens have been fooled in a number of different real-life settings: a boyfriend or girlfriend dates someone else behind their back; they can't figure out how a friend made a better grade on a *Hamlet* paper until they see a set of "Cliff" notes in that person's notebook; a supposedly wimpy little guy bench-presses fifty pounds more than anyone else.

Impress upon your kids that *those who think they can't be fooled are usually the easiest people to fool*. Why? Because they don't ask questions in their mind about what they're seeing. Their illusion of invulnerability to deception lulls them into a false sense of complacency. Kids who know they can be fooled, however, stay alert and think critically about what they're seeing or hearing.

DIFFERENT WAYS WE CAN BE FOOLED

Talk with your son or daughter about the different ways we can all be fooled: by what we see, by people we know and don't know, in sports, and so on. As your child tells you how she thinks she has been fooled or has seen someone else fooled, give her examples from your life, both when you were a young person and as an adult. This not only helps kids, but it also teaches them something about their parents—and kids like stories about their parents.

Emphasize that we should not be afraid to admit that we can be fooled, and that it's when we pretend that we can't be fooled that we let our guard down. Then it's even easier to be tricked, because we might not be paying close attention or asking enough questions. Here are some examples to help you get started.

Ages 4–6
- Fooled during hide and seek
- Thought something in a movie or TV program was real and it wasn't
- A magician's magic trick

Ages 7–12
- You became friends with someone you thought you'd never like
- A class was harder than it appeared at first
- When your eyes are bigger than your stomach and you eat too much dessert

Ages 13–17
- People who spend all their money on gambling or lotto tickets and think they will hit the jackpot
- A good-looking guy or girl, who you thought had a perfect life, actually has many personal problems
- A group of people seemed to be your friends, but it turned out they were really only interested in using your car or something you owned

WHAT IS DECEPTION?

Notice that up to this point I have not used the word *deceive,* as in: you will *deceive* your child with a trick. Instead, I've relied on the words *tricked* and *fooled.* This is because the words *deceive* and *deception* are usually interpreted as something inherently bad.

But the tricks I have explained *do* deceive the mind, just as Jerry Andrus' tricks deceived the graduate students. The reason we say, "I fooled Johnny with the apple trick," rather than, "I deceived Johnny with the apple trick," is because the word *fooled* sounds less harsh. So when Jerry reveals the deck of cards to be a block of plastic, we're more likely to say, "Jerry fooled me," suggesting that we're not talking about something bad or malicious, but rather a clever, educational trick.

Does this mean that being fooled is different from being deceived? No. It's just that for most people, the words *deceive* and *deception* are more emotionally charged.

Webster's Dictionary defines "deceive" as: to mislead by a false appearance or statement. "Deception" is defined as: the act of deceiving.

At a glance, both these definitions sound pretty foreboding. But as you will see, there are many deceptions in life that are good and are not harmful. That's why I prefer to redefine deception as: *the act of creating a mistaken impression in someone's mind.*

Good Deception Versus Bad Deception

In 1989, I spoke at a presentation for an international conference of the Young Presidents' Organization. Admission to the YPO requires that before you reach age forty, you become president of a company with at least fifty employees that does at least $4 million of business per year.

My opening remark to this group was, "Today, we're going to look at deception: when to use it and when to expose it." Instantly, a number of brows furrowed. These were hard-charging executives and entrepreneurs, yet (according to their evaluations afterward) they had never thought through the difference between using good deceptions and confronting and exposing bad deceptions.

This neglect is true of most people, because this idea is rarely addressed in schools or churches—places where one would expect this concept to be clarified because of the moral implications.

Most of us assume that deception is always harmful. Creating a mistaken impression in someone's mind, however, isn't necessarily a bad thing. Here are some common examples of deception that we usually don't think of as being deceptive—yet they are:

◆ Personal grooming aids. Manufacturers sell everything from paint, wax, powder, fake hair and eyelashes, and false heels to body-slimming undergarments so that women and men can try to deceive others about their actual looks, age, or body condition.

◆ Sports and trick plays. Sports are chock-full of good deceptions—what we call "trick" plays. A quarterback fakes to a halfback to freeze a linebacker, then drills a pass over the middle to a tight end, splitting a seam.

◆ Crime prevention. A more practical example of a good deception is something most families do when they go out for dinner: they leave lights on to deter would-be burglars. They want to create a mistaken impression that someone is home. Timers that activate lights, a TV, or a radio can complete the illusion.

◆ Surprise gifts. A heartwarming example of a good deception
is when the normally forgetful husband feigns that he forgot
his wife's birthday, only to surprise her with a special present.
Even though we don't normally think of this kind of thoughtful act as deception, deception does come into play.

We may not be consciously aware of it, but we do distinguish
between good and bad deceptions or tricks. For example, there are good
practical jokes and bad ones.

Here's an example of a practical joke that crossed over the line
because it violated rules that all parties involved had agreed to. This
trick, related to me by Jim Sundberg, a former catcher for the Texas
Rangers and the Minnesota Twins, was used in a baseball game.

In that game, with runners on first and third, a catcher suspected
that the man on first might try to steal second. So he loaded a small
peeled potato, which he kept in his back pocket, into his glove. When
the runner broke for second, the catcher threw the potato to second
base. The runner on third, assuming that the catcher had thrown the
ball to second—because he saw the potato in flight—broke for home.
The catcher then threw the actual ball to the third-baseman, who ran
down the lead runner and tagged him out.

Although the trick was amusing to the fans, the catcher was thrown
out of the game. His expulsion for breaking the rules made it clear it
was a bad deception.

RECKONING WITH GOOD AND BAD DECEPTIONS

If only the deceptions that can harm kids were as benign or isolated as
the catcher's poor judgment. But they're not. As U.S. Senator Patrick
Moynihan succinctly put it, "The world is a very dangerous place." And
deception is a key part of what threatens kids. It affects every aspect of
their private and public lives. This is why *for their own survival, they
must have a fundamental understanding of what deception is.* They need
to know how to tell good deceptions from bad ones and threatening
deceptions from safe ones. And they need to know how to respond.

The most immediate channel through which deceptions confront
kids today is in relationships with people they know. Questions that
can arise in this context are, "Who can I trust? Are they telling me the
truth? Do they really care about me, or are they just using me? Am I
being honest with myself, or am I just fooling myself into believing

something that isn't true? Is it really okay for me to sleep with this person who says he loves me? Since everyone else is doing it, does that mean it's okay—that it won't hurt me?"

Beyond personal relationships, external influences require kids to grapple with the distinction between good and bad deceptions. For example, kids need to be able to articulate why camouflage used in combat is a good deception, versus why a politician creating a false impression with deceiving words (or by omitting critical information) is a bad use of deception.

Additionally, kids have more mobility and the ability to communicate than their counterparts one hundred years ago. The advent of modern transportation and communications—faxes, modems, databases, teleconferencing, cellular phones, scores of TV channels—gives them the chance to do more and establish more relationships. While our increased mobility and communications can help save lives via 911, better inform us about weather, or help us evaluate the latest developments in the Mideast, a potential also exists for greater exposure to deception. This is why it is disconcerting that schools, churches, and other institutions rarely instruct on what deception is or how to distinguish between good and bad deceptions.

Although kids frequently come in contact with deception, we must resist a circle-the-wagons and retreat-from-the-world mentality. Only by positively engaging the world with a sense of street smarts can kids have a positive effect on their world. To do so requires that they have a balanced understanding of the difference between good and bad deceptions.

TALKING TO KIDS ABOUT GOOD TRICKS AND BAD TRICKS

So, how do you talk to kids about the concept of good and bad deceptions when most adults have never even thought it through?

First, for younger kids (approximately ages four to seven), don't use the word *deception*. It's too difficult. Instead, use the word *trick*. Explain that a trick is when someone or something fools them, and that some tricks are good and some are bad. The apple trick, for example, is a good trick; a crook tricking people out of their money is a bad trick.

For older kids, try using the word *deception* along with the definition: *creating a mistaken impression in someone's mind*. If they get hung up on that definition, try this one: when somebody believes something to be true that isn't.

When you talk about different kinds of good and bad deceptions, sooner or later your discussion will inevitably trigger the next question: How do you know when it is or isn't okay to use a good deception? Don't worry—we'll cover that a little later. But our first priority must be *to make sure that kids know that there are both kinds of tricks/deceptions: good ones and bad ones.* Here are some examples to help you reinforce this concept in your family.

Ages 4–6
♦ *Good trick*—by sleight-of-hand, a magician changes a one-dollar bill into a one-hundred-dollar bill.
♦ *Bad trick*—the magician uses the same trick to cheat someone out of money.
♦ *Good trick*—hide and seek.
♦ *Bad trick*—hiding a friend's toy and not giving it back.
♦ *Good trick*—a chameleon changes its color to protect itself.
♦ *Bad trick*—you trick people into believing that your parents are rich, hoping that will make them like you.

Ages 7–12
♦ *Good trick*—your mother uses makeup to make her look prettier (even though she really doesn't need it—right?).
♦ *Bad trick*—an older woman has a face-lift to trick a much younger man into thinking she is younger, so he will marry her.
♦ *Good trick*—army camouflage to hide a soldier.
♦ *Bad trick*—a seventeen-year-old boy tricks an army enlistment officer into believing he is eighteen so that he can enlist.
♦ *Good trick*—creating special sound effects on a record.
♦ *Bad trick*—a singer has another person sing for him on a record, tricking people into believing his voice is better than it really is.

Ages 13–17
♦ *Good deception*—a surprise birthday party.
♦ *Bad deception*—you tell a date you're sick, then go out with someone else.
♦ *Good deception*—you use mnemonics, an astounding memory system, to give the impression that you have a photographic memory.
♦ *Bad deception*—you read a classmate's paper and write

essentially the same paper, with a few changes, to give the false impression that you didn't plagiarize it.

◆ *Good deception*—an undercover drug agent with an assumed identity fools a dealer in order to make a bust.

◆ *Bad deception*—using a fake ID to get into a nightclub.

Now it's time to tackle the question: How can we know when it is or isn't okay to use a trick/deception?

MOTIVE, METHOD, AND CONSEQUENCE

In 1987, in the town of Midlothian, just southwest of Dallas, an undercover cop was murdered during an undercover drug sting in a local high school. The case received a lot of publicity because the officer was only twenty-one years old, and the youths who murdered him allegedly practiced a self-styled form of satanism.

Since the officer had a slight build and a baby face, his superiors decided that he could pass as a student. For several weeks he attended classes to locate the drug dealers operating out of Midlothian High. Usually the worst thing that happens in this kind of operation is that the undercover cop's cover is blown, and a lot of time is wasted. Not this time. A bullet to his head in a field ended his life.

A little over a year later, during the summer of 1989, I was presented with a decision of a similar kind that the police had faced, only felonies were being committed that were far worse than drug dealing. A young girl (I'll call her Kelly) from an upper-middle-class suburb in north Dallas was gang-raped by a cult-like group. After her release from a treatment center, she told me that she had also seen two and possibly three murders. She was too terrified to swear out a complaint because the group had made menacing threats against her and her mother.

I spoke with a contact at the Dallas Police Department, who said that unless she was willing to come in and swear out a complaint, there was nothing he could do. "Dan," he told me, "the best thing you can do is find an inside informant if you're going to investigate this thing. If you turn something up, let me know."

Like all big cities, Dallas is seething with crime, and these kinds of complex cases chew up a lot of man hours. Cops usually can't chase these kinds of cases without hard evidence; it's more productive to work on less complex cases in which they do have evidence.

In this situation my best source of information was Kelly. She gave me a list of teens who she said were involved. I considered surveillance of suspected perpetrators—called "perps" by cops—but surveillance without an informant to let you know what is going to happen and when is costly and often unproductive. Another option was to enlist as an informant a youth who knew those in the group. This option was tempting, because Kelly said that other kids were being similarly victimized, and it would have been the quickest way to get access to the group's activities.

To make a good decision, I had to weigh the fact that I didn't want to jeopardize a young teen informant's life against the fact that I didn't want to see any more kids hurt. Ultimately, my choices boiled down to two different deceptions: (1) I could have Kelly or one of her friends pretend that they wanted to be a part of the cult group to get information. (2) I could use a false name when I approached members of the gang to secure information.

To reach a sound decision, I used a method employed by many in law enforcement: I examined the *motive, method,* and *consequence* related to the two options. In doing so, I posed three questions:

The motive: Why am I using this deception?

The method: What type of deception am I going to use, and how am I going to use it?

The consequence: What are the possible outcomes of using this deception?

With this grid, if there is ever an unfavorable answer to any one of these three questions, then the deception under consideration must be eliminated. It's scrapped, and another option is sought.

Let's look at how I used *motive, method,* and *consequence* to evaluate the option of using Kelly or one of her friends as my informant.

First, my *motive* was a good one. I wanted to find hard evidence concerning those who hurt Kelly in order to prevent others from being hurt. Second, the *method* of using a teen to do undercover work was a bad one. The teen was not of legal age, was inexperienced, and might be harmed or killed. Finally, the *consequence* could have been a good or a bad one. However, because the method was unacceptable, I scrapped the idea.

Another deception that I considered employing was for me to assume a false name, like the Midlothian police officer. In this scenario, my motive remained the same, and so it was again a good one: *find out who hurt Kelly and prevent additional crimes.* The *method,* assuming a false name, was also acceptable: no laws would be broken and the public's trust in me as a journalist wouldn't be damaged. Finally, the *consequence* might be that I would successfully get enough information to write the story and turn incriminating evidence over to the police. There might also be a negative consequence, like what happened to the Midlothian officer. However, I am an adult who is experienced in this kind of situation; therefore, I could choose whether or not to take that risk.

In this case, I ultimately decided against using a fictitious name because the risk was too great. Since most of the members who floated in and out of this group were twenty-five or under, my appearance would be too conspicuous. Therefore, the use of an assumed name to do undercover work in this situation would be a bad use of deception. If the risk had been minimal, however, then it would have been a good use of deception.

For another example, suppose that in seeking an interview with a congressman, I falsely tell him that I'm with the *New York Times,* because I don't think he will talk to an independent journalist. This is an unacceptable deception because my *method* undermines the public's trust in journalists. And it is lying, which we'll look at in the next chapter.

This evaluation strategy works well in most real-life situations— including extremely difficult ones. If either motive, method, or consequence comes up negative, then the deception under consideration is discarded, another one is employed that does pass all three tests, or a deception isn't used at all. By weighing decisions on these criteria, you'll be able to make the right choice fairly quickly.

Evaluating motive, method, and consequence, however, is not situational ethics, in which individuals shift their moral or ethical base to achieve a desired outcome for a given situation. Stealing is stealing, and murder is murder. But by examining motive, method, and consequence, we ensure that we don't violate our morals, ethics, or civil laws by using a bad deception when we think it's a good deception. Answering these three questions will also help us know *why* a deception is acceptable or unacceptable.

Of course, these three questions aren't a formula that will guarantee perfect decisions. It's possible, for example, that we could make a bad decision because we didn't foresee a potentially negative consequence. Or out of ignorance, we might innocently violate a rule or law. But thinking through these criteria will minimize our chances of making bad decisions about the use of deception. And if we do make a bad decision, we'll know why it was bad, which will help us not to repeat the same mistake.

Most important, however, is recognizing that *the motive, method, and consequence technique will only work for people with a moral base who are honest with themselves.* People who are corrupt or dishonest with themselves may or may not make a good decision. Rather than basing their choices on their moral and ethical base, they will make decisions based on what is to their own benefit. For this reason, as one teaches kids how to use this evaluation strategy, emphasis must also be given to obeying the rules, laws, moral standards, etc.

EXPLAINING MOTIVE, METHOD, AND CONSEQUENCE TO YOUR KIDS

When explaining this concept to younger children (approximately ages four to eight), it's best to use words other than motive, method, and consequence. Instead of motive, ask, "*Why* do you want to use a trick?" For method, ask: "*How* are you going to do it?" And for consequence, ask: "*What* might happen if you do it?"

Here are a few examples:

Ages 4–7

The trick/deception: Review the following scenario with your child: Your child is trying to get you over to a neighbor's house, where a surprise birthday party has been planned for you. The trick is that the neighbors call and tell you that they have a problem, and they want you to drop everything and come quickly.

The motive: Your child wants to make you happy by giving you a surprise birthday party. This is a good motive. If the motive was not a good one, then he or she would have to stop here and either find another motive or not go any further.

The method: The neighbors make you think that they have a problem. This is a good method because no one is hurt and no laws are broken.

The consequence: You may go through a few minutes of needless worry or concern, but then you will be happily surprised and appreciate your child's effort. This is also good.

The decision: Since all three steps are acceptable, then this trick/deception can be used.

It's important that you emphasize to young children that they must be honest with themselves, and they must know the rules—such as safety rules or civil laws. Encourage children to take their time when thinking through their decisions, and if there is uncertainty, to get advice from an adult they trust.

Younger kids usually won't understand all of this concept right off the bat, but don't give up. With practice, they will.

Here are a few situations that you and your youngster can use to practice answering the *why, how,* and *what will happen* questions:

- ◆ A soldier who wears camouflage to remain hidden, versus a robber who wears a policeman's uniform to rob a bank.
- ◆ Tricks used in hide and seek.
- ◆ Tricks used in sports or games.

With older kids and teens, you will need to spend more time going over this lesson because they will come up with harder and more provocative scenarios. Hang in there—you'll get through it! Depending upon the maturity of your child, you may need to use *trick* instead of *deception* and *why, how, what* for *motive, method, consequence.*

Ages 8–12
- ◆ A police officer turns on the siren to his squad car simply because he wants to get home faster.
- ◆ A police officer who is out of ammunition tricks a crook into thinking he has bullets left so that he can make an arrest without anyone getting hurt.
- ◆ When TV news uses a re-creation without informing viewers that it is a dramatization.
- ◆ The use of special effects in movies, such as aging an actor or staging a car crash—compare both good and bad uses of this kind of trick and then compare with TV news using re-creations without informing viewers.

Ages 13–17
For this age group, it's best to compare one situation with another.

- ◆ The use of traps to catch animals—mousetraps versus traps to catch endangered game.
- ◆ The use of drugs to mask pain—drugs responsibly administered

by a doctor after surgery, versus a hallucinogen taken as an escape from personal problems.

◆ Techniques for food presentation—applying lemon juice to sliced apples so they continue to look freshly cut without turning brown, versus an advertising firm's use of a photo showing a big, thick, juicy hamburger when the actual burgers sold by that fast-food chain are thin and dry.

SUMMARY

The most important lessons to teach your kids about deception are:

1. We can all be tricked, because our mind and our senses aren't perfect.
2. Deception (or a trick) isn't always a bad thing. There are good deceptions and bad deceptions.
3. To determine if a deception is acceptable or not we have to examine motive, method, and consequence. This will only be an effective gauge when applied by honest people with a moral base for making decisions.

CHAPTER THREE

Secrets, Lies, and the Truth

◆

Secrets and lies have something in common: both involve concealing the truth. There are times I have to decide whether I should or shouldn't reveal my true identity when I'm investigating a crime case. When I do opt to assume a false identity, through the use of words—a verbal deception—I'm keeping the truth of my identity a secret, which we would call a lie. The word *lie,* however, which is normally used to imply bad intent, seems too harsh in this kind of situation if it has passed the motive, method, and consequence grid. Yet this is what we call a verbal deception. Does that mean it's wrong? Additionally, when is it acceptable to keep something a secret, and when isn't it?

In this chapter, we'll examine a number of thorny issues raised by secrets, lies, and the truth. Truth is a critical concept, and we must teach youths to cherish and protect it. To do this, they must develop a clear understanding of when it is and isn't appropriate to conceal the truth.

GOOD SECRETS, BAD SECRETS

Kids like secrets. But not all secrets are created equal. A simple definition for kids of a *good* secret is: hidden information we *aren't* supposed to share with a particular person(s). And a simple definition for a *bad* secret is: hidden information we *are* supposed to share with a person(s) we trust. Kids need to know which secrets are okay to keep and which are not.

This short, simple lesson will help kids in their everyday experiences, as well as provide a hedge of protection against threats from molesters, gangs, and others who might want to influence a child to keep a "bad secret."

Keeping Good Secrets

There are all kinds of secrets that are supposed to remain secrets. A teacher has to keep test answers secret until the test has been administered. People who work for manufacturers may have to sign a contract agreeing that they will keep product formulas a secret. Those who work in the military have to keep secret passwords and codes. A chef has to keep a special recipe a secret. When I joined the International Brotherhood of Magicians, which has about ten thousand members worldwide, I signed a code of ethics that I wouldn't reveal trade secrets to anyone except another magician.

Kids also have to keep good secrets. For example, Sally might tell Sarah to keep it a secret that she "likes" Joey. Keeping good secrets involves trust, and kids must be taught that if they don't keep a good secret, it will be hard for others to trust them. Most kids have little difficulty understanding this.

Even stories in the Bible talk about keeping good secrets. Jesus told a man He healed of leprosy to keep the miracle a secret temporarily, until he saw the high priest.

> When he [Jesus] came down from the mountainside, large crowds followed him. A man with leprosy came and knelt before him and said, "Lord, if you are willing, you can make me clean."
>
> Jesus reached out his hand and touched the man. "I am willing," he said. "Be clean!" Immediately he was cured of his leprosy. Then Jesus said to him, "See that you don't tell anyone. But go, show yourself to the priest and offer the gift Moses commanded, as a testimony to them." (Matthew 8:1-4)

Theologians have suggested many reasons why Jesus may have done this. Some have said that He may not have wanted to call attention to Himself at that time. Or perhaps Jesus wanted the man to contemplate what happened before he told anyone else. Whatever the reason, keeping a good secret a secret not only builds trust, but it also protects against the misuse of the truth.

Exposing Bad Secrets

The difficulty for most kids is knowing when they aren't supposed to keep a secret. I've taught the following principle to thousands of youngsters, always with positive results: *Never keep a bad secret because you are embarrassed or afraid.*

For example, when Jimmy comes over to play at Rob's house, he carelessly knocks over an exquisite china vase. He threatens Rob, "If you tell your mother that I knocked over the vase, I'll punch your lights out." Here, Jimmy uses fear to coerce Rob into keeping a bad secret.

Another example is when someone is the victim of a crime. In one case, an officer told me of a woman who was tricked by a con artist into believing that a candle had magical powers. The crook used tricks to fool the woman, who paid seven thousand dollars for the candle. When the woman realized that she had been duped, she was hesitant to come forward and report the swindle because: (1) she was embarrassed that she had been deceived, and (2) she was afraid that the swindler might come back and harm her.

Kids who understand the rule about bad secrets—don't keep a bad secret because you're embarrassed or afraid—will not only make better ethical and moral decisions in life, but they will also be less vulnerable to molestation and other criminal activities.

The daughter of a friend of ours was five when she participated in *Kid Tricks,* the children's video series I produced that was the original inspiration for this book.

With blonde hair, blue eyes, and gorgeous round cheeks, she became the target of a would-be molester, who beckoned to her from his car and urged her to get in and "keep it a secret." She remembered that her mother told her never to talk to strangers. She also remembered from her experience in the taping of *Kid Tricks* that you never keep a secret because you are embarrassed or afraid—and she was afraid of the man. So she started screaming before he could entice her into the car. He fled, and she was safe.

Another friend of ours didn't have such a positive outcome. His son, a high school football player I'll call Steve, was approached by a youth minister of a local church to have sex. Steve angrily refused but didn't tell his parents of the incident for two reasons: First, he was afraid that others might not believe him; second, he was afraid his father might do something foolish out of anger. The staff member was eventually caught and fired due to several incidents with other youths. But Steve, who didn't have a clear understanding of what to do with this kind of secret, needlessly suffered much anxiety.

Steve's example points out the need for kids to be taught from the time they're young when to keep good secrets and expose bad secrets and how to find a trustworthy person with whom to share a bad secret. This also applies to a youth who is told to keep a secret under the threat of abuse. A mother in Phoenix told me how a local gang in their suburb had been terrorizing kids and extorting money, without the knowledge of parents. Her own teenage son was a victim until he practiced the lesson in this chapter, refusing to cave in to gang threats to "keep your mouth shut." A similar application is in the case of a secret initiation rite that goes afoul, such as a hazing in a fraternity or club.

It's not enough, however, just to teach kids to expose bad secrets. Of prime importance is guiding them in who to turn to when it's time to tell someone.

Finding a Trustworthy Person
Kids need trustworthy adults they can go to when it's time to confide a bad secret. Parents, cops, teachers, Sunday school teachers, and neighbors are all possible sources of help—not foolproof, but at least a starting point. Kids must feel secure that the person won't expose them to increased danger and can assist them in getting help if needed.

A good place for kids to start is to seek help from someone who has helped them before. If this person isn't available, then they should think of someone they trust who is not directly connected with the situation and can provide help and assistance. Obviously, a child who is abused by an uncle shouldn't go to the aunt for help, because she might either be part of the criminal act or she might react by dismissing the allegation because of her inability to cope with the situation. Here, someone not connected with the situation is needed.

Because kids aren't always able to make good choices when they're afraid and might turn to the wrong person for help, they need assistance in determining who is safe. Ideally, as a parent you're the first person your child can turn to for help, but you might not be available.

The best preventive measure is to make a list of people, complete with phone numbers, whom you and your child know are trustworthy and who can provide assistance if called upon.

This list should include the following:

◆ A couple of teachers.
◆ A police officer. On a Saturday you might even take your child to a crime prevention officer just for a visit, to allay any fears in case a call is ever necessary. Many schools have such officers come and provide helpful presentations just for this purpose.
◆ A Sunday school teacher or minister.
◆ Two or three neighbors.
◆ A couple of trusted relatives or friends.

After you've made the list, review it with your child and keep it in a place where he can get it easily. Talk about who would be the most likely people your child would call for different kinds of problems. Avoid vivid details about negative situations that might needlessly frighten children. Instead, consider approaching the conversation more as a simple detective mystery. For example: "If someone at school, like a school bully, told you to keep a secret if you didn't want to get hurt, who would you go to?" Here a teacher, coach, counselor, or principal would be a natural choice. Or, "If you saw a gang of boys on the street hurt someone and they threatened you not to tell, who would you go to?" In this situation, a parent, police officer, or neighbor would be a good selection.

What's important is that you don't dwell on the danger that your child might be placed in, but rather on exploring together who might be a helpful candidate in different kinds of situations. By making a list of those people, your child will have already thought through the criteria for finding help, which increases the likelihood that he or she will make a good decision when confronted with a threat.

GOOD LIES, BAD LIES

Like the word *deception,* "lying" is an emotionally charged word. *Webster's Dictionary* defines a lie as: an untrue statement made with the intent to deceive. In this definition, the use of the word *deceive* seems to imply that harm is inflicted. But there are instances in which a verbal deception can be used for good.

Think of a teenage boy who suffers from severe acne going out on his first frightful date. Looking to his mother for support, he asks her, "How does my acne look?"

She carefully considers her response before answering, "Son, you look terrific."

Her statement hardly qualifies as a truthful description. She is lovingly withholding the truth from him at a moment in his life when he doesn't need to know every detail of what she's thinking. It's hard to think of this as something hurtful. Later, when he is thirty, she can tell him the truth. But when he is shaking like a leaf, he doesn't need to be reminded of his skin's true condition. This example illustrates that there can be a good use of a lie—what some call a white lie. Personally, I prefer to use another word for a good lie, which will be introduced later.

If there's such a thing as a *good* lie, then how do we define what a *bad* lie is? Consider the following definition that was proposed by a philosophy professor at a college where I was lecturing. He had derived it from various philosophers, and it's the best practical definition I have come across that is easily understood and applied: A bad lie is withholding the truth from someone who *has* the right to know.

Strictly speaking, this statement isn't really a definition, but rather a *condition* of when a verbal deception qualifies as a *bad* verbal deception. It's like an additional condition added to the motive, method, and consequence questions, falling under the consequence category. We could rephrase it like this: The consequence of using a bad verbal deception—a lie—is that the truth is withheld from someone who has the right to know.

Moving from this definition of a bad lie, we can define a *good* lie in these terms: a good lie is concealing the truth from someone who *doesn't* have a right to know.

Here's another illustration of a good lie. On Sunday mornings, when I'm in town, I teach a Sunday school class for kids from an inner-city environment. Many of them live with one parent in crime-infested apartment buildings. They often feel self-conscious because other kids are better dressed than they are. Consider a ten-year-old girl whose dress has obviously been passed down to her through several others. Can we call it a bad lie if I tell her, "You look very nice today," to put her at ease? I don't think so.

To the extent that my comment conceals my actual opinion of the condition of her clothes, my statement can be considered a lie. But it shouldn't be classified as a bad lie. She doesn't have a right to know what I really think. Just like the mom and her acne-ridden son, to tell the whole truth would be cruel. In both instances the motive, method, and consequence of using a verbal deception—a good lie—are appropriate. So the concealment doesn't qualify as a bad lie.

Now let's imagine that an overweight daughter is talking to her mother about taking care of herself. She's trying to assess the reality of her condition and then determine how to respond to it; she's not getting ready to go out on a date. She asks her mother if she thinks that she's overweight. If her mother tells her that she isn't, then this becomes a bad lie, even though it may be a small one, because the daughter is seeking her mother's help and has a right to honest, thoughtful, and gentle counsel.

How to Tell the Difference

Kids can quickly grasp the difference between lying about taking cookies from a cookie jar and a cop who has to give a fictitious name in an undercover sting. If a fifteen-year-old gains admittance to an R-rated movie by declaring that she is seventeen, she is obviously telling a bad lie. By law, the theater isn't supposed to admit someone underage. It has a *right* to know how old she is. However, Jews who escaped from Nazi Germany by concealing their Jewish identity, as well as non-Jews who protected them by lying to the Germans, were not guilty of using a bad lie. The Nazis forfeited their right to know the truth, since their goal was to unjustly sentence innocent victims to a concentration camp and a horrible death.

This raises the toughest question: *When* does someone have the right to know the truth? One simple guideline is that if laws or rules (established by government, school, home, etc.) are broken, then a verbal deception should not be used, because withholding the truth under these conditions qualifies as a bad lie. The exception, of course, is if those laws or edicts conflict with God's laws. The Nazi extermination campaign is again an example, because the law of the land legalized murder, forbidden by the Ten Commandments. Another example is when a family uses authority for odious ends, such as a father's sexual abuse of his daughter. If the daughter lied to her father in order to report him to the authorities, she would be using a good lie.

Of all the concepts described in this book, deciding when it is and isn't appropriate to use a verbal deception can present more potential gray areas than any other. To successfully make a distinction requires that one have an unchanging moral and ethical base. For this reason, I assume that the reader embraces the Judeo-Christian concept of law—i.e., the Ten Commandments. As discussed previously, without an unshifting moral and ethical base, any framework for evaluating when deception is or isn't appropriate becomes worthless. Even with this framework, there will still be times when a clear-cut answer won't be apparent. However, by using this framework, kids—and adults—will make fewer bad decisions.

Talking to Kids: Describing a Bad Lie
When explaining to small children what a bad lie is, try using the following definition: A bad lie is a bad trick that uses words to hide the truth from someone who *should* know the truth.

For older kids, seven to seventeen, use this definition: A bad lie is a trick or deception with words that hides or conceals the truth from someone who has a *right* to know, or *should* know, the truth.

To make it easier to grasp the concept, first explain the idea that a bad lie is a bad deception that uses words. Then explain the second qualifier—that it is withholding the truth from someone who has a right to know. Then go over some examples. Here are some to get you started:

- A child doesn't tell the truth when asked if he took the last piece of pie.
- A child tells his parents that he is doing fine in a particular class when really he is failing.
- A child says that she did her chores when she didn't.

Talking to Kids: Describing a Good Lie
For kids four to six, define a good lie as: a *good* trick that uses words to hide the truth from someone who *isn't* supposed to know the truth.

For kids seven to seventeen, define a good lie as: a trick or deception with words that withholds or conceals the truth from someone who *doesn't* have a right to know the truth. Explain that a good lie is a good trick or deception using words. Then explain the second qualifier that a good lie withholds the truth from someone who doesn't have a right to know the truth.

A Helpful Term
Although we don't think about it, we often use words to describe actions that are good deceptions, such as: fake, acting, pretend, feign, ruse, and trick. Here are some examples:

◆ A football player says, "He really *faked* me out with that last move."

◆ After attending a play, an appreciative critic writes, "Her *acting* is so superb that she really looks like she is ninety-five years old."

◆ A father instructs his kids: "Now make sure you *pretend* that you've forgotten Mom's birthday, so we can really surprise her."

◆ Two girls comment about a potential beau: "He *feigned* that he didn't notice me, but I know he did."

Although we have many words to communicate good *actions* that involve deception, there isn't a word in the dictionary to communicate a good *verbal* deception. My experience is that when the word *lie* is used to express both a good and bad verbal trick or deception, kids and adults are more easily confused. And personally, I've always been uncomfortable with calling a good verbal deception a "good lie" or a "white lie." I have always felt that the word *lie* should be used solely to convey the idea of something that harms, because most of us use the word *lie* juxtaposed with *truth.* The idea that a lie is opposed to the truth is justifiably imbedded in our psyche, and it should stay that way.

For this reason, I've coined a new word for a good lie, so we're less likely to confuse a good verbal deception with a bad one. Then the word *lie* can be reserved for the negative opposite of the truth.

This new term is *vrick,* which can function as either a verb or a noun. It's a combination of two words: "verbal" and "trick," and I've discovered that both kids and adults grasp it easily. The definition of vrick as a noun is: *a good verbal deception.* The definition of vrick as a verb is: *the act of using a good verbal deception.*

Vricks Versus Lies

Let's apply the word *vrick* in the example of a surprise birthday party. Your neighbor calls you and says that you must come over quickly. There is a problem. But when you dash over, you find out that a surprise party has been planned for you. In this situation it's too harsh to say that your neighbor used a lie or lied to you; instead, we could say that your neighbor used a vrick, or that she vricked you. That is, she used a verbal trick to get you over to her house.

Kids tend to grasp this idea more quickly than adults because they haven't been taught that there isn't such a concept or word. They will accept it at face value. Here are some more examples:

Vrick: You tell someone she looks good—like the example of the little girl with the hand-me-down dress—when she really doesn't. The little girl shouldn't know the truth about how her dress looks because it would only make her feel worse.

Lie: An overweight person asks for an honest opinion about her weight, as in the example above. Withholding the truth is wrong, qualifying as a bad lie, because she is seeking guidance and help and has a right to know the truth, while being told in a thoughtful way.

Vrick: A magician says that he put the coin in his hand, but he really hid it in his other hand. The audience doesn't have a right to know how his trick is done, unless he lies and says it is done through "powers" rather than by trickery.

Lie: A bank teller says that he gave a man all the money he counted, when he actually kept some back for himself.

Vrick: Your parents are out, someone calls on the phone, and you think he might be trying to find out if you're alone. Because the caller doesn't have a right to know the truth, it's the right thing to tell him that your parents are home and can't come to the phone because they're busy.

Lie: Your mother calls home and asks you if there is anyone with you. You are not supposed to have a friend over, but you have violated the family rules by doing that anyway. You tell your mother that no one is there.

These examples will trigger discussions about related issues that kids will inevitably bring up. For example, what do you do with people who might get angry if they're told the truth? Suppose a friend asks you, "Am I really hard to get along with?" Determining the appropriate answer here can be difficult. Do you risk telling the truth even though your friend will get mad? Do you tell him just part of the truth, because that's all he can handle? A real friend tells the truth and tries to help, and a wise friend knows how much to say at the appropriate time.

Another idea to explore with older youths is the idea of deceiving someone not by the deceptive words you *do* say, but by what you *don't* say—which is called "the sin of omission." For example, Ron backs into a neighbor's car, and he tells his friend Jim about it. Jim's father tries to help the neighbor identify who did it, and asks his son, "Jim, did you see Ron dent Mr. Smith's car?"

Jim answers, "No, Dad, I never saw Ron dent the car."

Although it is literally true that Jim never actually observed Ron backing into Mr. Smith's car, his answer is a form of a lie—a bad verbal deception. Jim knows that Ron did it but is withholding the truth from his father who has a right to know.

There is no perfect method for determining when it's right to use a vrick. However, we can clarify most situations by examining motive, method, and consequence, and by discerning when someone has a right to know the truth. Another important aid to help us avoid using a bad lie or being the victim of a bad lie is to have an understanding of *why* people lie.

WHY PEOPLE LIE

There are essentially two reasons why people lie. Kids need to understand what these reasons are so that they can spot deception more easily and also resist the temptation to lie.

The first and most obvious reason why people lie is that somebody wants something for nothing, or something to which he isn't entitled. Some examples:

- A person lies about his identity in order to steal money from someone else's bank account.
- A child lies to his mother that he didn't already have dessert in order to get an extra portion he's not supposed to have.
- A youngster lies about his age in order to gain admittance to a restricted ride at an amusement park.

A second reason why people lie, which is often harder to spot, is because of their fear of pain. They lie so they won't be hurt. This can occur whether someone is lying to another person or herself. Some examples:

- A parent asks her child a question, and the child lies out of fear of (legitimate) punishment—whether physical pain from a spanking or loss of freedom from being grounded.

◆ A youth lies about the size of her house to kids from a more affluent neighborhood so she won't experience the pain of rejection.
◆ A teenager lies to her parent about a grade on a test so she won't have to be held accountable.

The first reason why someone will lie is easy for kids to grasp because it's concrete; someone wants something for nothing. The second reason, which deals with a desire to escape pain, isn't as easy to grasp because it's more abstract. The easiest way to explain this idea to kids of all ages is by illustration and discussion. Encourage your child to come up with his or her own examples of ways that people lie to escape various types of pain: physical pain, accountability, rejection, loss of freedom, and so on.

Adults will discover new variations on this behavior as they grow older. Here are some adult examples:

◆ A person is sick, but he won't admit to himself that he needs medical care because he's afraid of the pain associated with an operation or proper treatment.
◆ Parents who are exceedingly harsh with their children won't accept their responsibility for damaging their children's self-esteem.
◆ A student musician is auditioning for a scholarship, but he feigns being sick because of a fear of failure.

These examples can become quite complicated. There is one simple concept, however, that will guide kids and adults away from lying when they fear the pain of telling the truth: *Love the truth more than you fear your pain.*

LOVE THE TRUTH MORE THAN YOU FEAR YOUR PAIN

There is tremendous power in the idea of loving truth more than fearing personal pain. It can help us conquer the temptation to lie to others or ourselves. It also applies to lying when we're trying to get something for nothing or something we aren't entitled to. If we really love and cherish the truth, we would rather feel the pain of disappointment than to get something for nothing. We must love the truth *more* than we fear physical pain, punishment, rejection, being held accountable, or even a loss of freedom—as experienced by those in repressive regimes.

This is one of the most important lessons in life for foolproofing youths to deception and lying illusions. Using examples given in this chapter, talk with your children about what it means to love the truth more than to fear the different kinds of pain we can experience. Help them to be able to express this important lesson in their own words and from their own experiences with fear. Even wanting something for nothing can relate to the concept of fear—we are afraid that we will somehow miss out on something if we don't get what we want. By helping kids express this concept in their own words and from their own experiences, this lesson will have concrete meaning—one they can apply for the rest of their lives.

When we explain to kids that they need to love the truth, we must also make a distinction between truth and *facts*. Two plus two is a fact, but it won't change our outlook on life or make a difference in our moral base. But foundational truth, such as the immorality of murder or the existence of God, affects the very essence of who we are. This doesn't mean that facts aren't important; they are. But to establish a reference point for the immorality of lying, we need to love truth, not facts.

As already expressed, this is why kids need an unshifting base from which to say what is true and what isn't. Without an unchanging base, one can play all kinds of head games and rationalize any behavior by allowing the idea of absolute truth to shift depending on how one feels. Without guidance—such as, "In everything, do to others what you would have them do to you" (Matthew 7:12)—we and our kids will be hopelessly left adrift on a sea of subjectivity.

PERSPECTIVE FROM AN UNSHIFTING FOUNDATION

The book of Exodus in the Bible recounts the story of the Egyptian Pharaoh's decree that Hebrew midwives were to kill all male Hebrew babies as they were born. He did this because he knew that the Hebrews were expecting a deliverer to be born (who turned out to be Moses). Morally, Pharaoh's edict was wrong, even though it had become the law of the land. Scripture tells us that the midwives disobeyed Pharaoh and then vricked the Egyptian ruler by telling him that they had been unable to carry out his order because the Hebrew mothers gave birth so quickly. As Pharaoh plots his next move, the chapter closes with God rewarding the midwives for their good use of deception, in which they risked their own lives to save the Hebrew babies.

Another example in the Bible of a good deception rewarded by God is told in the book of Joshua (chapter 2). The heroine is a prostitute named Rahab, who protected Joshua's spies when the soldiers of Jericho came looking for them. She vricked the soldiers by reporting, "they went that-a-way," while at that very moment she had them hidden on the roof of her house. In the New Testament, the writer to the Hebrews commends Rahab's faith (Hebrews 11:31), and James uses her story to illustrate the righteousness of faith in action (James 2:25).

These two examples bring us to a crucial point: Discerning between good and bad deceptions can be a force for good only when this discernment is in the hands of moral people. People who are committed to the unchanging standards of morality of the Judeo-Christian tradition as expressed in the Old and New Testaments. This commitment must be unwavering, even under pressure from the antagonistic forces of the prevailing culture.

William Shirer, the acclaimed CBS radio journalist and historian, called the years of 1930 to 1940, during which he lived in Germany, "the Nightmare Years." Shirer observed that it was during this period that Hitler realized that he could never attain absolute power unless he destroyed the base from which moral German church parishioners viewed the world and made decisions—the Bible. To do this, Hitler created the National Socialist Church, so that he could be the sole author of the moral absolute. He commissioned the truths of the Bible to be rewritten, the Old Testament erased, and all references to Jews deleted from the New Testament so that he could carry out his "final solution" to the Jewish "problem."

Pastor Martin Niemoeller, a former WW I naval hero and pastor of the Confessional Church in Dahlem, an affluent suburb of Berlin, believed that if Hitler carried out his wishes, it would destroy Germany. In 1937 Niemoeller organized many thousands to protest. For his stand, he was incarcerated in a concentration camp for seven years. By his actions he demonstrated that he loved the truth more than he feared his pain.

In Niemoeller's last sermon, before the ruthless Gestapo imprisoned him in Berlin's Moabit prison, he said, "No more are we ready to keep silent at man's behest when God commands us to speak. For it is, and must remain, the case that we must obey God rather than man." Niemoeller, like the Hebrew midwives, said with his life that he must stand on the side of good—good as revealed in the Bible.

Madmen throughout history have said that they must do "God's will" as they ravaged their peoples: the Ayatollah Khomeini of Iran;

Hitler's henchmen such as Dr. Hans Kerrl, minister of church affairs, who said, "Nationalism is the doing of God's will. . . . God's will reveals itself in German blood. . . . True Christianity is represented by the party." Because of their corrupt moral base, these doers of evil would twist any moral or ethical code to deceive and destroy.

For your children, the concepts presented here are worthwhile only when coupled with an unshakable moral base that doesn't change with the whim of a dictator or a misguided electorate. Affirming what one's moral base is and where it comes from is as crucial as giving kids thought-tools so that they are not deceived by evil.

SUMMARY

Successfully negotiating the difficult issues of lies, secrets, and the truth requires the following: (1) discerning how and when to keep good secrets and expose bad secrets; (2) understanding the difference between good lies and bad lies; (3) grasping the importance of loving the truth more than fearing one's pain; (4) basing issues of truth and morality on the unchanging foundation of biblical truth.

Because lies and secrets involve concealing the truth, kids need to know when they should conceal the truth and when they shouldn't. Using a concept such as "vrick" is not just a matter of juggling semantics, but rather a way of protecting a cherished respect for the truth.

A phrase that our kids embraced when they were much younger is, *you can fool my eye, but don't mess with my mind!* The fact that we're vulnerable to deception shouldn't be a point of fear for kids, but rather an impetus for building into their consciousness the need to think critically and ask questions. This doesn't mean taking a negative bent in life. It means that we accept the reality of the inherent vulnerability we all have, and take steps to foolproof ourselves against the inevitable attempts others will make to deceive or manipulate us.

In 1992 I lectured at universities in Western and Eastern Europe and interviewed experts in Hungary, Germany, Austria, and Switzerland about destructive social trends in each country. To a person, each said that youths must embrace the Judeo-Christian ethic as expressed in the Bible for those trends to be reversed. Some of these experts, themselves, didn't embrace Christianity, but they recognized the inherent need for there to be an absolute moral base.

Dr. Maria Kopp, head of social psychiatric studies at Semmelweis Medical University in Budapest, Hungary, who has documented the similarity of trends in the United States and Hungary—such as high suicide rates, divorce rates, and the increase in violent gangs—stated the following: "Without Christian values, we will eventually lose human values. And without human values, we will eventually experience anarchy or facism."[1] Her comments characterized what each of the other experts from diverse professions and beliefs said during my 1992 trip: Parents must unashamedly and with wisdom teach biblical principles to their children.

When kids are guided through the concepts of lies, secrets, and the truth with a biblical perspective as their moral, ethical, and spiritual base, they will rarely be deceived during the pivotal moments in life.

CHAPTER FOUR

Illusion and Reality: Checking Out the Facts

◆

Knowing the difference between illusion and reality is as fundamental as knowing the difference between a lie and the truth.

An illusion is actually a type of deception, because it occurs when something or someone fools us. It's usually linked with its opposite, the word *reality*—as, for example, in the case of a news story, when we must distinguish between the actual facts versus the created illusion we receive from a particular broadcast.

In popular use, we tend to think of deception as a deliberate act. But not all illusions are deliberate deceptions. Sometimes illusions are created simply because we don't have all the facts, as with a mirage.

The most important tool you can help your child develop for distinguishing between illusion and reality is *a positive curiosity that will stimulate them to ask questions and check out the facts.* Illusions are only potent when we don't have all the facts or when we don't want to know the truth.

Here are a few illusions that affect youths: Is a TV personality the same on and off camera? Do drugs really make you more powerful, or is it just a feeling of power? Does a particular group of kids really take care of you, or do they just exploit you? Is that attractive person the same on the inside as he or she seems on the outside?

With an understanding of illusions and the importance of asking questions, your child will become more discerning. Let's look at some foolproofing techniques in this area.

UNDERSTANDING WHAT AN ILLUSION IS

The first step is understanding what an illusion is. Here is a simple definition:

An illusion is something that isn't what we think it is when we first see it.

Here is a more complex definition:

An illusion is something different than what we perceive.

These definitions can be summed up this way: *An illusion is simply a mistaken idea.* Anyone can have a mistaken idea. As we learned in chapter 2, we can all be fooled because our mind and our senses don't work perfectly. But we can also be fooled simply because we don't have enough information.

When a magician performs a trick—creates an illusion—we're fooled because we don't know the secret. We don't have enough information to figure out how the trick is done. When a quarterback fakes a hand-off and our eye follows the wrong player, he creates an illusion that fools our eye. It's important for kids to understand that everyone can be fooled by illusions—it's not a question of gullibility.

Kids need to know that there are two different kinds of illusions: *active* and *passive*. An active illusion occurs when someone deliberately sets out to trick us. A passive illusion is when someone or something fools us even though there is no deliberate intent.

Active or Deliberate Illusions

Active illusions are like magic tricks or cinematic special effects. An example of an audio illusion is when a guitar mimics the sound of a snare drum. To create this illusion, you take one guitar string and pull it over the one next to it, and then hold down both strings with one finger. (I use the E and A strings, because they're the heaviest.) Then you do a tremolo—plucking the strings back and forth very quickly—with the guitar pick. As the two strings "buzz" against one another, they perfectly mimic the sound of a snare drum. This amusing trick allows a child to see how easy it is to create an illusion that can fool one of the senses.

There are also active illusions that fool the brain. Some riddles, tongue twisters, and puzzles will qualify in this category. The coin trick in chapter 2 is a good example of creating an illusion with words.

Make a list with your child of some illusions that fool both the mind and the senses, in which someone or something deliberately tries to create an illusion. Look for examples from all areas of life: nature, games, work, school. A creative example is when flowers simulate the appearance of an insect to attract insects to them for pollination. A humorous story from the Bible (Judges 7) recounts how Gideon and his men defeated the Midianites by using the sound of trumpets and smashing jars to create the illusion that they were a big army.

Passive or Non-Deliberate Illusions
There are many passive illusions in life that fool us, even though no one is trying to trick us. Here are some examples:

Optical illusions. The two line segments below are identical in length, but the direction of the arrowheads distorts their appearance, creating the illusion that one is longer than the other.

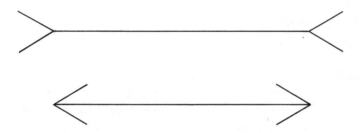

Another optical illusion occurs when the pavement on a dry highway on a hot day shimmers and appears to be wet. Actually we are seeing a reflection of light.

News anchor reading a teleprompter. When many youngsters watch a news anchor read the news, the illusion is created that the anchor has memorized most of what he or she is reading. No one tries to trick a youngster into believing this; rather kids are fooled because they don't have enough information: they don't know there is a teleprompter.

Illusions in speech. Words called homonyms—which sound the same but have different meanings or spelling, such as "tale" and "tail"—can create illusions. "Pool," for example, can mean a pool of water, a motor pool, or a pool table. If you're not aware of the whole context in a given discussion, a homonym can create the illusion of a completely different meaning. A youngster might hear his dad say, "They're putting me back out in the field," and mistakenly assume that his dad is being placed on a farm instead of an on-site location.

CHECKING OUT THE FACTS

For kids to discern what's real and what isn't requires three basic capacities:

- ◆ A desire to know what is true.
- ◆ A desire to discover the facts.
- ◆ Basic skills for checking the facts.

Kids usually have little resistance to seeking out the truth. Once youngsters have been fooled a few times, their natural instincts take over. They want to get to the bottom of what fooled them. When kids buy a toy they saw advertised in a TV commercial and they find out that it isn't "easy to assemble," they soon realize that the manufacturer created an illusion with the camera and clever editing to make the assembly look easy. After getting stung a few times, they'll make the connection that the reason the TV illusion was created was so that the manufacturer could make money.

Where kids need the most guidance is in learning how to check out the facts so that they can avoid being hoodwinked. How did the director of the TV commercial make it look so easy to assemble the game? Why did that candy bar look so good on TV—when one bite reveals that it doesn't have as many nuts as they showed in the ad?

Here are three basic skills for checking out the facts that most children can learn easily:

1. Ask good questions based upon what you observe.
2. Look for additional sources of information.
3. Consult with someone who can help you gather information or provide you with insight when interpreting the facts in order to make a good decision.

Ask Good Questions

In the example of a deceptive TV ad, kids can tape the commercial and look at it several times to see if they can get some insight into what was done that fooled them. They need to ask the questions a reporter asks: "who, what, why, where, and when?"

Who did this commercial? Does this manufacturer use these techniques in their other commercials? Who else has been fooled by this commercial? Do we all have something in common?

What fooled me? Was I fooled by the happy-looking faces on the kids, which created the illusion that the game was easy to put together? Or was I fooled by a special effect?

Why was I fooled? Did I want to believe that the game would be easy to put together because I wanted it so much? Or was I fooled because the manufacturer wanted to trick me into believing that the game would be easy to assemble so that I would buy it?

Where is this commercial airing? Maybe this will help me find out if other kids have also been fooled. Then I can ask them, and they might be able to help me understand why I was fooled.

When was I fooled? Was I fooled because I watched the commercial early in the morning after I had just gotten up, and I just wasn't paying close attention?

Look for Other Information Sources

Knowing how to ask the right questions is half the battle of figuring out what is real and what is not. The questions a reporter asks are a good starting point. Then if kids can't answer these questions on their own, they need to know that they can go to other sources to find the answers. In the case of a toy, they might check a consumer guide book, with the help of a teacher or parent. Perhaps the manufacturer has a history of making false claims.

In the case of the teleprompter, an on-site inspection of the news set would quickly give kids the information they need to figure out for themselves that the news person is reading from the teleprompter. They would also discover for themselves that they were fooled because they didn't have all the facts, and not because the anchor wanted to deceive them. Going to the set might also reveal that the anchor is really a short person and not as tall as they had assumed. With further inspection, a youngster might also discover that the set was *designed* to create the optical illusion that the news anchors are taller than their actual height.

In the example of the two arches that appeared to be different sizes, a youngster could check out the facts either by measuring each arch, or simply by putting one arch over the other.

Find Someone Who Can Help You

There are times, however, that we don't know what questions to ask or where to find sources of information (such as a consumer's guide) that can help us make a good decision. This is when a child needs to ask someone for help.

I recommend that you teach your child to use these two qualifications for identifying a person who can help:

1. *Find someone you trust, who wants you to find the truth.*

2. *Make sure the person you pick knows something about whatever it is you're checking out.* (If you don't know anyone who knows something about the subject, then find someone you trust who can help you find that resource person.)

The next time your child is fooled by an illusion, help her think through what kinds of questions she needs to ask to find out the real story. Then if she still can't find the answer, help her find someone knowledgeable about that subject. Let your youngster learn how to ask this person questions to get the answers or leads she needs to illuminate the answers.

Once kids have had experience solving a few questions on their own, they will gain the confidence that there isn't anything they can't solve (although we know that this is just another illusion, because we never can answer all questions in life).

THE STRONGEST DEFENSE

The strongest defense against morally corrupting illusions is to root kids firmly in reality and teach them to love the truth. This is why a child who regularly reads from the book of Proverbs, for example, is very difficult to con. Preserving "sound judgment and discernment" and seeking counsel are taught throughout its thirty-one chapters—one chapter for each day of the month.

When I interview a Christian family in which self-deception or denial is apparent, I usually find that this family rarely, or only selectively, studies from the book of Proverbs. They also tend to lack a fundamental discernment about life in general. In these families, parents don't encourage their kids to ask serious questions, such as, "what is real and what isn't?" and "what is true and what isn't?" Doing so would bring unwanted attention to specific situations in that family, which is why discernment isn't encouraged.

The kids I have observed during the past twenty years who are the toughest to deceive with harmful illusions have the following characteristics: They are taught to have an inquiring mind and to love the truth. They have developed a love for the Scriptures and a desire to live them out. And they regularly seek their Creator for His guidance in all situations.

During more than one life-threatening investigation, I have been unable to discern if someone was lying or telling the truth, or what the real story was and wasn't—even after I had spent days of analyzing the facts and consulting shrewd and experienced experts. In those situations, I believe that I was able to make good decisions because I did so after much prayer, and at least knowing the "good" as it is taught in the Scriptures.

This doesn't mean that I necessarily received a supernatural message telling me what to do. I wasn't relieved of the responsibility to ask questions, seek counsel, and do all within my capabilities to find truth. In fact, in most situations, I had to act without any clear signs. But making those decisions with honest motives and after seeking God's counsel has never brought harm to myself or anyone else. I have the non-illusory assurance that when I honestly look at any situation and seek God's will, He will not fail me or desert me in the face of any lying illusion. And truth—His unchanging reality—will eventually be made plain.

SUMMARY

A child's life must be firmly planted in reality, both physically and spiritually. Kids need to develop an insatiable desire to know the difference between what is real and what isn't. They also need to learn to ask questions and seek help when needed. In addition, they must have an unshakable moral base that will be their foundation. And they need parents to carefully nurture a love for the truth in the face of any pain. Then, when they are older, they will view their world with an insatiable hunger for the truth and a diminished susceptibility to lying illusions.

CHAPTER FIVE

Fantasy and Imagination: Where to Draw the Line

◆

Kids like to dream about many things: what they're going to be when they grow up; who they will marry; meeting their favorite sports or entertainment hero. These imaginative fantasies can be healthy outlets for the energy to dream and grow. Children's imaginations are inspired, in part, by the TV shows they watch, the books they read, and the games they play.

When I was an adolescent in the late fifties and early sixties, it was relatively safe to let kids select their own toys. About the only time a parent might have to step in was if the toy was potentially dangerous, such as a BB gun. By and large, a parent didn't have to be too concerned with negative values inherent in kids' toys and games. The same was true for most TV shows. It was a rare report when one would hear of a child jumping off a roof like his imaginary hero, Superman. Monopoly, hopscotch, baseball, books from the school library, Bugs Bunny cartoons, and dolls were the sorts of activities that usually fueled children's imaginations.

Unfortunately, those days are gone. Now there are games, cartoons, books, toys, and music targeted for kids that promote violence, the occult, early sexual activity, and a dangerous moral relativism.

And this trend is growing, not diminishing.

In this chapter we'll look at some ideas that will help you make good decisions about what is acceptable and what isn't for stimulating your child's fantasy and imagination. I have found that these simple guidelines—which have been accepted by many qualified mental health care professionals—can be applied almost universally. It may seem like a jungle out there at times, but you can take balanced action, without overreacting, to protect your youngster.

THE CORE PROBLEM

To many of those in the marketing business, kids are not children to be handled with care. They're consumers—marketing demographics to be exploited, no matter what the consequences. In 1989, the usually responsible *Dallas Morning News* ran the following photograph the day after Halloween:

5.1. Exploitative horror themes abound especially during Halloween.

Any caring parent should be filled with outrage at the sight of this small girl sitting by herself, needlessly being scared for the benefit of the camera. To their discredit, the photographer and the editor, who chose to run this picture, must have found it amusing to exploit this little girl's fears. No one seemed to care about the nightmares that would later visit her because of the "Freddie Krueger"-attired adult. (Freddie Krueger was the "star" of *Nightmare on Elm Street,* horror movies turned TV series unsuitable for anyone's consumption.) Regrettably, this photograph was taken at the East Dallas Health Clinic, which is supposed to promote, not undermine, the mental health and welfare of kids.

This photograph was not unique. The day before, the newspaper ran a photograph showing a small boy's terror at a chainsaw-wielding character at a "haunted house" exhibit. His parents allowed him to be frightened in this way. Why were they attending this function? Ironically, to benefit the Make-A-Wish Foundation, which grants wishes to kids dying of terminal diseases.

Kids' dreams, aspirations, and heroes should be uplifting, not cheap exploitations of their fears. The fact that you're reading this book right now may indicate that you don't agree with the direction our culture is headed in its attitudes toward kids. During the industrial revolution of the nineteenth century, treatment of children was abysmal as sweat shops abounded—the labor supply was stocked with youngsters who worked twelve- and fourteen-hour days with little pay under inhumane working conditions. When caring adults sat up and took notice, however, laws were passed, action was taken, and such sweat shops were banned in most communities.

Kids are easy to exploit. They have no money, political power, stature in community, or savvy to fight back. They rely upon adults to care for and nurture them. We must take a proactive role.

Here are three simple rules that will help you decide what is or isn't appropriate for your child to read, watch, listen to, or play with when it comes to appealing to their fantasy or imagination.

RULE 1—AVOID FEAR-PROVOKING ACTIVITIES

A healthy kind of fear motivates kids to responsible behavior—for example, "If you don't clean up your room, you will be grounded." Another type of fear helps protect them, such as the fear of being burned. A third kind of fear devastates kids by shutting down their ability to think, paralyzing and immobilizing them. This is the kind of fear the kids felt in the newspaper photos. Such paralytic fear is not only unhealthy, it can destroy a child's sense of well-being.

Over the years I have interviewed extensively a number of people who were the victims of torture when they were young. Almost all had in common a latent and unstated sense of fear about their lives. For some, their terror was so overwhelming that their brain literally shut down to protect itself. These people didn't even recall what happened to them until they were adults—similar to the post-traumatic shock syndrome experienced by veterans of war.

Many of these scarred people tend to withdraw, and there is often a "closedness" about who they are. They are very different from people who did have good nurturing and whose fantasies and imaginations were positively nourished. Individuals from good homes are usually more transparent, make friends more easily, exhibit greater productivity in their work, and enjoy a sense of general well-being.

But even kids who come from good homes are just as vulnerable to paralytic fears if their minds are filled with ideas that fuel a sense of terror in their imaginations.

Horror movies and TV shows, overdoses of cop shows that glorify killing, or even roller-coaster rides (for very young children) don't help kids; they tear them down by arousing pointless fear.

If you observe that a particular game, TV show, book, or type of music causes your youngster to harbor a destructive fear, then replace that activity with a positive one. Find and encourage activities that inspire your child's imagination toward positive achievement, creativity, healthy competitiveness, love, service for others, joy, and so forth. If a particular fairy tale scares your child, find another one. If a movie or TV show fuels their imagination to fear something they shouldn't, turn it off.

The apostle John wrote, "There is no fear in love. But perfect love drives out fear" (1 John 4:18). If you want your child to feel confident and secure, feed his imagination and fantasies with those things that will inspire what the apostle Paul wrote about in Galatians 5:22-23: love, joy, peace, patience, kindness, goodness, faithfulness, gentleness, and self-control.

RULE 2—AVOID ACTIVITIES THAT FOSTER AN OBSESSIVE DESIRE FOR POWER

As we will discuss in more detail in Section II, kids feel less secure today than they did thirty years ago because of deteriorating family conditions. When this happens, it is predictable that many kids will imagine that they have superhuman powers or an invisible friend who can rescue them from their pain and fears. In chapters 16 and 17, we'll look at how this desire pushes many kids into the occult and into cults. Most kids, however, will hope for and seek other kinds of powers to rescue them.

One TV drama portrayed the story of a seven-year-old boy stricken with AIDS, which he contracted from his deceased, drug-using mother. The program, "Christmas Presence," an installment of the former weekly TV series *The Equalizer,* was wonderfully scripted by Coleman Luck, a prominent TV producer who is a Christian.

In the fictional tale, the boy lives with his grandmother, and the two are forced to move from apartment to apartment because of threats by neighbors who are fearful of the boy's condition.

In the boy's bedroom hangs a poster of his hero, Mr. Manhattan, wearing a trench coat and fedora, standing under a streetlight on a darkened street. The caption reads, "Mr. Manhattan—he came from nowhere to save a dying world." When threatened by a menacing phone call or a rock through the window, the boy turns to his imaginary hero, whom he calls on his toy phone to come and save him and his grandmother.

Our kids watched this program and immediately saw the point of the story: We all hope that there is a savior to protect us. Imaginary heroes can't save us because they are imaginary, as the little boy discovered. Mr. Manhattan existed only in his mind. And earthly heroes, such as police officers—or, as in this story, the "Equalizer"—can't always save us. But our heavenly Savior, Jesus, can. And this is how the show ended: the boy's wayward father unexpectedly returned to his son, while the boy listened to Matthew's account of the Christmas story, read by the English actor, Edward Woodward, who portrayed the "Equalizer" character.

Although produced primarily for adults, children who have seen this specific story respond almost universally: *now the boy is safe; I hope there is a savior out there who can protect me.* The show didn't stimulate our kids to imagine that they could have powers or an imaginary hero who could save them from harm. Rather, they were left contemplating that there is a real Savior who has the power to save them. This story, however, was an exception.

Too many shows, games, and books sold for adolescent and teen consumption promote fantasies that kids can have their own personal power, or that they can turn to a dark and mysterious character for power. This can encourage youths to entertain the thought that occult or cult involvement can save them—or to develop a self-deceptive and warped way of looking at the world.

The Third Reich, China during the reign of Mao Tse-tung, and Cambodia under the Khmer Rouge are all examples of totalitarian and brutally repressive regimes during which people's imaginations were fueled with a deviant desire for someone with power to take away their pain—no matter what the cost. Even if it meant pretending—fantasizing—that evil was good.

Kids' activities should encourage an acceptance of what is real rather than an obsession with the hope for illusory powers or persons who can deliver them.

It isn't necessarily harmful, however, if a character in a story has powers. C. S. Lewis, the famous Christian author, wrote some of the most entertaining and thought-provoking fairy tales in all of children's literature. Some of his characters had good powers; others had evil ones. One such character is a witch with evil powers. She is the allegorical Satan in the story *The Lion, the Witch, and the Wardrobe* in Lewis' beloved *The Chronicles of Narnia* series. Lewis does not glorify her, however. She slays Aslan the lion—the Christ figure—but is defeated when Aslan is resurrected, and Narnia is restored.

Just as Jesus used parables to communicate truth, so, too, does Lewis through the vehicle of his fairy tales. His stories are told with clarity and reflect biblical truths, so that no child would want to seek the powers of one of the evil characters.

The Bible, of course, portrays many evil characters, chief among them Satan, who has the power to destroy and ravage. But the Scriptures do not inspire children to obtain powers like Satan's; instead, they teach us that God created us not to seek personal power for our own ends, but rather to seek ways in which we can serve Him and others.

The test for the inclusion of the theme of powers in a story for youths is whether or not the portrayal of those powers inspires kids to fantasize obsessively that they, too, can have similar powers. The *Equalizer* episode didn't fan a lust for power, but rather a desire for a chance to love, serve, and be reconciled to others. These themes and others—such as building confidence, overcoming adversity by hard work, and caring about others in need—are themes that should be carefully nurtured in a child's imagination.

A Word About Halloween

When I was a boy, Halloween was not terrifying. It was fun. In my neighborhood, occult themes weren't emphasized or overplayed the way they are today. In fact, most kids dressed up in costumes that depicted their favorite TV stars: mine was Jackie Gleason of the *Honeymooners*. Our fun came from going around the neighborhood and collecting candy.

Today, Halloween has taken on a twisted dimension in many neighborhoods, leaving parents wondering, *Should we let our kids go trick-or-treating?*

The idea of kids dressing up in costumes and getting sweets from the neighbors is fun. But it's a far cry from having to take candy sacks to local hospitals to be X-rayed because of the rising incidence of sabotaged treats. And the innocent disguises of past years have increasingly given way to costume themes centered on intense horror and the occult, such as those in the photograph we saw earlier in this chapter. These themes can terrorize kids. Much of Halloween is no longer harmless fun.

In our neighborhood, most kids don't dress up in costumes with an occult or horror theme, and their parents walk them door to door. There is a pretty clear understanding that dressing up in costumes and collecting candy is okay as long as it remains separate from occult and horror themes. If the majority of kids and parents didn't go along with this, we would find a replacement for trick-or-treating for our kids.

My advice is that if most of the neighbors approach Halloween this way, then it's okay for kids to go trick-or-treating in their neighborhood. Here are the guidelines I recommend that parents communicate to their kids: (1) no occult or horror themes in costumes, and (2) the reason for trick-or-treating is to have fun seeing the neighbors and sharing candy—not because of any belief or indulgence in the witches-and-goblins dimension of Halloween.

If your neighborhood does not provide the right environment for trick-or-treating, I encourage you to seek a positive alternative, such as those offered by many churches. In some neighborhoods, groups have taken it upon themselves to create their own fun-filled activities, without an atmosphere of fear or unhealthy curiosity in youngsters regarding dark powers.

RULE 3—DON'T IDENTIFY WITH NEGATIVE ROLE MODELS

The presence of a negative character in a story, game, or song doesn't necessarily mean that activity isn't suitable for young people. As pointed out, in C. S. Lewis' story kids are not encouraged to aspire to the witch's power. The acceptability factor depends on whether the reader/viewer is encouraged *to identify with a negative character*—to want to be like that destructive individual. A glaring example is the game sold to kids called "Dungeons and Dragons" (D&D).

In D&D, participants create their own characters—wizards, clerics with magical powers, paladins, assassins, and others. Magic powers and archaic weapons are used to fight in perilous scenarios invented and presented by the leader of the game, the Dungeon Master. The darker and more complicated the obstacles, the more imaginative the players must become to act out the character they have chosen.

D&D is not the root source of crimes and suicides, but many have taken place after a youth's involvement with it. Game expert Mike Stackpole notes that public pressure over this issue was in part responsible for the decision of TSR of Wisconsin, the manufacturer, to remove all references to demons in its second edition of D&D.

Although this was a good step, D&D still doesn't meet the bottom-line prerequisite of no negative role modeling: therefore, kids shouldn't play D&D. Stackpole says that game makers are stepping up their efforts to include advice on how to minimize violence and promote good outcomes. He also says that any fantasy role-playing game is escapist, joint story-telling—a form of entertainment in which everyone participates in creating the storyline. He warns that role-playing games are not appropriate for obsessive or alienated kids, because they may experience negative consequences. The risk is that such self-styled games may magnify these youths' problems, triggering a fixation on them. Additionally, some youths may blur the line between reality and the game they're playing.

The rise in the number of role-playing games started around fifteen years ago, about ten years after increasing divorce rates began unraveling the family fabric. It seems that for many kids, the absence of a stable family created the desire to pretend to be someone else in an effort to escape from their problems at home.

One extreme example of video games promoting violent and bigoted imaginative thoughts surfaced in 1990 in Austria and Germany. These video games—such as *Aryan Test* and *KZ Manager* (KZ stands for concentration camp)—extolled the virtue of being a Nazi, extracting gold teeth from and gassing prisoners. In one Austrian city, 39 percent of the students polled knew about these games and 22 percent had come in direct contact with them.[1] In the United States, video games like this haven't taken hold, although games with occult and violent themes that fuel kids' fantasies are common. On *60 Minutes,* one *eight-year-old* member of a Los Angeles gang compared video games to killing a competing gang member with his AK-7 semi-automatic machine gun.

Particularly in light of current social conditions, the only role-playing games that are appropriate—if any at all—are those which promote sound moral values, positive outcomes, and positive characters. With the large number of troubled kids today, the social risk of potentially harmful games is unacceptable.

If an activity invites identification with a character that doesn't further a Judeo-Christian moral view, then another activity that does should takes its place. If a video game, for example, featured characters who through occult powers do good acts whom youths wanted to emulate, this would be unacceptable. Even if a character seems to do good, more important for a child's imagination is the route by which that "good" is accomplished.

PROMOTING POSITIVE ROLE MODELS

The concept of promoting positive role models also applies to real people in public life—whether in sports, entertainment, politics, and so on.

When you notice that your child is beginning to identify with a famous person, do some checking to see if there is a strong moral tone in that person's life.

This brings up the distinction between *talent* and *character*—the second doesn't automatically follow the first. There aren't many public figures who model both. Look for those who are talented as well as moral in their approach to life. Then talk to your child about why he wants to be like that person. If his desire is simply to be talented like that person, point out that being talented is a good thing—but more important are the character and beliefs behind the person.

When kids have identified with someone who is not a positive role model, encourage them to find another. Here, the lesson distinguishing illusion from reality would be a good one to review, raising the question: Is this person all that he or she appears to be?

For example, one of my sons wants to be a performing magician— at least while he's in school. When we see a magician on television, we first discuss the magician's talent and if there is any technique my son should learn. Then he will usually ask me, "Dad, is he a good person?" If I know that the person is—such as my good friend André Kole, one of the world's premiere inventors of magicians' illusions— I'll tell him. Then my son knows that it's okay not only to like the magician's talent but also to like him personally, and that it's probably okay to be around him if he ever meets the magician.

If the magician is not a moral person, my son won't even inquire about meeting him. He'll just observe the magician's talent and take in what he can from a distance. Fortunately, our kids have found that occasional person who is talented and morally sound.

A good friend of ours is a professional baseball player. My boys each have a bat he has used in a game. They avidly follow him in the daily box scores and watch him whenever he's on a televised game. What the boys appreciate most about our friend is that he is a Christian man who maintains a moderate lifestyle, even though he earns over $750,000 a year. A veteran of several years, it was only this past year that he splurged and bought an old Corvette and fixed it up. Before that, he drove an older-model Toyota. My boys took note of this when we went to his well-appointed, but certainly non-extravagant, home. But even more than his modest lifestyle, what really impressed my boys was how our friend carried himself on the field in one tense inning.

In 1990, his team made it to the playoffs, and the opposing team was brutally dominating. We were all riveted to the set as we saw our friend's team fight for a chance to play in the World Series. As we watched, we all had the feeling that our friend, an excellent hitter, would have to bat in a crucial situation. And he did.

It was the top of the ninth, and his team was down by two runs. There were two men on base, and our friend came up to bat. The boys tensed up and shouted encouragements at the TV set in front of them, as if somehow their exhortations could reach him. But on this day, the other team's pitcher was unstoppable. With over fifty thousand opposing fans screaming at our friend to strike out, the pitcher blew a fast ball by him. He struck out. The game was over. His team wouldn't make the World Series.

Our boys stayed focused on our friend, a fierce competitor, to see how he would react. He didn't curse or throw his bat or helmet, as other players had done earlier in the game. He simply grimaced and walked back to the dugout. One son said, "Dad, he's a good sport." And the other added, "Yea, and that's more important."

To my sons, our friend is a hero because of who he is on the inside, not because of his talent or how he performed in a particular situation.

It's okay for kids to fantasize that they will one day develop a talent like a great sports hero, singer, artist, teacher, or scientist. But more importantly, kids need to be encouraged to question who the person is behind the talent. Today, it's easy to be fooled by cleverly edited media reports and video releases. However, if discussions of talent and character are a regular part of family life, role models can be a healthy source of inspiration in kids' lives.

HOW TO SAY NO: OFFER AN ALTERNATIVE

It isn't a certainty that every child will be harmed by participating in a negative role-playing game or watching a cartoon with a subtle occult theme. So how do we explain saying *no* when a child justifiably objects, "but it hasn't hurt me," or "my other friends don't seem to be hurt by it"?

First, *parents must clearly articulate for their children what is objectionable.* Does the activity stimulate excessive fear? Does it encourage an obsessive desire for power? Does it promote identification with a negative role model whose morals are contrary to Scripture's teachings? *It is up to parents to be certain that there is no doubt about what is objectionable.* As child psychologists often point out, kids do like to be given limiting parameters, even when they complain. It shows that someone cares.

Second, *parents should explain that even if the activity hasn't visibly harmed anyone, participating in it may harm someone else.* I have interviewed students, for example, who have played D&D with no apparent ill effects. These same students were in agreement that it could negatively impact their friends who were looking for an escape from problems at home.

Third, *parents should put the focus on other activities that are healthy and reinforce good values.* There is so much available today that appeals positively to young people's imagination that no youth should be left wanting.

SUMMARY

We all have the ability to imagine and create, and it's healthy to nurture a child's imagination and fantasies in positive directions. While following the three basic rules, be certain to emphasize the positive with your child. Kids who are simply bombarded with what they shouldn't do, and are not given a healthy assortment of positive alternatives, will often become inordinately rebellious when they grow older.

For parents, the chief task is not only to monitor with sensitivity what kids are taking in, but also to be attuned to their desires and aspirations. This can occur only with regular and open communication.

CHAPTER SIX
Tricks or Powers?

◆

Something about claims of supernatural or paranormal powers unearths issues at the essence of who we are and what we aren't. And these claims can be seductive for kids, appealing directly to their active imaginations. Kids may want power to stop someone from hurting them, to feel special, or just for fun—such as the power to fly.

The desire for powers is particularly acute when the social fabric is coming apart. Feelings of powerlessness in the face of what is painful or threatening—whether from an internal or external source—increase the likelihood of seeking powers. This is the case in Western culture today. I have observed kids in the United States and Europe destructively seeking supernatural or paranormal powers to overpower, mask, or act as a distraction from what they perceive to be threatening. And, as is to be expected, there are those who want to exploit that pain and offer their own brand of powers as the antidote.

In this chapter we will take a quick tour through various supernatural and paranormal power claims that are pitched at kids. In a later chapter we'll look at how these claims of power relate to the cults and the occult. (For additional perspective, see *Powers: Testing the Psychic and Supernatural* and *Tricks or Powers?* in the appendix.)

PSYCHIC POWERS OR MIND GAMES?

For most of this century, scientists have conducted experiments to determine if the human brain has the ability to predict the future, read someone's mind, move an object without touching it, and other alleged mind powers. The term *extrasensory perception* (ESP) was coined by one such researcher, Dr. J. B. Rhine, to refer to these hypothetical powers. Another term used to express these alleged *mind* powers is the word *psychic,* which should not be confused with the word *supernatural.* Psychic implies a *human* ability, while supernatural implies a power from an *external* source, such as God.

However, as far as science has been able to determine, these *brain* powers do not exist. Although tens of millions of dollars have been spent on such research, no one anywhere in the world has ever been discovered to possess these abilities.

For over twenty years, I have investigated claims made by psychics, fortune tellers, psychic detectives (who claim they can solve crimes), psychic surgeons (who claim power to operate on people with only their hands, remove tumors, and instantly seal incisions), and many others. Many of these activities have been dumped into what is popularly called the New Age Movement (see chapter 16 for more on this subject). I receive weekly calls to my office about these types of persons espousing mental powers, and not one has ever proved genuine. These reports, however, have always turned out to be a fabrication, an exaggeration, an instance of self-delusion, or an outright fake.

When I started to investigate these individuals, I didn't know if our brains possesssed such powers or not. It didn't matter to me one way or the other. I do believe in supernatural power, which we'll get to in a minute, but brain powers? I just didn't know.

With the passage of time, I have become convinced that we were never created with such mental powers. I've come to this conclusion not because I wanted to disprove their existence, but rather because to my knowledge no one anywhere in the world has been able to demonstrate them. If such a person surfaces, I will report it.

Why is this issue so important for kids? Because TV shows, newspapers, magazines, and even kids' publications such as the *Weekly Reader* regularly feature stories about people who make these claims, and kids believe them to be true.

In 1981, James Hydrick, who was allegedly the world's leading psychic, snared many kids into following him with his claims of powers. As referenced in chapter 1, I produced a television special about him, *Psychic Confession,* which aired in 1983. In it I exposed how he used trickery to deceive millions on national television. Hydrick confessed on camera to his deceptions as well as what he did in people's minds to deceive them, enabling him to form a cult-like following. Currently, Hydrick is serving a prison sentence for several counts of child molestation.

I have found that a common denominator with many of these "psychics," including Hydrick, is sexual abuse. Virtually every fraudulent female psychic I have interviewed, for example, was sexually molested by her father. And nearly every fake male faith healer I have investigated who has lived during the past fifty years had either an overly oppressive father or no relationship at all with his father. It seems that their motive for faking power is rooted, in part, in a desire to protect themselves—obtaining power over their pain—and to feel important in the eyes of others.

I don't necessarily advise detailing the sexual abuse factor to your child, but I do recommend that you first point out that scientists have never found anyone who has these *mental* powers. Second, without exception, whenever a report has surfaced that a scientist has discovered someone who does have these powers, within a short period of time the claim is proven to be a mistaken one—and almost always because of trickery.

Kids must be taught to ask, "Has this person been investigated by someone who knows how to check out the facts? Is this an illusion, or is it real?" In this context, a scientist is no match for a clever and corrupt trickster, as history has repeatedly demonstrated. One such trickster is Uri Geller, who claims that he can bend metal just by lightly stroking it with his finger. Even though his trickery has been exposed, famous persons such as journalist Barbara Walters and Senator Claiborne Pell of Rhode Island, head of the Senate Foreign Relations Committee, have been fooled by him. Senator Pell even took Geller to nuclear arms negotiations in Geneva during the early 1980s to beam positive thoughts to Yuli Voronstov, the Soviet arms negotiator!

The lesson is clear: If adults can be fooled, so can kids. However, when kids are taught that no one has these powers and that we must check out the facts, their vulnerability to these people plummets.

THE QUESTION OF SATANIC POWERS

Because I'm a journalist with expertise in exposing those who make fraudulent power claims, I am regularly asked by those who do and don't believe in God: "Do you believe that Satan exists, and if so, do you believe that he has supernatural powers?" This question is asked because of media stories and the recent development of the teen satanism trend, detailed in chapter 16. Although much could be discussed about this question, you may find the following helpful toward developing a non-fear-driven perspective.

First, I do believe that Satan exists. Second, I believe that he has supernatural powers. As a journalist, I can't prove that what I believe is true in the same way that I can prove someone is a fake by using videotaped footage. My thoughts about this are based on cases I have investigated and on studies of Scripture.

In the book of Job we find that Satan, *after* asking God for permission, was able to inflict disease upon Job. Additionally, in the book of Revelation is predicted the rise of a false prophet who will work with the Antichrist and even call down fire from heaven:

> He exercised all the authority of the first beast [the Antichrist] on his behalf, and made the earth and its inhabitants worship the first beast, whose fatal wound was healed. And he performed great and miraculous signs, even causing fire to come down from heaven to earth in full view of men. Because of the signs he was given power to do on behalf of the first beast, he deceived the inhabitants of the earth. (Revelation 13:12-14)

Throughout Jesus' ministry, the Scriptures state that demons had the ability to inhabit people—what is called possession or demonization—and manipulated their behavior and that Jesus had power over these demons. For Christians, it is accepted by faith that the above accounts are true and that there are real supernatural demonic powers. But how often do these powers manifest themselves today, and what effect can Satan have on people through his powers?

A key to answering these questions lies in Jesus' description of Satan in John 8:44.

> He was a murderer from the beginning, not holding to the truth, for there is no truth in him. When he lies, he speaks his native language, for he is a liar and the father of lies.

Most people think of Satan's first act of deception as tricking Eve into eating the forbidden fruit in the Garden of Eden. Not so. According to the Scriptures, it was his *third* act of deception. His first was conning himself into believing he could be like God. His second act was seducing a third of the angels into following him. In all three cases he used lies to deceive.

In over twenty years of investigating reports of supernatural demonstrations of Satan's power, such as levitation, I have yet to find even one case that could be verified. This doesn't mean that Satan doesn't have powers, but I believe that for whatever reason, God has put a cap on Satan's ability to use his supernatural powers.

I'm not saying it isn't possible for Satan to manifest his powers, but it doesn't seem to be common in the United States or in Western culture. If this weren't the case, I would find numerous examples because of the number of calls my office receives. Regarding possession, I do believe that it occurs, but it is very rare; in twenty years, I have seen only two actual cases.

What this means for parents is that they shouldn't worry that Satan is going to use supernatural power over their kids to control their behavior and make them do strange things such as levitating. Although I believe possession occurs infrequently today, I don't believe it's something you should fear for your child. Even in teen satanic groups I have investigated, possession or manifestations of supernatural power are not at all common.

From the Bible, we know that Satan is a liar. It seems he would rather deceive with a lie than a power, because through a lie he can remain concealed. If he were scaring the wits out of people with his supernatural powers, he would drive them toward God. Also, the passage in Job suggests that he can't randomly use his powers: he must receive permission to do so.

I would advise any parent who believes that they have encountered an actual manifestation of satanic power to use the utmost restraint before taking action. I have observed a number of youths who were needlessly traumatized by an "exorcist" trying to cast out demons.

Dr. Paul Meier, a noted psychiatrist who believes in the existence of Satan, warns that many kids go through developmental episodes in which they become obsessed with sexual thoughts, compulsively lie, and so on, but this doesn't mean that they are possessed. Problems at school, a recurring nightmare, or just plain rebelliousness, common in most kids, should be considered first. He recommends that if parents are uncertain about their child's condition, they consult a qualified mental health care professional as well as a spiritually discerning pastor or lay worker who has a proven track record in working with youths.

But what of power claims involving *God's* power?

SEEK SERVICE, NOT POWER

In the Bible, accounts of God's supernatural powers abound: Moses watching the Red Sea split after he stretched his rod over it; Peter walking on water to Jesus; and Jesus Himself healing the sick. When we teach kids about the miraculous nature of God, however, the emphasis should be on how we *serve* a miraculous God, not that we ourselves should aspire to have the same powers.

This doesn't mean that we can't teach how God helps us when human help fails. Any Christian who has been faithful for some years can testify to His intervention. But in our hurting culture, *it's a terrible disservice to teach kids that we can do something to trigger God to act supernaturally.* This is how many aberrant movements have sprung up in Christendom through the ages, as misguided people have sought some formula to unleash God's supernatural power.

Kids need to be taught to live a life of faith, as did Shadrach, Meshach, and Abednego in ancient Babylon. These Israelite overseers refused to obey King Nebuchadnezzar's command to worship the golden idol he had erected. Enraged, Nebuchadnezzar tried to coerce them into compliance by threatening to burn them alive. The three stood fast in their reply:

> O Nebuchadnezzar, we do not need to defend ourselves before
> you in this matter. If we are thrown into the blazing furnace, the
> God we serve is able to save us from it, and he will rescue us
> from your hand, O king. But even if he does not, we want you to
> know, O king, that we will not serve your gods or worship the
> image of gold you have set up. (Daniel 3:16-18)

Kids need to be taught to live by faith as did these three men. If God chooses to deliver us, fine. If He doesn't, that's fine, too. If we are afflicted by a disease and He heals, we are thankful. And if He chooses not to heal, then we will still worship Him and serve Him. Period. No preconditions.

Outside the church and inside the church, there are many who offer supernatural power to those who are hurting, when it is only God who can give such power. I believe that as we reach the end of this century—the end of the second millennium—we will see fake claims and promises of supernatural power continue to escalate dramatically. This has happened many times throughout history. There is something about the finishing of a century that increases an expectation for change; and when a culture like ours is in pain, many with reckless abandon will seek release from pain through "powers."

While kids learn biblical lessons that God can heal us and deliver us from evil, with an even greater emphasis, we must caution young people not to go chasing after those who promise powers or the ability to tap into God's power. Such a pursuit is just another form of idolatry, replacing faith in God with our own pursuit of power.

For Shadrach, Meshach, and Abednego, God would have been no less God if He hadn't saved them from the furnace. Many of the prophets, and eleven of the twelve apostles, were martyred for their faith. The Bible recounts that sometimes God acted miraculously to save His servants, and sometimes He didn't. What was constant, though, was the faith of His servants, regardless of whether supernatural powers were dispensed or not.

SUMMARY

During the next ten years, the numbers of people making power claims and the various ways in which they will promise power to those seeking it will probably rise. Kids will be affected by this trend. Since the latter half of the 1980s, and for the first time in U.S. history, a perceivable demographic of teenagers on their own (without adult leadership) have sought power from Satan in cult-like groups. There have always been a few kids who have done this throughout history, but not an identifiable and predictable demographic as we are seeing today. This unprecedented trend is the most extreme and negative expression of kids seeking supernatural powers.

What currently affects the greatest numbers of kids—and adults— are claims of mind powers. Fortunately these claims are easier to address because of the inability of psychics and others to demonstrate their many "powers." For this reason, after the 1983 airing of *Psychic Confession,* cultic groups and figures, like Hydricks, died out in the United States and Europe.

The best defense against these kinds of "power" trends is for kids to be taught to live as did the three men confronted by the inferno, with parents leading the way by setting the example—without fear or panic.

Although kids are often more vulnerable to deception than adults, they are also often more resilient to hard times. They bounce back quickly.

In my work, there is a certain risk factor that at times can be life-threatening. As a family we don't focus much time thinking about it, and neither do I act foolishly to invite harm to come my way. But like others whose professions present a certain amount of risk—such as firefighters and police—it is a part of my job.

Our family does acknowledge that my profession is what God wants me to do with my life, and so we trust in Him for protection. There have been several situations, though, in which I know that I received an additional "boost," and for His help I am thankful. But if there comes a day when His invisible hand doesn't in human terms seem to redeem the situation, we will accept that as well. We hope that we have infused in our kids the concept that belief in God should not be conditioned on His performance of supernatural miracles. We live by faith.

The offer of supernatural powers can be tempting, but more assuring for kids, and a stronger force in their lives, is a parent who loves them and purely reflects the love of Christ in their life. The power of this supernatural love provides our true security and ultimate hope.

SECTION II
THE FAMILY
FACTOR

One of the most important factors in shielding youths from harmful trends is a stable home environment. Although it is crucial that kids receive education on how deception affects us and deceptive trends that can harm them, even the most astute teaching can be undermined when family life is disrupted.

Growing up in a single-parent or in a dysfunctional home doesn't mean that kids will automatically fall prey to harmful influences or repeat the unhealthy patterns of their parents. However, when the family unit is shattered, youths are predictably more vulnerable to harm from threatening trends. Therefore, in the challenge of meeting unexpected threats, the family is the first line of defense.

This section will cover the importance of the family role, trends negatively affecting the family, how to improve parent-child communication, and teaching kids the decision-making skills necessary to develop and exercise discernment.

CHAPTER SEVEN

Family:
The First Line
of Defense

◆

News reports often quote statistics that reflect the increasing numbers of troubled kids—at-risk kids—in our society. But in general, we rarely hear any honest appraisals of the one thing that has the most powerful potential to reverse these negative trends among today's youth: *parents' relationships with each other and with their children.*

When was the last time you heard someone say, "If parents learned to get along better with each other and their kids, then many of our social problems could be successfully addressed"? Is this opinion just wishful thinking? I don't think so.

When I was reviewing studies on teenage sexuality, compiled by the Department of Health and Human Services' Center for Disease Control in Atlanta, one definitive study revealed that the most significant factors that will determine the age of the first sexual contact were: the educational background of the mother, religious affiliation, and family stability. In other words, "The lower the mother's education, the weaker the religious affiliation . . . and the less stable the family at age 14, the earlier the age at first intercourse."[1]

If this is true, and if much of the pressure on a youth to have premarital sex can be curbed within the family, then why isn't this solution loudly trumpeted? Sex education and distributing condoms in the schools get top billing, but have you ever heard a news report or a television special on teen sexuality mention the most important deterrent—the family factor? Probably not. Why? In part, *because a collective guilt complex exists throughout our culture,* fostered by millions of broken homes during the last twenty-five years.

Imagine a politician, battered by a stack of social ills on his desk, standing up and saying, "Parents, you have a moral obligation to be better spouses and parents. The family is bedrock. Look at the problems you're fostering because of your selfishness and neglect! Important decisions that can affect the family should be made *after* asking: Will this help or hurt my family?" If there were such a political pronouncement, it would most assuredly presage the end of that politician's career. The guilt felt by parents who neglect their reponsibilities would quickly translate into denial, and then into an unleashing of anger at the legislator for being "insensitive" and "shifting the blame." But this is in fact the real story when we look at our Western culture as a whole.

CHANGING FAMILIES, DEVASTATING CONSEQUENCES

In 1960, Mom and Dad lived together with their kids—in what's called the "nuclear family"—in 44 percent of the families in the United States. In 1989, this dropped to 27 percent. In 1960, only 13 percent were single-parent families. In 1989, that number had jumped to 27 percent. In 1940, there was only one divorce for every six couples married. In 1989, the rate soared to one divorce for every *two* marriages.[2]

Dr. Paul Amato, professor of sociology at the University of Nebraska and a regular reviewer of *The Journal of Marriage and the Family,* estimates that 31.7 percent of all adults in the United States are either children of divorced parents or are themselves divorced. If the current divorce rate continues into the future, 50 percent of the population will be so affected, and 50 percent of the children in the U.S. will come from divorced families.[3]

For years, many in the various counseling disciplines have down-played the severe emotional damage suffered by children from divorced families. That perspective has rapidly eroded under the pressure of hard data. Dr. Judith Wallerstein's ten-year study of sixty divorced families confirmed and quantified what many suspected: *Divorce shreds young lives, and its effects stretch long into adulthood.* Dr. Wallerstein wrote:

We were able to see clearly that we weren't dealing simply with the routine angst of young people going through transition but rather that, for most of them, divorce was the single most important cause of enduring pain and anomie in their lives.[4]

In another study, one woman said in an interview:

You accept as an article of faith that your parents will stay together until they die . . . and then they pull the rug out from under you and you want to scream out and ask, "How can you break the very rules you yourselves wrote?"[5]

Clinical psychologist Dr. Diane Medved had prepared to write a book on how to evaluate a decision to enter into a divorce, but scuttled her well-planned project after evaluating the statistics and her personal anecdotes. Instead she wrote another book, *The Case Against Divorce*, in which she explained:

I had to face the fact that writing a "morally neutral" book showing divorce to be just another option—a life choice no better or worse than staying married—would be irreparably damaging to the audience I wanted to help.[6]

Is the disintegration of the family damaging to our social fabric? Law enforcement and mental health care experts think so. The National Center of Health Statistics recorded that between 1983 and 1987 alone, juveniles arrested for murder soared 22.2 percent. This means that there's more criminal activity out there to ensnare kids. And for kids who don't harm others, there is another deadly trend born of despair: suicide.

In 1990, *more than one out of every four teens contemplated suicide,* according to the 1991 Centers for Disease Control survey of high school students. And one in twelve—8 percent—actually attempted it. Sixteen percent said they had made a specific plan. *Since 1950, suicide rates per capita have quadrupled.* And one-third of all homosexual and bisexual male teenagers have attempted suicide at least once, according to a 1991 year-long study by the University of Minnesota and the University of Washington.

Where are Mom and Dad?

Half of all mothers with children under a year old now work, yet a 1991 Roper poll showed that 48 percent of children ages eight to seventeen want Mom to stay home from work.[7] Another study claimed that nearly *half* of all divorced fathers hadn't seen their kids in more than a year.[8] And when you take all kids into consideration, 12 percent, or 7.5 million young people, are considered to have mental disorders.[9]

With all this acknowledged damage, why is it surprising that there are so many traps waiting to snare youths by taking advantage of their pain and apprehension? Most juvenile officers will tell you that repeat offenders tend to come from troubled homes. When I'm trying to find the reason a youth has become involved in an occult group that is committing crimes, the first ones I want to interview are the parents.

This doesn't mean that every case of destructive youth activity is the result of absent or negligent parents. There are some kids who just choose to do wrong, beyond the ordinary range of adolescent rebellion. And there are loving parents who aren't responsible for their present or former spouse's irresponsible behavior. When you take our culture as a whole, however, there is no question that parents are failing in their most important responsibilities in the home.

QUALITY AND QUANTITY TIME

One area of misunderstanding and failure on the part of many parents is the lack of time spent with their kids. We expect that some hardened businessmen will chase the buck, leaving their families chasing after them. But this neglect occurs even in Christian ministries. Here the pursuit is not material gain but ministry goals to reach greater numbers of people. Consider what happened to a friend I once had, whom I'll call Bob.

Bob worked for a Christian ministry that tried to help families. His job responsibility was setting up conferences, and he traveled three out of four weeks every month. I was troubled by the large spans of time he spent away from his family, so I asked him if he shouldn't travel less.

"Well," Bob replied, "God has given Sherry a very special capacity to handle my situation as well as the kids." I was skeptical, and I raised the issue a couple more times with him and his wife. They both said that they were doing okay.

Within a few years, however, the dam broke. Sherry couldn't adapt to shifting from the lead role when Bob was on the road to a supportive role when he was home. They began to drift apart simply because they hadn't taken the time to get to know each other; and the kids drifted away from their absentee father.

Eventually, Sherry couldn't take it any longer. She went to Bob's boss and pleaded for him to take Bob off the road. His boss wouldn't listen. Bob wouldn't listen. Within a year they were divorced.

Despondent, Bob eventually lost his job. The ministry wasn't sensitive to the needs of his family. The mission to get the job done—and many other families were helped—had been the most important goal. He continued to decline in spirit as he moved from one job to another.

Sensing the need to confront my friend, I told him I thought he was suicidal and offered to assist him in getting help. He refused. The denial he had practiced for years on the road had become his only partner. Tragically, he was found dead in his apartment because he wouldn't take medication for a health condition he'd had since childhood. He was a kind person, and I miss him, but not nearly as much as his wife and kids do.

A tragic irony in this story is that a family ministry bought into the idea that the "cause" was more important than the staff's own families.

In my interviews, single parents who have gone through the throes of divorce often emphatically state that in traditional—i.e., nuclear—families, mothers shouldn't work while the kids are at home, and fathers should make business decisions only after they have considered the impact on the family.

Debbie Blair, who was divorced and remarried, says that the first fifteen minutes after school are crucial. "That's when the kids are bubbling over about what happened that day. After fifteen minutes, they either start processing it all themselves or simply shelve it." Kids need Mom there for them. My wife has a small business, but she didn't start it until our youngest entered first grade. She schedules her work so that she is home 95 percent of the time when the kids come through the door.

Remember the statistic I cited earlier on the effect of a mother's education level on her teen's sexual activity? Mom needs to give time to her kids so that her influence can help shape their lives.

But this also applies to fathers. Troubled over my friend Bob's death as well as my own increasing career opportunities that could take me away from my family, I sought an older friend who was head of data processing for I.B.M. in the Middle East and Europe. His marriage was thriving and his kids were well-adjusted. "How do you do it?" was my simple question.

"I put my family first," he responded.

"I know that, but *how* do you do it?" I repeated.

"I just told you—I put my family first," he replied. "If I was faced with a job transfer that would have disrupted our kids or with responsibilities that would take me away from home more than was appropriate, then I took action. I either found another way to get the job done, or another person who wouldn't be negatively impacted taking that responsibility. I had predetermined that I was fully prepared to leave I.B.M. if there was ever a threat to my time with my family."

His stake-in-the-ground commitment was the reassurance that I needed to forego career opportunities that would have taken me away from my family.

A few times a year my work requires me to travel for one or two weeks at a time. When this occurs, I spend additional time with the family before and after each trip. I even take one of the kids with me on at least a couple of short trips every year. I want my kids to know that I will be there when they need me.

In the mid-seventies, when I was just getting my career off the ground, Sandy, my wife, worked as a nurse. After our first child, Carrie, was born, Sandy continued to work for three years. We coordinated our schedules so that one of us was always at home with Carrie. It was a financial sacrifice, but our priority was Carrie—not our standard of living.

Don't believe the lie that quality time is more important than quantity time. Both are important. Lee Dogoloff, the executive director for the American Council for Drug Education, says that "quality time is a yuppie invention."[10]

Quantity time doesn't mean hours in front of the television. Turn it off. Do things together. Take time to ask the kids how their day went. Ask two or three times in different ways, because most kids don't unlock the interesting stuff until they've been prodded a little. That's just how they think. Try it: How did it go today? Anything exciting happen? You look a little down. What all's going on? You want to talk a bit? You look like you're feeling good—what happened after school?

Don't forfeit these moments. They're opportunities that will soon be lost forever—opportunities to know who your child is and what he or she is experiencing. If you have to change jobs to keep your family number one, do it. *In the long run, nothing will be more important to you and your family.* It's okay to live in a less expensive home, drive a ten-year-old car, and forego the latest-name labels. When they're older, kids who are cared for won't remember this or regret the lack of an extra bathroom. What gives kids reassurance and warm memories are the times spent with those they love, not things they used to own and have discarded.

"Time. The four-letter word identified second only to love as a cornerstone of family cohesiveness."[11] Cherish it, and so will your kids.

FOR SINGLE PARENTS

If you are divorced, whether single or remarried, you may find it difficult to accept what a number of surveys today clearly indicate: ruptured families increase risk to kids. In support of this opinion, most *divorced* parents I've interviewed during the past few years agree that this consequence is indeed true. Denying this fact will only delay awareness and obstruct sensitivity to these kids, passing on the problem to future generations.

One single parent told me, "Look, it isn't my kids' fault that they're living without one parent. For me and my former wife, our responsibility is to make raising our kids our number-one priority. My own personal comfort is secondary. Period."

Single parents also repeatedly tell me: We must make every effort possible for our kids to go home to *somebody*—either in their own home or someone else's. Although most single parents work, a neighbor, relative, another single parent, or someone from church are all options to greet kids when they come "home" from school. When this isn't possible, to a person each single parent with well-adjusted kids said something like: "Don't let the kids become married to the TV." Unsupervised, television is not something that can be trusted to help shape young minds.

According to these parents, most of the time single parents have after work and household duties should be spent with their kids. One single mother said that she set aside one night a week for herself, which she needed, but the rest were for her children. She said that for her kids, this was her expected act of love. Daycare centers, the government, and schools aren't parents and should be relied on for assistance only as a last resort. Only *parents* are parents. What's important is that they make an intense effort to spend quality time with their child, and that the child senses the parent's commitment.

Fathers separated from their families need to see their kids—often. Kids need their fathers, unless they're abusive. Studies show that kids are more stable when an abusive father is *not* in the home than when he is present. This is not to encourage divorce, but it indicates that separation might be helpful to a child while a father is receiving counseling and is working to correct his abusive behavior. If a former wife angrily makes visits disruptive or punishes kids for seeing their father, fathers should see their kids as much as possible and work to find other creative ways to stay in touch—to let their kids know that they love and care for them.

Lisa, a single mother, raised her three kids from ages five to nine in Iowa City. She worked a full-time job while studying for her bachelor's degree in management and human relations. Now her kids are ages twenty to twenty-four. They are all well-adjusted, and none did drugs.

"I was frazzled, but the kids never seem to remember the burden of my hassle when we talk about our days in Iowa City," she recalls. "There were three things I did that I think were responsible for their well-being.

"First, we found a local church and became active. I didn't have a lot of money, so we took advantage of their activities. The church also helped reinforce good moral values.

"Second, I gave them each individual attention and stayed tuned into what they were experiencing and feeling. When they came home from school, they went to a neighbor's house. Then I came home, prepared dinner, and spent time with each of my kids individually. I also talked with them before we went to bed. We not only talked openly, we were also real. We never skirted important issues.

"Also, every month I found a special activity for each of my kids that only they and Mom would do together. Not only was it fun, but it gave us more opportunities to communicate. I didn't want all of my kids lumped together all the time when we talked. Yes, it was hard finding sitters or someone to keep the other kids, but it was worth the frantic running around that was sometimes required.

"And third, I always let my kids know that I loved them—both by my actions and by telling them so. Too many parents don't verbalize their love along with hugs and acts that show they love their kids."

SECRETS OF THE BEST FAMILIES

During the past several years I've read hundreds of clippings and books and interviewed as many kids and parents related to different cases I was researching. One book, though, stood out from them all: *Back to the Family* by Dr. Ray Guarendi. This book is the cumulative effort of the

Children's Hospital of Akron, Ohio, and the National-State Teachers of the Year Organization.

The hospital wanted to identify the best traits of families where the parenting reflected the "highest commitment to family life and whose children collectively showed strength of character." To assist, the hospital asked one hundred of America's top teachers to recommend families from students they'd taught. The hospital correctly expected that teachers, who spend more time with kids than anyone else outside the home, would be the best qualified to find the finest families for the survey. Asking for assistance by the Teachers of the Year ensured only the finest nominations of family candidates.[12]

Many of the teachers had known the nominated families over a period of years, having taught more than one child from the same family. After careful screening, each family member was interviewed, both individually and collectively.

The families were from many socioeconomic backgrounds and stations in life. In one family, both father and son were learning-disabled. Another family was led by a single mother who raised a son and a seriously handicapped daughter. Another couple had a son at M.I.T.

One of the couples was Jay and Mary Willett of Phoenix, Arizona. Jay briefly played professional football and is now an artist and high-school teacher. Mary is employed part-time as a substitute teacher. How much the Willetts loved their child-rearing years was evident during the interviews.

They proudly spoke of their two children: Jason, age nineteen, who is in pre-law at the University of Arizona; and Meisha, age twenty-one, an honor student and college sophomore class president, and "very wholesome," according to her dad. The Willetts feel a special gratitude for their children, because each nearly died in their young lives. At age eighteen months, Jason needed an emergency tracheotomy to breathe, and at age ten, Meisha survived open-heart surgery.

Throughout, the Willetts' interview was marked by tears and intense emotion. At one point Jay's voice began to tremble, and soon he was sobbing. Mary, too, began to cry. After regaining his composure, Jay said, "Forgive me—as you see, I'm a very emotional person. When you asked me what are my fond memories of my children, it suddenly hit me that I could no longer hold and protect my son and daughter in my strong arms. The days of childhood are gone."[13]

Taken together, these families all had similar enduring qualities that were far more important than material gains or status. Of the 387 children in these 100 families, "none have ever been in serious trouble with the law. . . . None have been suspended from school. None have an alcohol problem. . . . This unblemished record is even more impressive considering the reality that some kids by their nature are just hell-bent on learning about life the hard way, no matter how good their parents are."[14] How many of us parents wouldn't give all we possess to make such a claim when watching our last child take off on his or her own—for better or for worse?

What made these hall-of-fame families unique? Here are some of the common qualities they shared:

◆ The parents showed their kids unconditional love, and they let each child know that they were loved, demonstrated by actions, words, and hugs.
◆ The parents had the will to discipline and teach with clarity. Contrary to what is in vogue, well-placed spanks on the rear for youngsters were often used.

(In our family, spankings ended about the time the kids reached age nine, depending on the child. Before the spanking, we sat down and calmly discussed why they were being punished. Then they received their licks with a thin strap or spatula on the rear or thigh as they place their hands on the dresser, so that another part of their body wouldn't be hurt if they jerked away. We carefully spanked only with a safe inanimate object—because hands are for loving. After a spanking, we would sit on the bed, hold them, pray with them, and reassure them that we loved them and that they were forgiven. Then we asked them if there was anything they wanted to talk about. Sometimes a good cry helped to bring out something completely unrelated to their punishment that they wanted to talk about.)

◆ A youth's self-esteem was carefully nurtured as he or she was taught absolute standards of right and wrong that didn't change on a whim.
◆ Nearly 90 percent of the families held that their spiritual beliefs were paramount. One family said, "Our strong religious background is the center of our family, because if you're a Christian and you trust in God, then everything else will fall into place. Our parents really believe that God is the one that is going to see us through and that we should seek throughout

our lives to trust God and to find out what God really wants us to do."[15]

Another family commented, "We always have our morning devotional . . . we have been taught to place all of our worries in the hands of the Lord and to remember that everything has a purpose—'Thy will be done.' "[16]

◆ Quantity and quality time were both important.

◆ Parents expected the "personal best" from each child, not the parent's arbitrary standard of perfection.

◆ Open channels of communication were a primary focus, particularly when kids started going through their "changes."

None of the parents laid claim to being perfect; in fact, just the opposite was true. All readily admitted their shortcomings—an indication of honesty and confidence that they could still be good parents. And not one claimed to have a magical or God-given secret or talent for "sizing up children and immediately finding the psychological 'cure' for a troubling situation."[17] They also fended off unasked-for advice, instead choosing to seek out other parents who had tackled child-rearing problems successfully, in order to fine-tune their own child-rearing skills.

I cannot recommend this extraordinary book strongly enough. It's loaded with candid insights from parents themselves. I find it reassuring that they all share solid common sense—and recent studies show that these values and approaches are time-tested solutions that will reduce a youth's vulnerability to deception from harmful trends. While this book isn't specifically about child-rearing and development, I hope the insights from it will reassure you that *how you raise your child is your best first line of defense against deceptive trends.*

SUMMARY

It is a ruinous lie that parents don't have to stay married, or stay married happily, in order to protect their children. While some kids might escape unscathed, most don't—as proven by statistics, and more importantly, the individual kids themselves.

Keeping your family healthy and intact by investing the time and energy to make child-rearing your foremost responsibility will do more to protect your child than any other factor.

Single parents, or those who are divorced and remarried, must make whatever sacrifices are necessary to compensate for the deficit most kids experience as a result of divorce. The intolerably high divorce and dysfunction rates in families makes parenting even more critical now than ever because more at-risk kids knowingly or unknowingly pull down other kids from healthy families.

The good news is that bedrock concepts of parenting, which have been dismissed as outdated by pop psychologists, do build and sustain families—even during our tumultuous times. As one friend of mine optimistically put it, "We don't have to raise our kids properly . . . we *get* to. *It's our privilege.*"

Finally, 90 percent of the families interviewed in *Back to the Family* recognized the critical need for spiritual values in the home. This perspective is even taking hold in the mental health care profession. At the American Psychological Association's 1991 meeting, numerous papers were submitted touting the importance of "religious" beliefs to resist temptation, overcome drug addictions, and aid in therapy. One such study of more than twenty-five hundred Stanford University students found that 57 percent of the students who embraced the following statement were able to resist the temptation of cheating: "I believe in a God, creator of the universe, who knows my innermost thoughts and to whom one day I will be held accountable."[18] It is reassuring to see this recognition of bedrock beliefs from a profession that doubled its number of family therapists during the last ten years.

In the next chapter we'll look at how to teach a child to make good decisions—an important step toward discernment.

CHAPTER EIGHT

Decision-Making:
The Path to Discernment

◆

Learning how to make decisions is a pathway to discernment. Kids need a clear and practical framework for making decisions when their parents aren't there to tell them what is right and what isn't. In this chapter we'll examine the relationship between commandments, principles, and allowing kids the freedom to make their own decisions.

The guidelines we'll explore are not themselves foolproof. The inevitable presence of human error means we'll all make bad decisions at one time or another. But a solid framework can reduce the chances that kids will yield to the pressure of the moment or fail to recognize that they're being deceived.

COMMANDMENTS—SET IN CONCRETE

Commandments are the elementary building blocks for restraining evil, promoting the good, and providing the solid moral foundation for decision-making. They don't change. Stealing and murder, for example, are forbidden—not to be contested. These building blocks lay our foundation—in concrete. As journalist Ted Koppel and others have noted, God called His law the Ten Commandments, not the Ten Suggestions.

Most kids have at least heard of the Ten Commandments, even if they can't recite them. These unchanging divine laws provide clear moral guidance. The Ten Commandments are different from commands (small "c")—the rules and laws we establish in our families, organizations, and governments—in that manmade rules and laws can change while the Ten Commandments don't. Simple family rules might include: curfews, telling the truth, unacceptability of foul language, etc.

The Ten Commandments and morally sound rules and laws are good for kids because they clearly draw the line between right and wrong, are a deterrent to unacceptable behavior, and provide a sense of security by demarcating boundaries. When kids transgress against them, discipline can be an effective teaching tool.

In the New Testament, the Ten Commandments are put in an important context, recorded in Jesus' answer when questioned about which of the commandments was most important:

> "The most important one," answered Jesus, "is this: 'Hear, O Israel, the Lord our God, the Lord is one. Love the Lord your God with all your heart and with all your soul and with all your mind and with all your strength.' The second is this: 'Love your neighbor as yourself.' There is no commandment greater than these." (Mark 12:29-31)

The commandment that we aren't supposed to steal is far easier for youths to grasp and live out than Jesus' commandment, which shapes the very essence of who we are. Making good decisions where the boundaries aren't as clearly and decisively drawn—especially related to issues of character—is where most of us have difficulty; and this is where applying *principles* with discernment can be most helpful.

PRINCIPLES—"TRUTH GUIDES" FOR DECISION-MAKING

Principles are not as precise as commandments. They're more like ideas than specific applications, but they're just as fundamental for building character and making good decisions. The difference between principles and commandments should be made clear to youths: commandments are absolutes that must be obeyed; principles are "truth guides" that we must consider when making decisions. While we are to be *firm* in maintaining a principle, we must be *flexible* about our method for applying it.

As already suggested, the book of Proverbs in the Bible is one of the finest sources for sound principles we have. Here are some examples from Proverbs: When pride comes, then comes disgrace, but with humility comes wisdom (11:2); he who brings trouble on his family will inherit only wind (11:29); hard work brings a profit, but mere talk leads only to poverty (14:23); a man of knowledge uses words with restraint, and a man of understanding is even-tempered (17:27). Here are two additional examples from the Bible: "I will set before my eyes no vile thing" (Psalm 101:3); "Watch out that no one deceives you" (Mark 13:5).

Now let's set up a possible scenario. The psalms passage clearly tells us to avoid whatever is corrupt or impure. Soft-porn movies would clearly fit this category. But what about a movie based on the Holocaust, which features a carefully and sensitively crafted scene of nude people entering a gas chamber? Both movies have nudity: but one is created to exploit, while the other is intended to communicate in a realistic way the horror of an historical event. It is unlikely that someone who watches the latter will be sexually tempted.

When Proverbs counsels us to "preserve sound judgment and discernment" (3:21), it means that we are to judge and discern the difference between good and evil, between right and wrong, between what is acceptable and what is best. We are to discern whether our own behavior, as well as others', is or isn't acceptable. It is *not* our responsibility, however, to judge the innermost part of a person's heart; this is left for God. We are to hold only the conduct of others to account.

The apostle Paul addressed this issue when he provided guidelines for preventing excessive or abusive argumentation in cases of honest disagreement: "Accept him whose faith is weak without passing judgment on disputable matters" (Romans 14:1). For example:

> One man considers one day more sacred than another; another man considers every day alike. Each one should be fully convinced in his own mind. He who regards one day as special, does so to the Lord. (verses 5-6)

Paul gives a principle here that each person must follow by making his or her own decision. One person might consider Sunday morning sacred as a time for worship. But a nurse or utility worker, who is required to work Sunday mornings in order to be of service to others—the nurse for medical emergencies; the utility worker to keep a power plant operating, which allows the church to conduct services—might set apart Sunday evening as sacred. In this example, it is acceptable that each person makes a different decision regarding time set aside for worship.

At a seminar I conducted on ethics for a group of internal auditors, I was asked, "You've talked about the need to be consistent when we apply our industry's code of ethics, but which moral and ethical code do you personally subscribe to?" I said mine was the Judeo-Christian moral and ethical perspective communicated in Scriptures.

Apart from my spiritual convictions, as a journalist I can honestly say that the Judeo-Christian ethic is the best one in practical application. For this reason I have used it as the basis for this chapter. However, when God gave His law to humanity, he didn't engrave it on skyscraper-tall monolithic stone monuments to be viewed for all time. He knew that we would probably worship the monument rather than the Giver of the law. Instead, He planted His law within us, as the Old Testament prophet Jeremiah recorded:

"I will put my law in their minds and write it on their hearts. I will be their God, and they will be my people." (31:33)

We can help kids to be honest with themselves by reminding them to ask the question, "Do I love the truth more than something I want, or more than I fear the pain?" This powerful question can cut through such obstacles as fear of rejection by friends or fear of honestly confronting a situation when making a difficult decision.

We can be encouraged by this promise: "You will seek me and find me when you seek me with all your heart" (Jeremiah 29:13). In addition to its primary meaning, this verse also implies seeking and struggling to find the truth; and kids need to be encouraged and given the freedom to struggle to seek the truth.

GIVING KIDS THE FREEDOM TO DECIDE

All of us need the freedom to struggle in making decisions. This is particularly true with kids. The younger a child is, the more direct input we need to provide through teaching and admonishing. As children grow older, however, parents should loosen up on the reins and become more tuned in to listening rather than telling.

Kids need increasing freedom to struggle with decisions for themselves in order to develop character strength, because in the days ahead

Mom or Dad won't be around to help make their decisions.

But encouraging kids to make good decisions on their own doesn't require suspending or relaxing family rules or responsibilities. As Dr. James Dobson (founder of Focus on the Family and former associate clinical professor of pediatrics at the UCLA School of Medicine) points out, when children raise the question (either verbally, or through their actions) "Who's in charge?" responsible parents must always affirm that the parent is in charge. Firm teaching and stable authority provide the appropriate context in which parents can teach their children how to protect themselves, in preparation for adulthood and for their possible roles as eventual parent or protector of others.

You might find the following list of questions helpful as you and your child explore how to answer the question, "Am I making a good decision?" They can also provide helpful checkpoints when you're deciding what is and isn't acceptable for your child:

1. Does making this decision violate any commandments, rules, or laws?
2. Will it violate any scriptural principles—that is, broad biblical concepts? In other words, does this decision honor God and strengthen me, or is it an offense to others?
3. What are my responsibilities when making this decision? (For parents: What are my responsibilities in allowing my son or daughter to make this decision?) What do I have to do to carry out my decision?

It's usually in life's "gray" areas that young people most need a basic understanding of the principles taught in the Bible. They know murder is wrong, but they need discernment to decide on which movies they should see. Family Bible studies, in addition to individual study time, will undergird kids with biblical principles to support good decisions.

One hot summer's day, my sons helped me cut down some dead limbs from the twelve-foot-high bushes lining our back yard. My sons laughed at a number of tall, skinny limbs that drooped over once the dead limbs were removed.

"Boys, see how weak these limbs are?" I pointed out. "What happened is that as they grew taller, they were held up by these dead limbs. Instead of growing strong on their own, sturdy enough to withstand severe thunderstorms, they grew up puny.

"This is how we look when we don't struggle against difficult things in life," I explained. "Some people let others do everything for them and make all their decisions. Eventually, when they face something tough in life, they droop like these weak limbs.

"That's why it's actually a *good* thing when God lets us deal with tough times—so we can become strong and not weak like these limbs. The older we get, the more we have to be able to make tough decisions. And to do this, we have to know what God expects from us."

It's not easy to strike the right balance. Sometimes parents are too permissive, letting kids do whatever they want. Sometimes they're rigidly legalistic, depriving kids of the freedom necessary for growth. The former lets a child run wild; the latter props up a child, making him grow up weak. Neither position builds discernment.

What most helps kids develop the ability to make good decisions is *thoughtful and balanced nurturing*—the best safety net.

THREE STEPS TO BALANCED NURTURING

Fred Crowell, formerly head basketball coach at the University of Alaska, owns and runs Northwest Basketball Camp in Spokane, Washington. Fred—who just turned fifty—and his wife, Susie, have degrees in counseling and proudly raised two children of their own (one is now married). They have vigorously invested their lives in young people.

Each summer, twenty-five hundred youths and coaches attend Fred's camp, which has earned a reputation among coaches as the finest summer basketball camp in the Northwest. Adding to the camp's uniqueness are the evening meetings in which Fred sensitively presents Christian values, which thousands of players have accepted and now practice in their own lives.

Because of his successful track record in working with kids, Fred is often asked to speak to parents on how to teach kids to make good decisions. He breaks this into three areas: (1) teach by example, (2) clearly explain what you expect from your child, and (3) discipline your child when necessary.

"When they hear these three points, most parents lock on to discipline," Fred comments, "because discipline usually requires the least amount of time or energy expended. Taking time to set an example and teach young people exactly what is expected of them is hard work. But without the first two, discipline is weak and usually ineffective."

Let's take a closer look.

Set a Good Example

Kids are sharp. They soak up everything they see us do because we're the big people they desperately want to become. If Mom and Dad teach one thing but do another, kids are less likely to make good decisions on their own.

The next time you sit down with your child to teach him something, ask yourself, "Do I observe this in my own life?"

For example, do you screen the types of TV programs that *you* watch, to be consistent with the message you're communicating to your kids? If you tolerate gratuitous sexual themes, don't expect your child to follow your instructions about TV watching when you're gone. The not-so-subtle message a youth picks up is, "If it's okay for them, there's no reason I can't do it."

Do you tell your child not to abuse drugs—and then have one or two drinks too many? Have you ever considered abstaining from alcohol so that you're not an inadvertent stumbling block to a friend who may be a closet alcoholic? Imagine the power of your example when explaining to your child that you have chosen to abstain because too many people are closet alcoholics. Your action would far transcend a simple "no alcohol" rule for your child, and inspire in him or her a heroic concern for others.

I believe that *teaching our kids by example is one way that God silently teaches us to clean up our own act.* Desiring the best for our children, and then carrying out a commitment to put our own actions on the line, is the most powerful sermon. As parents, we ought to have a healthy dread of our children growing up to realize that Mom and Dad were phonies—teaching one thing and doing another. A good, consistent example, when reinforced in a family context, however, becomes habit-forming. It will be a catalyst to good decisions—even those made quickly under pressure.

Teach with Clarity

Setting a good example paves the way for the second step to balanced nurturing: *individual instruction.* This means taking time out with kids to explain clearly what is expected of them.

Of course, teaching responsibility can be as simple as delegating household tasks at family meetings or posting lists on the refrigerator.

But teaching discernment emphasizes *concepts* and how they apply to specific situations. This requires family meetings as well as individual time with a child, away from siblings. Individual attention says, "I care about you," and it enables parents to tailor their remarks for each child's specific needs.

In our family, when we teach important concepts we talk about examples from everyday living, review with each child how he or she has handled specific situations, and often discuss these incidents in light of biblical principles. It's an ongoing process.

If teaching doesn't come naturally for you, don't be discouraged—it doesn't come easily for most people. But if you make it your goal to love your child and teach your child *clearly,* you will prevail. Parents who take their teaching assignments seriously, ask questions of other parents about what works, and abide by scriptural principles are able to teach their children with clarity about even the most difficult issues.

The key is to *take the time to think about what your child must learn.* Create opportunities to speak with your spouse or another parent about examples and the best approaches. Talk to your child in an unhurried way, and answer his questions. Almost *nothing* will replace your investment of time—for you, spending time will help clarify what you're teaching; for your child, spending time says that you care.

Another source of excellent teaching and encouragement is an effective church youth ministry. This is why my wife and I are committed to helping in this area at our church. But as helpful as they are, church ministries should provide a *supplement,* not a *replacement,* for the time parents spend teaching their kids.

Discipline and Motivate
There's plenty of good material on disciplining kids, so I'll just touch on a few key points here.

For kids up to nine or ten, effective discipline methods include spanking, withholding of privileges, or just a good stern talking-to. For older kids, grounding is effective for serious problems. We've found that for most "minor" offenses, however, "aerobic discipline" works great. For behavior such as forgetting to do a chore or making a sassy remark, our kids do pushups or situps—usually twenty-five to fifty at a time. This accomplishes two things: (1) the kids quickly learn what is expected of them, and (2) the exercise burns off their anger or frustration when punished.

Effective discipline can help shape kids' decision-making skills by instilling in them the recognition that there are negative consequences for bad decisions. Discipline is most effective when kids are nurtured by parents who teach by example and establish clear expectations. In this context, discipline doesn't become a cause for resentment, but a demonstration of love and caring. A child raised in this kind of home will even tend to remind his parents when he needs to be disciplined for something he's done wrong. That's because he has the assurance that his parents really do love him, the discipline is best for him, and it will help him become a better person.

Fred Crowell comments, and most psychologists agree, that just as important as punishment in the process of discipline is praising good decision-making and motivating kids to want to do good. Fred suggests the following dialogue as an example of the kind of parental attitude that can motivate kids:

> *Parent:* Don't expect me to get excited about what excites you unless you're willing to get excited about some of the things that excite me.
> *Youth:* What do you mean?
> *Parent:* Well, when you come up to me on a Saturday morning and ask me to take you somewhere, how do you feel when I'm too tired? When I don't express any enthusiasm for something you want that's important to you, how do you feel?
> *Youth:* I'm disappointed.
> *Parent:* Sure you are. But I'm also disappointed when you don't show enthusiasm for doing your chores or being on time for dinner. Or you give me a look like I'm an ogre. So we'll have a lot more fun if you get excited about those things that excite me. That's only fair, right?

An important part of being a parent is *looking* for opportunities to encourage and motivate kids.

Kids need praise and encouragement. If they don't get it from parents they'll seek it elsewhere. Peer pressure is a strong influence on kids, but even stronger is the effect of caring parents who nurture their character in a balanced way. Buying material things isn't sufficient to communicate, "I'm proud of you." Kids need praise when they do make the right choice . . . when they have struggled to deal with a tough situation.

Remaining silent communicates, "What you do doesn't matter." Parental neglect or withdrawal does not give kids freedom to develop character; active caring does. Stay involved with your kids, and you'll help them develop the discernment they need for lifelong decision-making skills.

SUMMARY

These two character qualities are the least present in our Western culture: (1) discernment in decision-making; and (2) honestly being able to confront pain. Both involve making choices.

To develop discernment, kids need an unshakable base of truth from which to make their decisions. Those who customize their own moral base can be easily swayed. Embracing the Scriptures as a moral base may be unfashionable in some circles, but it will give steady guidance to kids through the challenges and difficulties of growing up.

Kids should be taught to cherish commandments and principles through personal example, lucid teaching, and, when appropriate, discipline. Additionally, as kids get older, they should be given greater freedom to make their own decisions. This freedom is essential for kids to develop into discerning adults.

SECTION III
KNOW THE STREETS

Developing skills in confronting deception and shoring up the family defenses are crucial foolproofing measures. But to be streetwise, you need to know the streets.

This section will provide you with an overview of many of the harmful activities threatening kids today. Not every trend may be prevalent in your community, but most will. The next ten chapters supply what you need to know about these activities and how to counter them with positive alternatives.

As you read each chapter, think back to the first section for relevant concepts that might be helpful to review with your kids. For example, if there's a gang threat in your neighborhood, review chapter 3, "Secrets, Lies, and the Truth," and chapter 4, "Illusion and Reality: Checking Out the Facts." Gangs are often driven by secretive behavior and the illusion of acquiring power. Checking the facts reveals that gangs don't deliver on their promises.

This kind of review will help reinforce kids' understanding of *how* to think. As you talk through these issues, don't dwell on the negative—face it honestly, but let your emphasis rest on the positive. Together, you and your family can develop a balanced and healthy perspective, without fear, on the issues of greatest importance to you and your family.

CHAPTER NINE

A Streetwise Approach to the Entertainment Media

◆

*For practical reasons, the basic ingredients of movies
are action, sex, violence, and stars.*[1]
Richard Zanuck
producer of *Driving Miss Daisy*

◆

*I think films are important, and because I think they're important,
it seems to me an act of total madness [for a filmmaker]
to create a society you don't want to live in.*[2]
David Putnam
producer of *The Mission* and *Chariots of Fire*

◆

*There's got to be a time somewhere, OK, when someone can
turn on a television program and find something that they feel
won't be offensive to them or their children.*[3]
Howard Rosenberg
TV critic for the *Los Angeles Times*

It's no longer news that grossly immoral programming is being beamed up on movie screens and into our homes. Nor is it news that kids are at risk because of it.

But it *is* news that programming with objectionable content for kids is no longer relegated to late-night hours or cable stations. Respect for children and families expressed through television and movies has virtually vanished from our culture.

One *New York Times* editorial opined: "Parents cannot possibly control television with its titanic omnipresence."[4] But despite all the negatives, television is part of the process of staying informed about the world, and entertainment in wholesome, limited doses is acceptable. It's critical, however, that kids learn discernment concerning what to watch and what to turn off.

In this chapter we'll look at what our response as parents should be in light of the moral decline in the entertainment media industry—both movies and television. Most of our attention will be directed at television, since it is a more powerful force in kids' lives than the presence of movie theaters. (In chapter 10, we'll explore how kids can stay up on what's going on in their world through the news media.)

THE DECLINE OF THE MEDIA

People often say, "The media have become too liberal," or "The news media are biased." When people say this, they don't realize that the word *media* applies to every form of mass communication, from print media (such as newspapers, magazines, and books) to visual media (such as movies, television, and videos) to news media (which broadcast stories on both television and radio and also put stories in print).

Media is a big word. We tend to use it to express the idea that someone is trying to tell—and often sell—us something through one of the above mediums. And it is usually used negatively. But regardless of which media we're talking about, there is a general consensus that the entertainment media, the subject of this chapter, are in a state of moral decline: its soul is driven by a desperate revenue generating juggernaut. And this reckless disregard for moral values and absolutes has a damning effect on kids.

Actor Hal Holbrook observed, "Show business has become so corrupt, it's one of the most disgusting forms of endeavor on earth today."[5]

Actor Mel Gibson straddles the fence. "I think there is a level of violence in films that's unacceptable," he states.[6] He also remarks that he won't let any of his six kids watch the violence-laden, R-rated movie *The Road Warrior,* in which he starred.

Prior to 1934, many movies were bawdy and featured nudity. In response to pressure from grass-roots organizations and local churches, Hollywood established a Production Code in 1934, which remained in force until 1966. By and large, during this time the industry corrected its excesses. Films with explicit sex or excessive violence, or movies that incited racial bigotry, were prohibited. Although film prints of movies with unsuitable content had been preserved, they were largely inaccessible to the average person. Now, however, with the introduction of videotaped movies, even if all producers went clean tomorrow, the repository of morally unsound videos is available to titillate people cheaply for years to come. That is, unless people say, "No!" Unfortunately, that seems unlikely.

It's a sick industry that frequently features young kids and toddlers in PG-13 and R-rated movies with overtly sexual themes and debasing language. Through these movies, industry moguls proclaim: as long as we can make a buck, kids don't matter.

One ABC television show, *American Detective* produced by Paul Stajonovich, features live footage of police work. It regularly runs long and gut-wrenching shots of kids crying for their parents who are being taken into custody. No blocking out of these innocent kids' faces to protect their privacy—just grotesque exploitation. But the heartless intrusion into kids' lives doesn't stop here.

Over the Christmas holidays in 1991, I took my kids to a clean PG movie. During one of the previews of coming attractions, which are supposed to be suitable for viewers of *any* age, the narrator loudly proclaimed, "The b---- is back." Later that month, the box-office hit was *The Hand that Rocks the Cradle,* in which the central female adult character grabs a young boy about six years old in a schoolyard and threatens, "I'm going to tear your f------ head off!" What kind of a sick director would allow such a line to be delivered to a child or allow a child to be shown in a scene like that? But the real punch line to this story was delivered later, when I discovered to my amazement that the production company for this movie, Hollywood Pictures, is a division within the Disney organization! More on this later in the chapter.

These and numerous other examples tell parents that the entertainment media has taken the gloves off in the fight for profits—and they don't care where the punches land, or whose child they abuse, along the way.

Is It Possible to Reverse the Decline?

Much of what's in the media has become so offensive that some parents don't watch or read any of it, losing immediate touch with what's being sold to kids. Other parents, weary of fighting the battle, give up, leaving all the choices to their kids.

For most of us, the media become a behemoth that seems impossible to move or change. And as long as the moral slide continues in the United States, so, too, will the same tone in the media. No one can predict whether or not our country will acquire Judeo-Christian values. That's not something we can have direct control over. We can't control the behavior of other people.

We can, however, control our own behavior. We can teach our kids to stay informed about what's going on in their world. We can also teach our kids that it's okay occasionally to be entertained by movies and programs that wholeheartedly endorse our Judeo-Christian values.

Contrary to some opinions, the main problem for parents is *not* the producers who create movies and television programs that have explicit sexual messages and images. Rather, it's parents themselves who stand idly by and let offensive programming come into their homes via television and the videos they rent. Even in the church, significant numbers of Christians who teach Sunday school consistently go to see and rent R-rated movies designed to titillate, with little concern for the example they're setting for their kids. The owner of one Blockbuster Video store near us said that affluent parents are the worst offenders when it comes to renting R-rated videos for their kids. "They rent as many as five and six at a time," he said.

A steady diet of programs that promote immorality desensitizes parents so that they downplay what their children are watching. Remember, Jesus didn't rail against the Roman system of government, which had been given the earthly power to have Him crucified: He condemned the sin in a person's heart that gives rise to corrupt forms of government.

If parents made better choices and set better examples for their kids, perhaps the various media would change. But then again, they might not respond. If there are enough people who don't embrace Judeo-Christian values and continue to watch their programs and read their materials, media moguls might say of the abstainers, "They're morally uptight. Who needs them? Earnings are high enough without them."

So even though change for the good is unlikely, it is still possible. In the meantime, we can lodge our protest by refusing to watch unacceptable programming and movies and sending in letters of protest to sponsors—in addition to refusing to buy their products.

Chicago Tribune columnist Bob Greene assailed the parents of America for not registering their outrage at the Madonna concert that aired on HBO in 1990, which glorified filthy language and masturbation. Greene wrote:

> What is amazing is not what came across the screen. . . . The surprising thing was that an insignificant number of parents called HBO to object to the show. Apparently, the parents of America have totally given up on hoping that they can control the entertainment environment their children are exposed to. . . . It's about a country that has been so beaten down by a lessening of standards for what is acceptable in public and what isn't that something like the Madonna concert can be telecast to millions of families, and it doesn't even cause a ripple of controversy or complaint.[7]

One reason that outrage wasn't expressed against this cable TV show is that many parents who embrace a moral view of life don't subscribe to the premium cable channels like HBO, Cinemax, and Showtime, which often feature morally debasing programming.

Even if we do lodge appropriate protests and the media don't respond to our moral choice, this doesn't absolve us of the responsibility to set a good example for our kids. We need to teach them how to be informed, how to draw the line between moral and immoral entertainment, and how to establish parameters on how much time is appropriate to spend on entertainment. Am I advocating censorship of thought in the media? No. But I *am* advocating that parents assume their moral responsibility.

As an investigative journalist involved in both print and electronic media, I often see the seamy and unseemly side of life. I am not a prude, nor are those in my family naive. Our family doesn't hide from the unpleasant parts of life. We recognize them, and we respond accordingly.

The decline of moral standards in the media has even caused a number of critics within the media to express their outrage. Even news reports are documenting this decline.

INDUSTRY SELF-CRITICISM

A segment of the *ABC World News Tonight* report on November 2, 1990 addressed the entertainment industry's changing standards. It was anchored by Peter Jennings, who delivered his voice-overs with a tinge of cynicism. Jeff Greenfield was the ABC commentator who presented the report. The segment replayed numerous sexually explicit video images from TV shows. Peter Jennings opened with the following:

> Finally here this evening, television and taste. Not too long ago we would have automatically suggested that at the very least you might not approve of your children seeing the behavior and hearing the language in this last report. Now, even though we may be personally offended, we would feel a little foolish. For what you see in this report by Jeff Greenfield is what you get . . . *every night* on television now.

With Jeff Greenfield's reporting interspersed, the segment flashed explicit dialogue as well as images from prime-time television shows covering everything from sexual experimentation among teenagers, to graphic anatomical references in casual conversations, to gratuitous sexual scenes. Greenfield explained,

> All through primetime this season there are words and pictures that would have sent network executives into shock just a few years ago.

The following clips provide two examples from the segment:

9.1. Scene from ABC sitcom *Roseanne*, 8:00 p.m. CST:
Teenage Girl 1: "Did you get felt up?"
Teenage Girl 2: "No!"
Teenage Girl 3: "I did!"

9.2. Scene from CBS sitcom *Murphy Brown,* 8:00 p.m. CST:
Murphy Brown (interrupting two feuding men in the middle of a newsroom): "Why don't you guys just pull down your pants? I'll get a ruler, and we'll settle this once and for all."

"It didn't happen overnight," Greenfield commented. He went on:

> It wasn't any one episode of any one program. But the journey from *Ozzie and Harriet* through *All in the Family* through *Hill Street Blues* to *thirtysomething* and *Rosie O'Neil* has given us a television climate in which the once unthinkable is now unremarkable.

After a series of comments from industry executives, producers, and critics on the realities of competition among networks and cable stations for viewers, changing levels of acceptability, and their varying views on the desirability of these changes, Jennings concluded:

And there is this to think about. Recently, Howard Stringer, the CBS Broadcast President, told a gathering of industry executives that the change in standards on television has not been punished—by the marketplace, by the audience, or by the critics.

Relatively unchallenged, the slide has continued until, as Greenfield stated, "The unthinkable is now unremarkable." A month later, on December 5, 1991, ABC's *Nightline* aired, uncensored, pop star Madonna's new video, "Justify My Love," which depicts graphic nudity and sadomasochistic themes.

In response, *Dallas Morning News* TV critic Ed Bark wrote,

Network television lost its virginity . . . sponsored by the likes of Allstate Insurance and the United Negro College Fund. . . . 220,000 households in the Dallas-Fort Worth area witnessed a woman in suspenders, with her nipples exposed, rubbing a man's cr----. . . . Madonna did make at least one sound argument. Sexually suggestive videos . . . air at all hours of the day on MTV, she said. I was replaying *Nightline* at 9:30 A.M. Tuesday when she said this. No better time to tune in and take a look. What did I see on MTV? Donny Osmond—the new, leather-clad sneering Donny—singing "My Love Is A Fire," while women in various stages of undress writhed around him.[8]

Significantly, the Madonna video wasn't shown on HBO or Fox TV, noted for risqué themes, but on *Nightline,* an ABC news show usually characterized by dignified taste. To give the show a ratings boost, ABC's *Monday Night Football* heavily promoted the upcoming Madonna video, which aired one hour after the game.

Of even greater significance is that ABC chose to run the Madonna piece as a part of its regular programming just six weeks after *ABC World News Tonight* ran its news segment on the offensive nature of programming that airs every night before 8 p.m. As Peter Jennings himself had noted, CBS President Howard Stringer pointed out that the trend of declining standards hadn't been punished by the viewers, the critics, or the marketplace (i.e., sponsors).

One *New York Times* critic observed that there are even TV commercials that should be given an R rating:

There is no question, of course, that sex among teenagers is more prevalent these days and that virginity is at a premium by age eighteen. But there is a question of whether the social realities are being merely reflected or actually created by television, not only through programming but also *the Calvin Klein-type commercials that merit an R rating of their own* [emphasis added by critic].[9]

The following photo provides an example of such advertising fare:

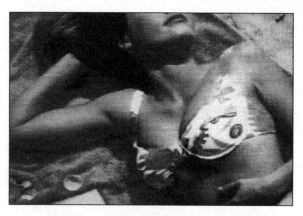

9.3. From a commericial aired before 8:00 p.m. CST.

Offensive advertising is not limited to television, however. On December 12, 1991, our local newspaper, the *Dallas Morning News,* ran a sexually explicit advertisement for Foleys, a local department store. The full-color lingerie advertisement featured unairbrushed photos of see-through garments, clearly showing women's breasts. This kind of advertising has become common in most metropolitan newspapers. Now many local hometown newspapers can't even be trusted to be responsible. The day may come when a parent will have to scour the newspapers before kids can get after the sports page or comics.

I did some further checking and found out that several years before, the *Dallas Morning News*—which has received several Pulitzer Prizes in the last few years—had included a similar insert for a now defunct department store. It was far more graphic because it was printed on slick sheets, rather than on newsprint stock, which obscures detail. The staffers at the *Dallas Morning News* said the paper received a lot of flack from the insert, and had vowed not to include any more explicit material that could be seen by youngsters. So much for trust.

As noted by the *Los Angeles Times* critic Howard Rosenberg, we should be able to turn on the television or open our local newspaper and not have to worry about finding something offensive to families with young children. Rosenberg's comment is especially significant because he is not a right-wing critic, but a liberal reviewer who was simply observing the obvious.

If offensive material appears in movies shown at local theaters, we can at least keep the kids home. But what do we do when the programs are being shown on network television in our home? The following section describes how our family has dealt with this deluge of immoral programming and movies. Perhaps you will find it helpful for establishing your own family response to entertainment media.

RESPONDING TO THE DECLINE

In 1986, I told my nine-year-old daughter that because the language in the movies was getting worse, there might come a day when we wouldn't be able to go to the movies more than once or twice a year. She nodded her head and said she understood.

Several times, our family had gone to a movie rated PG and heard language that only a couple of years before would have garnered at least a PG-13, if not an R, rating. (Although the quality of TV shows was on the decline during this time period, there were still a number of clean shows before 8:00 p.m., and our kids knew which shows were and which ones weren't.)

About a year after that conversation with my daughter, we went to a local theater to see a PG-rated movie. Before we bought our tickets, I had checked the ratings guide and even called the theater—and was told that there was no objectionable language, nudity, etc. But only a few minutes into the show, the language was so uncalled for that our kids objected. We left the theater and received a refund.

Since that time, we go to the movies only once or twice a year. In place of trips to the theater, we occasionally rent a movie from a video store. Before renting, we check the ratings book and inquire of the store owner. Still, this screening process isn't perfect; several times we've had to turn off a movie and take it back. (We're even leaning toward junking the whole video store concept because of the thousands of cassette covers flaunting risqué material as customers scan the aisles looking for an acceptable movie.)

Please understand that we're not movie or entertainment addicts. We just like to enjoy a good movie together as a family activity. Most we see are G-rated. We do occasionally watch a PG-rated movie, such as *Driving Miss Daisy,* or an historical movie such as *The Mission.* Both have uplifting messages and reinforce positive morals and values.

For our home, screening is a family process. We eliminate the obvious: gratuitous and excessive violence, foul language, sexual themes, and occultic themes. Then, as needed, we point out the why behind our "no." I believe that in most situations it's better to help youngsters understand *why* they must turn from bad programming, rather than just saying no. Here are some examples of how to discuss these issues with your kids.

Talking to Your Child About Content

Excessive violence. Explain that studies show that kids who watch too many violent scenes on television are more likely to commit acts of violence. Use an article in the newspaper or from a TV news segment that depicts kids committing crimes to make your point.

Another idea is to point out a couple of the local neighborhood bullies. Ask your child what kinds of programs these kids watch. In all probability, they watch shows with excessive violence. TV violence isn't the root of criminal activity, but it does add fuel to the fire. "As a man thinks in his heart, so is he," warns the author of Proverbs (23:7, KJV).

Foul language. This issue can be easily stated: "We don't talk like that in our house, and we won't have that kind of language coming in through our television." Most kids don't need a more elaborate explanation.

Sexual themes. For kids five to seven, a simple no without explanation is sufficient. After seven, it's usually necessary to point out: "What they're showing or talking about isn't the kind of love God wants us to have for one another, unless people are married." How you address this to each child will depend upon how specifically you have discussed sexuality. By the time our kids were eight, they'd had their "talk" about sex.

Occult themes. Here, reinforce the ideas from chapter 5, "Fantasy and Imagination: Where to Draw the Line," and from chapter 6, "Tricks or Powers?"

Drug themes. The explanation here is obvious: drugs are harmful. When you establish which shows are and are not acceptable, be sure periodically to watch those shows you've approved, because they can change. Many times we have watched a good show turn sour as it entered a second or third season simply because the writers were drying up. Gratuitous titillation is often turned to for the cheap laugh—the lazy person's path to success. Producers of the show will often rationalize the slide by claiming, "Hey, everyone has to do it."

When screening movies, I've noticed that it's easier to overlook coarse language on the big screen at the theater than at home on a small TV screen. This is because big-screen visuals often overwhelm the sound. Especially in action sequences, we're more likely to get caught up in what we're seeing than what we're hearing. On television, however, the words are far more noticeable and important.

I realized this phenomenon when my wife and I saw the movie *The Hunt for Red October,* a Cold-War movie rated PG. When we saw the movie at the theater, we didn't catch the three or four instances of coarse, unacceptable language because we were mesmerized by the visuals of submarine interiors. As we left the theater, we said to each other, "Now that was a clean movie the boys would like to watch."

A few months later, I checked out the video to watch with our kids. I was embarrassed when they turned to me when the first rough language surfaced. Although the language was on the lesser end of being offensive, it was still unacceptable. We turned off the TV set, and they asked me why I checked it out. I said that I never heard the "curse" words at the movies. Later, when I reviewed the objectionable scenes, I could see that the visual in those scenes overpowered what was being said.

So, when you get an appraisal from a friend of whether a movie is acceptable or not, be careful. Even thoughtful viewers might not catch something if they viewed the movie on the big screen. If parents have been consistent, however, an occasional blunder will not have a negative effect on their kids.

Knowing When to Make Exceptions

Occasionally, if there is a very specific educational reason, our family makes an exception to our content rules. As a boy, I remember being shown documentaries of the Holocaust that vividly depicted the horror of the Nazi concentration camps in which millions were exterminated. Today, if those programs had been released theatrically, they would have received an R rating. Still, I would want my kids to see them as long as we followed their viewing with careful discussion.

When my oldest son was ten, we showed him *Mississippi Burning,* which portrays the 1964 slaying of three civil rights workers. He had never before been exposed to racial hatred, and he was initially gripped by fear when we showed it to him. But with careful discussion, his justifiable fear subsided. We felt it was important for him to see this film because some of his friends at school were African-Americans. We wanted him to understand what his friends or their parents might have had to face.

Other programs we have shown our kids include *The Holocaust* and *War and Remembrance*. Both were made-for-TV miniseries and dealt with the extermination of the more than six million European Jews. If either miniseries had been released theatrically, its realistic scenes of people gassed in the death houses—nude men, women, and children herded with less dignity than cattle into "shower rooms"—would have drawn an R rating. Again, with careful nurturing and discussion before and after each program, our kids learned important lessons without harmful and negative aftereffects. Few kids will complain about establishing standards when they're handled in this manner.

It's important to emphasize to kids that corrupt material comes from corrupt minds. Drug and alcohol abuse, sexual immorality, and foul language are common for people who produce offensive programming. As needed, point out news clips that depict this kind of behavior. By showing kids what critics in the entertainment industry have to say about their own business, they will know that this is more than just Mom's or Dad's opinion. This way they can make the connection between the lifestyles of those who produce these shows and the shows themselves. Then, when kids go to a friend's house, they will have the conviction to ask that the dial be turned when an inappropriate show comes on. And if the friend refuses, they will have the courage to leave rather than stay and watch, because they'll know they're doing the right thing.

On the positive side, look for "good guy" producers, directors, and actors who participate in wholesome programs. Draw attention to articles indicating stability in their personal lives and positive themes or treatments in the programs they produce. Kids aren't dumb. When they realize that greedy people with corrupt morals usually produce like programming, they reject more than just the program. They reject who is behind the program. And the reverse is true. Kids will embrace good guys who produce good programs.

Here are some questions you can use to help your kids evaluate for themselves if a program is one that they should watch:

◆ What is the key message of this program?
◆ Is the message a good one?
◆ Does it conflict with the principles in the Bible?
◆ Who is trying to sell me something, and why?
◆ Do the people who produced this show seem to like kids? Do they have good marriages? Are they on drugs? Do I trust them?

Deciding Who You Can Trust

Sadly, there are no networks and few cable networks that can be trusted with kids. In the early 1980s, then Disney president Ron Miller said that Disney would never produce anything more than a "soft PG" movie for fear that "You'd get some church leader standing up and saying, 'Don't go to Disneyland. Stay out of Disney World.'"[10]

Times have changed. Disney now produces R-rated movies—the most recent and shocking example of which is the movie I mentioned earlier, *The Hand that Rocks the Cradle.* And just this year, Disney announced plans to produce a nationwide lottery game show for television—promoting gambling to an already addiction-prone society. In response, my kids at their own insistence now do what was unthinkable ten years ago: they screen which Disney movies they will watch. This began after I took them to see *Who Killed Roger Rabbit?* If Walt Disney ever saw a film like this, in which Mickey Mouse was featured with cartoon characters that used foul language, no doubt the current regime would have been summarily dismissed. Much of what Disney produces is still wholesome, but they're no longer trustworthy the way they primarily were in the past. Old man money is hot after Disney's morals.

Even some stations that purport to be Christian/family stations have taken a slide. One example is channel 39 in Dallas, which is owned by Pat Robertson. They regularly air shows such as *Sex and the Single Girl, Single Bars—Single Women* (although these are relatively tame in contrast to explicit network shows), and "infomercials" (half-hour paid commercials) from people such as Anthony "Tony" Robbins, a firewalker who espouses many of the themes common in the New Age philosophy (see chapter 16). When Nelson Flannigan, director of programming for this Dallas station, was asked if he thought that this programming was suitable in light of his station's history of providing family entertainment, he said, "Yes, it's evidently something we would run because we've run it. We've run it a number of times. I chose to put it on the air. . . . We're just like anybody else. We're trying to pay the bill."[11]

There are a few organizations—such as Focus on the Family—that provide reliable reviews, movies, and TV programming, but they're the exception. The best method we've found for reviewing programming and movies is: (1) check the reviews of a reliable critic; (2) check the ratings; (3) talk to other parents who have seen the program or movie. When these measures fail, turn the set off; if you're at the theater, leave and ask for a refund.

If you're a single parent, monitoring programming content may be difficult because of time constraints. In this case, find someone you trust to help you. Also, load up your kids with extracurricular activities and projects, so they won't be tempted to turn on the television while you aren't home. Don't let the television become a surrogate parent. If they absolutely must hear or see something while you are not home to diminish their fear and isolation, give them good reading materials, programs you've taped, and recordings of clean musical artists, such as Raffi, Michael W. Smith, or Natalie Cole's *Unforgettable*.

THE QUESTION OF TELEVISION

I mentioned that in 1986 I talked to my nine-year-old daughter about why we wouldn't be seeing many more movies in the future. In 1989, as we watched the standards on network television continue to plummet, our whole family had a talk. I explained to the kids that the downward trend was getting so bad that just like the movies, we might have to turn the TV off, with the exception of news or an occasional entertainment program. There were no complaints.

We continued to coast along until the critical ABC news segment on November 2, 1990. We felt that the kids needed to see the report, and so we showed it to them.

"Remember when I told you about a year ago that there might come a day when we would have to turn off the TV?" I began. "Well, that day is here. The people who put these programs together don't care about us, and we don't have to watch this stuff. We'll find other things to do for entertainment."

The kids then each recalled numerous times that a producer unexpectedly threw in gratuitous sex or foul language in a show that started out clean. They unanimously went along with our decision.

With their own eyes, our kids learned a hard lesson: for the most part, *the media world just doesn't care about kids*. Even with the death sentence of AIDS looming large, most programmers continue to promote promiscuity among youth. (It is a fact that the *younger* teens become sexually active, the *more* sex partners they have per year, and the *faster* sexually transmitted diseases are spread.)

We still watch the news and no more than about an hour a day—if that—of entertainment programming. What's been the impact on our family? Our kids will tell you we haven't missed a thing.

How Much Is Enough?
The average child watches *four hours* per day, according to the A. C. Nielsen Company. Yet *one* hour a day of after-school television entertainment is sufficient for most youngsters. Most kids spend more time in front of a television than in any other activity besides sleeping and school—during the school year.

In these large doses, television dries up a youth's creative abilities and interactions with others. Playing with friends, hobbies, homework, chores, games, reading, and all kinds of other activities should fill their time. Sure, there are exceptions, like when a child is home sick or there are a couple of really good shows airing on a Friday or Saturday night. But those times should be *the exception,* not the rule. If kids are given good activities to cut down on their idle time, they usually won't miss the mind-numbing experience that most television brings them.

Watching less television has only been a plus for our family. We dialogue more, attend my daughter's recitals, play ball after work, take walks, play an occasional game, and participate in the kids' hobbies when we can. Nothing bad has happened as a result of watching less television, because we have replaced that time with other activities and more meaningful time together.

Another favor that your family can do for itself is, *never leave the television on to be heard like music in an elevator*. It numbs the brain and stifles communication between family members. Have you ever tried to have a meaningful conversation in a home where the television blares incessantly? Eye contact is snatched away by the moving picture.

Even if programmers cleaned up their act, *we would still need to watch less*. We don't need to be *entertained* more, we need to *serve* more. Massive consumption of television is a selfish action. It rarely gives anything back to others. It does, however, aid in lowering our moral standards, and its thousands of commercials create an intense desire to buy and feed self. Some may argue that this in turn stimulates the desire to work and earn more money. For some it may do that, but in most cases it is work driven by greed.

Most commercials don't encourage themes such as volunteering time to work in inner-city communities, helping the handicapped, becoming more literate, or studying harder in school. Those that do should be applauded. Don't be afraid to encourage your kids to "zap" (mute the sound of) the ones that are inane or offensive.

Take Control—Use Videotape!

About half of the news and entertainment shows our family watches we've previously taped. If a program becomes offensive, we turn it off and put in another program we have taped. On Sunday afternoon, my oldest son and I scan the local TV directory that comes with the Sunday paper and mark which shows we want to tape. Sometimes we don't watch any television for days or even weeks at a time, except for news.

By taping shows and keeping a small collection, you can cut down on your kids' temptation to flip the dial and watch "whatever is on."

AN ANTI-JUDEO-CHRISTIAN MORAL BIAS

Only on occasion are Judeo-Christian perspectives treated kindly by the entertainment media. Movie exceptions include *Places in the Heart, Tender Mercies,* and *Chariots of Fire.* There are a handful of television exceptions, but for the most part Judeo-Christian viewpoints are dispatched with hostility, or Christians are portrayed as nitwits.

Michael Medved, PBS movie critic and host of the TV show *Sneak Previews,* pointed out that the movie *The Last Temptation of Christ* openly courted this anti-religious sentiment. This blasphemous film, which featured Jesus nailing someone to a cross and even depicted the Savior having an affair, is an abhorrent illustration of the hostility in Hollywood to religious values. Medved said about one reviewer who gave this film a glowing report:

> I remember a conversation with one of my colleagues who had prepared what I considered an unaccountably generous review. He explained himself with surprising candor. "If I was too rough on the film," he said, "then people would associate me with Jerry Falwell"—and that was an association he could not accept.[12]

Medved points out that even though the movie industry is driven by the bottom line, most movies that are antagonistic toward religion, such as *Agnes of God* and *Monsignor,* are box-office flops, while sympathetic shows such as *Tender Mercies* usually do very well.

> The movie industry's resounding endorsement of *The Last Temptation of Christ* is only the latest and perhaps the most grotesque illustration of the overt and pervasive hostility to religion and religious values that has taken root in Hollywood.
>
> It is hard to escape the conclusion that there is a perverse sort of idealism at work here. For many of the most powerful people in the entertainment business, hostility to traditional religion goes so deep and burns so intensely that they insist on expressing that hostility, even at the risk of commercial disaster.
>
> Moviemakers can't stay away from religious themes because of their deep-seated desire to be taken seriously; religion offers one subject which everyone acknowledges as fundamentally serious. If writers and directors take a swipe at religion in one of their films, no matter how clumsy or contrived that attack may be, they can feel as if they've made some sort of important and courageous statement. . . . By sneering at zealots and deriding conventional religious beliefs, a filmmaker can win the respect of his peers, even if his work is rejected by the larger public.
>
> It's easy for most moviemakers to assume a patronizing attitude toward religiously committed people because they know so few of them personally. If most big screen images of religious leaders tend to resemble Swaggart or Bakker it's because evangelists on television are the only believers who are readily visible to members of the film colony.[13]

Medved added that a 1982 study by the University of Maryland revealed that only 3 percent of the key decision-makers in the movie business attend church or synagogue on a regular basis, while over 50 percent of the general population attend services regularly:

> This means, of course, that the movie business is also out of touch with a huge portion of its potential audience. Statistics prove the point. In the 1940s, over 90 million Americans—close to two-thirds of the country—went to the movies every week. Today, the number of filmgoers is less than 20 million per week, and more importantly, surveys show that close to 40 percent of the American people don't even go out to a single movie in the course of a year.

Tens of millions of Americans, in part, have given up on contemporary movies because they see their own deepest values so rarely reflected—or even respected—on screen.[14]

Our family falls into this category, and there appears to be no end in sight for the entertainment media's open hostility to family or to Judeo-Christian values.

SUMMARY

With balanced parental encouragement and nurturing, kids can control what they view. It's okay to be entertained in moderation, and it's essential to stay informed—the subject of the next chapter. The downward moral decline in the media shows no signs of reversing itself any time soon, and so parents must remain vigilant.

Parents will be most effective by issuing a firm but balanced "no" combined with providing alternatives for their kids—and a willingness to monitor and enforce viewing decisions. Television is powerful, and its influence must be restrained. It can and will negatively change what our children believe unless we take the necessary time and measures to teach our children how to be selective.

When appropriate, we must lodge our protest to networks, programmers, and sponsors. This won't guarantee that there will be a change, because there may be more people who *don't* share a moral perspective, but it is our responsibility.

The most basic guidelines for a streetwise and foolproof response to the entertainment media are:

1. Watch less.
2. Watch selectively.
3. Remember that you don't have to buy.
4. Learn how to be informed.
5. Stay informed.

CHAPTER TEN

Learn How
to Use the News

♦

It may seem that television is turning into a vast wasteland, but information programming can still be valuable. When carefully examined, local and network news, news specials, and documentaries can provide useful information that is relevant to youngsters. The war on drugs, pollution, crime, new inventions, medical breakthroughs, weather, personal interest stories, and sports and hobbies are just some of the reports kids find interesting.

The sheer number of news sources and issues combined with occasional biased reporting, however, can make news confusing to kids. For these reasons, kids need to be discerning about how to stay informed and evaluate news and information.

Additionally, kids need to learn how to use the print media—newspapers, magazines, periodicals, journals, etc. The print media will give them a broader base of information and a countercheck of what they hear on TV news.

Certain news stories, though, can be terrifying for youngsters, such as the 1991 war in the Persian Gulf. This is why a parent is often best suited to teach a child the necessary lessons for checking out the facts without being overwhelmed emotionally or buying into seductive trends. In this chapter we'll look at some simple guidelines and exercises that you can use to help you and your child become streetsmart about the world of news.

WHAT'S THE NEWS?

For many people, "the news" is simply whatever's in the local paper or presented on network and local television stations. Discovering how "the news" gets to us through the news media is a big part of learning how to use the news.

Here are some definitions of "the news" that I've found helpful:

Preteen—News is defined as events that take place in our world that we need to know about, which are reported on television and radio, in newspapers and in magazines.

Advanced—News is defined as events and things that happen to people that are reported in the electronic and print media. (Not all stories that are important are reported, nor does every news source carry every important story. Often, news is something that a news producer or editor feels is important to report, rather than something that is really important to most people.)

This brings up the question of how the news media present the news. Fundamental to understanding the news is knowing *why certain stories are reported* rather than others, and recognizing that *the stories are reported in a particular order*.

The producer or editor is the one who decides which line-up of stories will get reported and in which order. The order in which stories are reported on TV or are given prominence in the print media is determined by international, national, state, local, and family issues—in that order. A news producer or editor asks, "Is it safe in my world?" During the Persian Gulf War, the answer was "no," so it led most news reports. If the answer for the day is "yes, it is safe in my world," then one asks, "Is it safe in my country?" And so on. Whatever story is the most important to the greatest number of people is the story that will go before another, and usually receive more coverage.

Because this is how news stories are often selected, it can appear that all the news stations have the same producer. If you were to switch stations, you would notice that the story order is often identical. The same is true of newspapers, when there are more than one in the same town. The important stories get more coverage and prominence and are usually run on the front page. It's not because there's a conspiracy, but rather because this method of story selection is what is taught in universities. This is also the natural order in which people usually prefer to watch and read news coverage.

When watching as a family, change stations during the evening news to other broadcasts and point out how the order of the reports is usually similar. Also, compare newspapers—if there's more than one in your town—and point out which stories get the most coverage. Emphasize that the editor and producer select which stories will run in which order, rather than the reporter.

Here is a suggested list of the kinds of stories that youngsters should start to follow:

◆ Pollution and the environment
◆ Inflation and recession
◆ Developments in the sciences such as medicine and genetic engineering
◆ Moral issues such as abortion and euthanasia
◆ Drug abuse
◆ Positive trends in education
◆ A simple understanding of which countries in the world have and don't have power and why
◆ Parts of the world where there is unrest (but not too much, or a child will develop an unhealthy fear)
◆ Stories about kids in other living conditions
◆ Censorship
◆ Negative and positive trends in entertainment and news

Now let's look at eight guidelines—"foolproofing tips"—that can help parents and kids use the news to stay informed and aware.

EIGHT FOOLPROOFING TIPS FOR USING THE NEWS

Question the Facts

Facts are facts—or are they? One of the first rules of thumb for becoming a discerning reader or viewer is, *never take any one newsperson's word about the facts.* Kids need to be encouraged to find other sources to confirm what is being reported: other TV news broadcasts, newspaper and magazine accounts, and specific journals related to a given subject (for example, on medical issues, check the medical journals).

Even good journalists will make honest mistakes. This can occur because they were given wrong information, they don't understand a particular story, or they are biased. When the first two reasons occur, most good news sources will often broadcast or publish a correction.

Some news reports get the facts wrong because of exaggerations. An example simple enough for most kids to understand is estimates of people killed in a major catastrophe, such as an earthquake. Usually the initial estimates are far more than the actual numbers, because relief agencies and local officials want aid to pour in. Also, they're less likely to be criticized for overestimating casualties than underestimating them.

To illustrate, pick one such story and follow it with your child for a couple of weeks. Point out the different estimates from the broadcast and print media, including radio news. Then ask your child why the estimates seem to vary, and the possible reasons: people exaggerate when scared, officials want more relief money, and so on.

Another area of inaccuracy is omission of information from a story. One example was when Lee Attwater, President George Bush's ruthless 1988 campaign manager, died in early 1991 of a brain tumor at age forty. A significant part of the story was that prior to Attwater's death, he embraced Christianity. On his own, Attwater sought out and asked for forgiveness from various politicians whom he had wronged, including the former governor of Massachusetts and Bush's Democratic opposition in the 1988 election campaign, Michael Dukakis. Many newspapers reported his conversion and true repentance. But some, such as the *New York Times,* made only a brief mention of this important change in his life. Why the sparse treatment? Because some news sources don't think that stories of spiritual consequence are important.

Then there are the news reports in which the journalist adds to the facts—hyping or distorting the story. An exaggerated example is the supermarket tabloids, in which writers boldly lie and make up quotes. (Sadly, the *National Enquirer* is purported to be the number-one periodical in the world.) Fortunately, this error is not as common in the legitimate press as the first two kinds of errors, exaggeration and omission.

It's important to remember that *reporters are only human.* Kids—as well as adults—are easily buffaloed into thinking that teleprompter-reading reporters know everything. In fact, at most stations, the news anchor doesn't even write the copy. Another staff person does this. Many news anchors, particularly at local stations, are really actors rather than reporters.

In most cases, the reporters in the field are the people who are actually doing the stories. They write their own copy, select whom they will interview, tell a camera operator which shots to get, and even help editors edit the footage from a remote truck on location, which is then beamed back by satellite to a station.

In other cases, a news producer at the station writes the basic story. Then the producer sends out a reporter with the exact copy they are to read on location. Very often, the producer also tells the camera operator which shots to get.

Most kids don't realize it, but even when news anchors are interviewing someone live during a newscast, the questions being asked are often fed to them by the news producer through their earpiece. This is why a news anchor may sometimes appear to be uncertain. The anchor is trying to listen to the interviewee and the producer. This is often necessary because the anchor is not an expert on a particular issue and needs assistance, or the producer is telling the anchor which shot is coming up next.

To help your child get a feel for what this is like, have someone role-play the interviewee and sit in front of your child, who will be the reporter. Now, to simulate a question fed through an earpiece, whisper a question in your child's ear, which he must ask of this person. Then, while the person is answering the question, whisper another your child must ask that relates to the answer being given. Do this for a few minutes, and your child will quickly get an idea of what's going on in front of the camera. It can really be confusing if you aren't on your toes!

Here is another way to point out that TV reporters are fallible. Compare how smoothly reporters can file their report when they're reading their copy from a teleprompter versus another report that is ad-libbed. The ad-libbed report is almost always rougher, and the "uhs" become apparent.

Don't Rely on TV News Alone

It's easy to take in the news from television. All you do is watch and react; you don't have to think as much as when you read a newspaper. Walter Cronkite, the former CBS anchor, remarked that TV news is usually nothing more than a banner headline service, because the average report is usually under a minute and twenty seconds. TV news reports usually amount to no more than the headline in a newspaper plus a couple of paragraphs.

In such a short span of time, it usually isn't possible to communicate more than just the basic theme of a story. Unfortunately, most people rely on TV alone for their news. This is one reason why it's so easy to change what people believe—especially kids. People base their opinions on a brief impression rather than a detailed knowledge of the facts.

The better informed we are, the harder it is to change what we believe with quick presentations or shallow and inaccurate facts. That's why we must teach kids when they are very young to do more than just watch TV news.

Follow a Story and Compare News Sources

To help your child understand that he will need more than TV news to get good information, pick a news story and follow it for one month. Select an ongoing national story of interest to your child that is being covered locally and nationally in both the broadcast and print media. It can be something light, such as a sports or entertainment story, or something more intense, such as a drought in California or a nuclear weapons facility that is illegally dumping hazardous waste. To see how the story develops in the various media, do the following:

Tape and watch both local and national TV coverage. When possible, if you have just finished watching one local affiliate report its story, change to one of the other local stations and compare the coverage. Then compare local and national coverage and what each emphasizes as the important points.

Follow the coverage in a local newspaper and in one out-of-town newspaper. I recommend the *New York Times* or the *Los Angeles Times* for out-of-town coverage. Again, compare the details in each. Point out that the local paper is less thorough on national stories, unless the national story comes from your town—and then the local paper will usually have more coverage.

Also, local newspapers often subscribe to news services, such as the Associated Press and Knight-Ridder. These news services have reporters all across the world. Then the local newspaper, which doesn't have reporters in a city where a story is breaking, can buy the news service's reports. This is usually indicated at the top of the news story or at the end. Sometimes a newspaper will combine a local reporter's interviews, which are done on the phone, with a report from a news service. There are some newspapers, such as the *New York Times,* that have so many reporters they provide reports to other newspapers, just like the Associated Press does. Of the national newspapers, I like to read the *New York Times* for raw information. It's usually the most thorough, although I often disagree with the opinions expressed on the editorial page.

Check news magazines for additional coverage. Take one or two national magazines, such as *Time* or *U.S. News and World Report,* and compare how different magazines cover the same story.

Read the editorials. Explain to your child that the editorial page is the place where a newspaper can give its personal opinion about an issue, also providing a place for people to write letters to the editors. Take a look at the editorial section of each newspaper or magazine and see what opinions they offer on the story you're following.

Sometimes a news source's editorial opinion will affect what the newspaper prints. Explain that the editor of a paper can tell a reporter how to report a story, and that sometimes the reporter won't object because of concern for keeping his or her job. Ask your child's opinion on whether the newspaper biased their story because of their editorial viewpoint.

Check electronic media against print media. Now compare how each of the various electronic and print media differ or are the same. Teach your child to ask questions such as:

- ◆ Why does this news source spend so much or so little time on the story? Is it for ratings? Is it because they can or can't afford to send a news team to the location?
- ◆ Does one news source seem to have changed its mind about how it is covering a story?
- ◆ Which news source or combination of news sources make it easier to understand the story?
- ◆ Which combination of news sources seem to get the facts straight more often? When a news source gets the story wrong, is it because the reporter got the wrong facts or because he or she deliberately misreported a story?
- ◆ Do the pictures in newspapers or the video images on television make it easier or harder to understand a story?
- ◆ Which type of news source, broadcast or print, gives the most details?

Common News Terms
These are some terms that kids should be familiar with:

News producer. The person in the electronic media (radio and TV) who puts together a news program and has charge over the reporters, editors, writers, anchors, etc.

Managing editor. In the print media, such as a newspaper, this editor decides which stories will be included on a given day and which ones won't, and also oversees other editors, such as the editor of the editorial page.

Journalist, reporter, or correspondent. This person reports the story on television or radio or in the print media. The word "reporter" is usually applied to a person who works every day for a news organization, while a "journalist" or "correspondent" may or may not work on a full-time basis for a particular news organization.

News anchor. This person reads the news from a teleprompter. Sometimes anchors are actual reporters; other times they are simply readers with acting ability. On radio, this is the person who reads the stories.

Video editor. The editor takes the raw footage, selects the segments that will be shown, and edits them together.

Copy editor. In the print media this editor takes out unnecessary parts of a reporter's story or adds something the reporter missed, as well as correcting grammatical and spelling mistakes.

Wire service. A news organization, such as the Associated Press, that covers stories, which subscribing media—newspapers, magazines, radio, and television news organizations—use in their reports. There are also major newspapers that send out their stories in a similar manner.

Documentary. A film or video program produced to educate and inform, which often has the same reporting standards as a regular newscast. The documentary, though, is usually in a longer format.

The Visual Part of a Story

Videotaped pictures on television and photographs in print news sources can enhance our understanding of a story. They also have a powerful ability to *shape* our thinking about a story, so it's especially important to understand their role in how the news is delivered.

Still photographs. A still photograph is like freezing a moment in time, which can be carefully looked at and thought about. Photographic stills usually try to convey one emotion. When a person is on trial and there is a public perception that he or she might be guilty, the newspapers will usually run a photograph that makes that person look mean, dishonest, or depressed. However, if the public perception—or an editor's perception—is that the person is innocent, the newspaper will often run a picture that makes the person appear to be valiantly fighting for his or her rights and reputation.

Unfortunately, most of us form our opinion of people from the pictures we see in print stories rather than from a careful reading of the facts. This is one reason why many large companies hire public relations firms to get positive pictures of their products or people in the print media.

With your child, compare still photographs of the same person or situation from different news sources and talk about the different impressions created. Then discuss whether the news source painted a fair visual picture of the situation.

Video images. These function differently than photographic stills. The action in a video image makes an event come alive. What kids need to know is that the video image is only an illusion of what really took place, because . . .

Video images show only a portion of the actual event. We don't see the whole event—what happens before and after the video clip. We also don't see what's happening away from the lens of the camera.

Editing changes reality. An interview of an hour or two might be condensed into twelve to fourteen seconds of broadcasted remarks.

How people or events are visually shot can alter what we think, how we feel, and how we respond to a story. For example, a shot taken from a helicopter of a refugee camp, which makes the refugees look like tiny ants, will not have the same emotional impact nor be as real in appearance as ground close-ups of starving kids. However, if one is trying to show how many people are in a camp, it might be more effective to use the helicopter shot, similar to the one used by the networks to show how many Kurds fled from Iraq after the 1991 war.

Camera technique can alter our impressions. How tight a camera operator zooms the lense in on a person during an interview can affect our interpretation of that person's remarks. On *60 Minutes,* the camera is often so tight on a person's face that the top part of the head is cut off. This lets the viewer focus solely on the mouth and eyes—and catch any flinch or twitch. If the same interview were aired with a long shot, which shows the whole body, it is often not as dramatic or revealing. These tight shots, however, are sometimes misleading because they can make natural nervousness appear to be deceitfulness; while a long shot, which doesn't reveal as much detail, wouldn't give the same negative impression.

To illustrate the power of the close-up, do a mock interview with your child. Ask your child a question on something he feels strongly about that will require more than just a yes or no answer. Videotape this answer with a close-up shot. Now repeat the same question, and ask your child to repeat the answer with the same level of conviction, but tape this second response using a long shot, showing the whole body. When you compare the two, your child will quickly get the idea of how a producer or camera operator can change what a viewer feels about a person being interviewed.

Explain that this doesn't mean that changing the shots is necessarily bad, because each shot is for a different reason: tight shots are for more important and revealing answers and insights; long shots are usually used to establish location and context. The next time you watch a news report, ask your child why different kinds of camera shots are being used, and whether the kind of shot selected is good or bad for reporting the story.

Some video images can have the opposite effect of what was intended. I've found that when there are numerous images of violence or starvation on news broadcasts, over a period of time youngsters can become numb to what that suffering means. Since there isn't immediate contact with it, over time it can make a child indifferent to what real suffering is.

Our family has overcome this numbing effect by participating in church projects to meet the needs of those who are suffering. Serving Christmas Eve dinner in a downtown mission or helping kids in a children's home are two good examples in which kids can relate to the fact that others are suffering, but in a context in which they feel safe.

A Weekly News Diet
Think of your child's appropriate levels of exposure to the news in terms of a weekly news diet. How much is enough? How much is too much?

Children ten and under need only about an hour or two of news per week. Since their vocabulary is limited, most of their consumption will be limited to TV, bolstered by an occasional article from which they can read underlined highlights you have prepared for them.

For this age group, limit exposure to news stories conveying death and destruction to moderate doses, with a parent or an older sibling present to answer questions. The Persian Gulf War revealed that even watching stories with the family can bring on nightmares. Each child is different, so pay close attention to how he or she responds.

After kids see something traumatic, it's important that they have an opportunity to talk about how they think and feel. We can't completely shield kids from these kinds of stresses, so as parents we have the responsibility to help them feel safe, or at least be there for them.

The press perceives itself primarily as a watchdog, which it should be. To counterbalance the negative, be certain that there is a dose of good positive stories that reflect positive values and situations. This is best done by taping and screening news broadcasts so that you can have control over what your child sees. For print stories, clip out articles from newspapers and magazines. There *is* a good side to life, even in the worst of times, and stories that reflect the gentler and safer part of life often get lost in the shuffle. Kids, however, lap up these stories, and usually like to watch them more than the negative ones.

For older teens, twenty minutes a day of news from TV and some from reading a newspaper is a good rule of thumb. This will also help them put into context much of what they are learning in school. Kids need to learn in the larger context of what is happening in the world. Sadly, few public schools have classes that explain how the news media work and provide tips on how to be informed, even though we are in the midst of what we call the "information age." Perhaps you might be able to get a class started in your school.

Particularly disturbing is that the majority of college students, whom I meet when I lecture on campuses, don't stay informed at all. Every college in America should make it mandatory for students to keep abreast of the major current issues, which would make their education more relevant. Most professors, deans, and students agree, but little is done to make this a priority. This lack of being informed is one reason that people are so easily swayed en masse, which reporter/commentator Bill Moyers carefully articulated in his PBS series *The Public Mind.*

Recognize the Money Factor
Network news anchors now earn over $2 million a year each, or about five times what our president is paid. News is about making money, not about people informing us out of the goodness of their hearts. While there are journalists who are committed to the integrity of their craft and not just money, many aren't. And even when a journalist works hard, the need for advertising revenues can cut a story to the bone.

Recently, a newspaper reporter from a metropolitan city spent several hours interviewing me to do a feature story that was to be about thirty or forty column inches. (This means that if the copy in each column were put in one long vertical line, the length would be thirty or forty inches.) However, the Persian Gulf conflict required so much space while it was being covered that advertising space had to be cut back. This meant that the newspaper actually lost money, even though it sold more papers.

When the reporter interviewed me, she said that her paper was over two hundred pages behind in advertising space, and that her report on my investigative efforts might be cut back. She was right. It was cut to only twenty inches. Not only was the meat of the story cut, but the article was choppy, jumping from thought to thought between paragraphs due to an inept editor. The reporter apologized for this and even sent me a copy of the uncut version.

For these reasons, I limit my number of interviews for the print or broadcast media. As a journalist, I can usually figure out if a reporter is being straight with me, but neither the reporter nor I have control over financial matters that can trim important elements of a story.

While watching a news broadcast or reading the local newspaper with your child, point out the number of ads and how important it is for these media to sell us something. It's easier to control the impact of sales messages in newspapers, because if we don't want to read them we can simply skip over them. But this is harder to do with TV commercials, unless we mute them out or switch to another station until they're over. But if we try the latter strategy, we'll quickly discover that the news stations run their commercials at almost the same times during a half-hour broadcast to prevent viewers from going to another station's newscast and missing the commercials.

Distinguish Between News and Entertainment

It's okay for news to be entertaining as long as the goal isn't simply to entertain. Today, however, people want to be entertained *more* than they want to be informed.

The benchmark of this trend took place in the early and mid-eighties. In most television markets, *Nightline* aired after the late evening news. It was a unique program in which anchor Ted Koppel interviewed individuals about important issues in an uncut format. His treatment was usually fair and extremely informative. Koppel was the first to master the appearance of talking to a person the viewer could see on the TV screen—Koppel saw only a small monitor off-camera. The illusion was created that he was looking at the same large picture the viewer saw.

Then *Entertainment Tonight (ET)* became popular, airing right after *Nightline*. Local programmers noted that more people wanted to watch *ET* than *Nightline,* so *ET* was moved up, with *Nightline* airing after *ET*. This was a bad indicator of days to come, because *Nightline* represented one of the first successful efforts by a network to provide longer discussions of critical issues after the evening news. Initially, because of the unique format, many had watched the informative and entertaining news program. When the novelty wore off, however, so did the viewing audience. (And as I noted in the previous chapter, even *Nightline* has lowered its standards by bowing to the need to entertain, as evidenced by airing the Madonna piece in 1990.)

Producers who noted that viewers wanted to see more real pictures in an entertaining format started producing what are called "reality shows." These are shows that dramatize real-life events—*911, Unsolved Mysteries, America's Most Wanted,* and *Top Cops* are some current examples. To kids, these shows can appear to be the same as a news program because they deal with real-life events. Kids have to be taught that these dramatizations are produced to entertain and not to inform. If these programs do inform, to the producers that's an extra.

This doesn't mean that something good can't happen from one of these programs: By watching *Rescue 911* a child might learn how to clear a blocked passageway in a choking victim, or a dangerous killer might be captured because someone sees a mug shot on *Unsolved Mysteries.*

However, what can additionally blur the line between entertainment and news for youngsters is when they see the local news announce that a criminal was apprehended because someone recognized them on one of these "reality" shows. Kids must learn to distinguish between *real footage,* which shows what is happening through the eyes of the camera lens, and a *dramatization,* which portrays what may or may not have actually happened. This is important because every year, stories appear in both the electronic and print media in which a TV reporter staged something for the camera that wasn't real, or a print reporter completely invented a story. I believe that these incidents will continue to increase as the pressure to entertain mounts, combined with even greater pressure for profits.

In the electronic media, we have seen the explosion of what are called "tabloid news" shows. *Inside Edition, Hard Copy,* and *Current Affair* are three examples. These shows deliberately blur the line between news pieces and outright fiction, just as the *National Enquirer* does. What is terribly disconcerting is that most adults don't recognize the difference between these tabloid shows—which are produced to entertain and not inform—and their local news.

Before one of these shows became prominent, it appeared that it was going to avoid the tabloid and entertainment route. In 1988, the producer of this show asked me to produce some segments, and I agreed to do so. However, after I put together the rough cut for my first piece, he told me that they wanted to reedit it to give it "their own special twist"—bending the truth to sensationalize. At that point I bowed out.

Don't allow your family to watch these tabloid shows, even if there is an occasional story that does have some news merit. For children, watching these programs is a seductive way to get them to buy into unreality and believe it is reality—not to mention the sleaze factor. Shows such as *Rescue 911* are okay as long as the content is acceptable, because these shows don't try to pass themselves off as news.

Watch for Slants
There are organizations hired by politicians and marketeers that assemble what is called a "focus group." A focus group is made up of people like you and me who are assumed to be representative of the rest of the United States.

During political campaigns, the focus group participants are asked what issues they consider important. During the 1988 presidential campaign, flag-burning was mentioned in one group, and one of the image-makers for George Bush latched on to this. Many of Bush's campaign appearances placed him in front of large flags, and even in a flag factory, to sell the visual image that Bush was patriotic and supportive of the flag. This wasn't bad, except that most experts agree those visuals, constructed to elicit an emotional response, dominated the campaign, instead of a discussion of the issues. I voted for George Bush, but I thought, *What if a candidate with an insidious agenda used the same techniques to sway emotions?* Hitler successfully did this through his propaganda machine that churned out movies glorifying the Third Reich and comparing Jews to rats.

On another level, some political speech writers and campaign managers have implemented a unique technique. They place a focus group in a room and have them watch a candidate's speech. The viewers are each given a small button to push when they think that what the speaker says is engaging. If the speaker isn't saying something that they relate to, they let up on the button. Then the results are tabulated and a computer-generated graph is plotted over the actual words of the candidate. In this way the tacticians can determine which group of words, and in which order, will elicit the emotional response desired—an *emotional* response that they hope will motivate a voter to select their candidate.

In Bill Moyers' revealing PBS special *The Public Mind*, these sophisticated techniques were detailed. And it appears that we will have more of the same in the future.

Our kids will be vulnerable to this kind of manipulation—especially if we hit a time of great financial distress—unless they are taught now, while they're young, to be discerning in their evaluation of the news, to distinguish the difference between illusion and reality, and to understand what it is that drives the various media.

A LIBERAL, ANTI-JUDEO-CHRISTIAN CONSPIRACY?

I often hear the complaint, "There is a liberal conspiracy in the press," suggesting that all the news media are controlled by a clandestine group. While the suggestion of a conspiracy among the thousands of news stations, newspapers, and magazines isn't true, there is a liberal bias, as there is in the entertainment media. Polls show that fewer than 4 percent believe in God or attend a church or synagogue, and most reporters favor abortion. So we can expect that even the most ethical reporters will sometimes taint their fact-gathering and reporting because of a built-in bias.

On a daily basis, though, most individual news stories move too quickly to be manipulated en masse by a small central committee. (If our press were state controlled this would be possible, but we have a free—albeit liberal—press in the United States.) Often, for example, footage shot of a Palestinian protest on the West Bank in Israel is beamed by satellite from Tel Aviv to the networks and edited as the broadcast is airing—that's how fast news footage and print stories are generated. This makes it difficult to control the slant of every story. But reporters and producers do regularly slant how broad issues are covered, such as abortion.

If we want to correct this bias, we need to encourage bright kids driven by integrity to become part of the press. Scholarships and grants need to be made available. Although there aren't many journalists with a Judeo-Christian world view, there are a few who *have* made a positive impact—not by slanting a story, but rather by giving fair coverage. Al White in New York City and Peggy Wehmeier Woods in Dallas are shining examples.

SUMMARY

Kids must be taught to ask thoughtful and penetrating questions without fearing the truth. This learning process should take place at home and in school so they can be guided with love and concern. Most kids need to watch less entertainment and spend more time being better informed as the world becomes more complex. Only informed citizens can make good choices during elections and effectively respond to issues as needed.

In times of great stress, our kids will be susceptible to following the images of what they see as a reaction to what is visually shown to be the truth. Ten-second sound bytes, however, don't provide the depth youths need to understand their world. I believe that in the future, those who can control the flow of information and visual presentations of the same will be able to manipulate the masses—particularly during times of great distress. Kids need to be savvy about how they can be swayed, so they won't be vulnerable.

Additionally, to reinforce the concepts in this chapter, review the following chapters of this book: chapter 2, "Deception: A Misleading Word" (especially helpful when talking about undercover reporting); chapter 3, "Secrets, Lies, and the Truth" (especially for addressing questions of when a news story should or shouldn't be reported); and chapter 4, "Illusion and Reality: Checking Out the Facts" (particularly for understanding the nature of an illusion as deliberate or non-deliberate).

CHAPTER ELEVEN

Music Trends You Should Know About

◆

Music often mirrors what kids feel inside—from Beach Boy joy to melodic melancholy to soaring spiritual experiences. It also enhances their emotions and is one of the most powerful mediums for influencing their behavior.

Studies estimate that between seventh and twelfth grades, on average kids listen to over *ten thousand hours* of music—about the same amount of time they spend in the classroom from entering kindergarten until graduating from high school. One study of kids aged eleven to fifteen found that "successful students, including those from low socioeconomic backgrounds, exhibited a preference for mainstream music, and less interest in [punk music—a form that often has violent themes]," while students who did poorly gravitated toward punk and similar forms of alienated music.[1]

Some call music "the soul's open window." It shouldn't be threatening to youths, but today it often is. Although many performers use this medium sensitively, plenty of others don't—churning out lyrics that debase women and glorify sadomasochism, or producing videos in which they outrageously simulate sexual acts in blatant disregard of the AIDS threat. Critics of this downward trend are no longer limited to church and civic leaders, as critics from the music industry itself have joined in crying foul.

It used to be that a parent only had to hear a recording to determine if an artist's music was suitable for their child. That has changed. Music today is often image driven by videos, not melody or lyric driven. Many artists now release recordings that are suitable for listening, but their concert performances, videos, or personal character are objectionable, making it necessary for parents to evaluate the whole package of goods being sold. Fortunately, a wealth of music is still produced that is suitable for youths.

In this chapter we will look at some dominant forces that have driven these destructive trends, how and why they have manifested themselves, their effect on youths, and how to respond with positive alternatives.

TRACING THE ROOTS OF DESTRUCTIVE TRENDS

In the sixties, musicians such as Janis Joplin and Jimi Hendrix introduced a raw, jagged-sounding music into popular culture, and the mass appeal of this sound still exists today. It was inspired by the technology of electric guitars and blaring amps, the availability of drugs, and the discontent seeded in part by American families splitting up.

This new music was an *enhancer* of the social discontent at an energy level that also acted as a *mirror* of the high-energy level of youths. Joplin's raspy and often angry voice was like a shout distorted by a defective mixing board, and Hendrix's runs exemplified the high-voltage energy of the times. Tragically, Joplin died of a drug overdose, and Hendrix asphyxiated on his own vomit in the back of an ambulance on September 18, 1970. News reports noted the presence of barbiturate drugs in his system.

Consider other tragic stories from rock musicians of the sixties and seventies, such as the popular group Fleetwood Mac. In 1990, Mick Fleetwood dispelled rumors that the original group was going to reunite for a twenty-fifth anniversary concert. Fleetwood explained that this was impossible because the original three guitarists were all in desperate situations: Danny Kirwan lived in a hostel for the homeless in England; Jeremy Spencer was a member of the Children of God cult; and Peter Green was "just not in the proper state of mind, to put it bluntly."[2]

Drugs and Music—An Inseparable Pair

The combination of drugs and music became inseparable for many musicians and their fans. The mind-altering chemicals that the Beatles and millions of others ingested offered the lying promise of an instantly changed reality that would be exciting and pain free. Of course reality didn't change, but many young people "fried their brains" pursuing this lie.

While I was in college in the late sixties and early seventies, my fellow students and I were openly courted by professors to "give it a try" and "don't knock it until you try it." To object to the craziness was to become an object of scorn. I watched many friends deteriorate with frightening speed as common sense vanished. Simultaneously, parents in record numbers abandoned the sacred vows of marriage and strapped their families on the rack of divorce. As the parents rebelled, the not-so-subtle message to the youth was that they too should rebel—and they did.

Although my generation experienced the proliferation of divorced parents, our grandparents still retained the memory of a stable and secure home. For most of us there was at least a choice of relatives to turn to for reassuring warmth and security. But the concept that the family was a sacred place from which children derived part of their identity was losing ground.

The catch phrase "do your own thing" permeated our culture. Not all students who did drugs and listened to the Rolling Stones wailed "I can't get no satisfaction" to mask their internal pain. For some it was just a more intense, permissive expression of the ageless teen rebellion. Since the culture said it was okay to be permissive, they did just that, and a "sexual revolution" followed.

Other youths sought a numbing experience, using high-decibel music to drown out their conscious problems and drugs to create an altered state. They did so to mask their pain or to distract themselves from that internal pain, born of severe problems at home—or the lack of a home to go to.

While the Beach Boys crooned about "good vibrations," the Beatles, who altered the sound of the music we listen to, popularized the combination of Eastern mystical spiritual pursuits and drug use. This blend is not unique, nor was it new. In the New Testament, the Greek word *pharmakos,* sometimes translated as "sorcerer" or "magician," referred to an occultist who dispensed magic potions and cast spells at the same time. (It comes from the root word *pharmakeia,* from which we get our modern word *pharmacy*.) The idea here was that occultists gave drugs (potions) and cast spells to create the illusion in followers' minds of supernatural spiritual powers.

The New Generation of Rootlessness

In the eighties, the illusory promise of power offered by drugs alone wasn't enough to satisfy a unique generation of American youth. For this unprecedented generation, the positive collective memory of family was gone.

For many of these youths, in addition to having divorced parents, it was no longer uncommon to have a host of aunts, uncles, and even grandparents who were divorced. As the numbers of these kids have grown, so too have the numbers of those on the edge for whom the pain is intolerable.

This is the fundamental reason that in the late seventies and early eighties we began to see increasingly bizarre behavior in youths, often characterized by strange spiked hair. These hairdos were a cry for help from hurting individuals who silently pleaded, *Pay attention. Look at my pain.* Other youths pierced their ears with rows of small safety pins, sending out the message: *Listen to my pain. I want to know someone loves me.* In the late eighties new music forms, such as industrial and new wave, often reflected this despair in a jarring and disjointed sound.

The music that drew in many of these on-the-edge youths violently expressed their despair. In movements such as hard-core, punk, and thrash, violent acts on stage and even in the crowds became commonplace. Performers smashed their guitars and amps during concerts, while kids wildly slammed into each other, causing bodily injury.

At the same time, teen satanism surfaced in the mid-eighties, declaring, "All right, you don't want to listen? Then this is what I think of you!"

Teenagers do things dramatically. It's their nature. It's no different when they're expressing pain. This is especially true when the source of the pain is a fragmented family life. When these stresses are piled on young people who are already going through intense hormonal changes, it's a recipe for disaster. Enter the nineties.

TODAY'S VIOLENT MUSIC

As millions of teens today drown in a pool of substance abuse, the music they listen to has become so violent, lewd, and overtly sadomasochistic that local communities are passing laws—which federal judges are upholding—to ban or censor the sale of this music to minors.

I'm now going to quote lyrics excerpted from music of the eighties that has set the tone for the nineties. I'm sure it will offend you—but what you *don't* know *can* hurt your kids.

Ted Nugent, "Violent Love"[3]
Took her in the room with the mirrors on the walls,
Showed her my brand new ship . . .
Screamed as she started to slip.
Give me a dose
Of your violent love.

Mötley Crüe, "Tonight (We Need a Lover)"[4]
Slide down my knees, taste my sword.

Mötley Crüe, "Ten Seconds to Love"[5]
Touch my gun
But don't pull my trigger . . .
Shine my pistol some more . . .
I got one more shot
My gun's still warm.

Judas Priest, "Eat Me Alive"[6]
Squealing in passion as the rod of steel injects. . . .

Carnivore, "Predator"[7]
I sense that living human beings dwell below my feet
an important source of protein you are what you eat . . .
broken splintered bones, boiling blood
torn and bleeding skin
blackened burning flesh melting fat
amputated limbs
eviscerated, lungs torn out
heart ripped from the chest
decapitated, a meal of vagina and breasts.

There is no statistical proof that violent forms of music actually cause a student to commit crimes. Reliable studies are difficult because the youth culture changes so fast. By the time a new trend is suspected of inflicting harm, it has often transformed itself into many splinter variations or disappeared altogether. But there is little dispute that *for kids who are troubled, destructive forms of music reinforce their anger and rage, making it more acceptable to act out that rage, increasing the likelihood of violent acts.* We don't find youths committing crimes after listening to Brahms, but it is apparent with heavy-metal music, exemplified by some of the lyrics just quoted. In fact, a number of convenience-store owners across the United States have started piping classical music inside and outside their stores. They have found it to be an effective deterrent to kids hanging around who have violent tendencies. Kids leave because the music is too passive.

Although it's not the underlying cause, music clearly does affect behavior. For example, studies have revealed the following connections:

> Of chemically dependent adolescents, 60% named heavy metal
> as their first music of choice. . . . In a laboratory study of the
> effect of music television (MTV) [it was discovered that] 7th
> and 10th graders, after watching 1 hour of selected music videos,
> were more likely to approve of premarital sex compared with
> a control group of adolescents. . . . Another behavioral study
> found that violent music videos desensitized viewers to violence
> immediately after viewing.[8]

The mixture of sex and violence is not new to our race. Throughout this century, "art houses" have featured X-rated movies, and pornographic magazines have supplied a steady output of material that debases women. But what is unprecedented today is the wholesale marketing of morally abhorrent material to young people. And probably no group is more vulnerable or susceptible than teenagers.

One retired executive in his sixties expressed shock that this music even existed, since he couldn't understand the blaring lyrics. He asked, "Did they crank up the volume of the instruments and synthesizers to make it impossible to understand the lyrics, so they could get by with this stuff?"

To understand the lyrics in these songs, a youth has to listen to the music over and over. The masking of the words by the monstrous volume of the "melody" may have crossed some producer's mind, and some youths laugh at those adults around them who are unaware of what the lyrics say. But a more likely explanation is that the loud volume, which started rising in the fifties, works commercially because for some youths it drowns everything out, creating a comfortable, pulsating cocoon, while for others it mirrors their internal rage.

VIOLENT LYRICS, VIOLENT ACTS

Robert Hicks, a criminal justice analyst for the Virginia Department of Criminal Justice Services, said that as a professional it is out of bounds for him to make any pronouncements about the value or lack of value of heavy metal or any other kind of music. But when Hicks, who is single, was asked, "If you were a parent, would you want your child to go into a heavy-metal music shop?" his succinct answer was "no."[9]

Kenneth Lanning, a special agent for the FBI's behavioral science division and one of the FBI's leading experts on sexual crimes against children, voiced a similar sentiment. Lanning comes out of the law enforcement tradition of upholding the law without making value judgments. Yet he said that he believes some music contains "messages that are dangerous and anti-social when combined with displaced loners."[10]

That many youths feel isolated and alone is reflected in the suicide rates cited in chapter 7: more than one out of four youths have contemplated suicide and one in twelve have actually attempted it. Yet the lure of profits have driven some musicians to produce music that directly appeals to these despondent youths. Some experts believe, with good cause—as evidenced by the following lyrics—that mindless exploitation even reinforces this suicidal trend.

Ozzy Osbourne, "Suicide Solution"[13]
Breaking laws, knocking doors
But there's no one at home
Made your bed, rest your head
But you lie there and moan
Where to hide,
Suicide is the only way out
Don't you know what it's really about?

Suicidal Tendencies, "Suicidal Failure"[14]
Father forgive me
For I know now what I do,
I tried everything
Now I'll leave it up to you.
I don't want to live.
I don't know why.
I don't have no reasons,
I just want to die.

In the eighties, music forms such as punk, thrash, and heavy metal became dominant forces that embraced violence and "macho/sexist/fascist/absurdist" excesses, as one music critic labeled them. The most dominant of these "headbanger" genres was heavy metal, a phrase coined by music critic Sandy Pearlman.

Consider one reporter's account of a heavy-metal concert held in Salt Lake City and attended by over thirteen thousand, which featured festival seating—in which there are no reserved seats on the stadium floor, and so youths jostle for position:

> Jimmie Boyd Sr. barely earns enough as an auto mechanic to feed and clothe his family, but when his 14-year-old son, Jimmie, Jr., pleaded for $18 to go to a heavy metal concert here last weekend he acquiesced.
>
> He drove his son to the Salt Palace where the Australian group AC/DC was performing and returned later to pick him up at the appointed corner. No Jimmie.
>
> Hours later, as if in a nightmare, two police officers arrived at the Boyds' door. Jimmie was dead, they said, trampled and suffocated by a surging crowd that pressed toward the stage as the band played "Thunderstruck."[15]

Jimmie was one of three people trampled to death. Some observers said that the band continued to play even though parts of the crowd at the front chanted for them to stop. One security guard estimated that the band, one of the most popular in the world, continued to play for over a half hour after the trampled mass was observed. He said that kids are trampled at virtually all heavy-metal concerts he's seen and that these kids are "passed hand to hand like rag dolls, over the heads of the crowd, until they reach a paramedic station at the rear of the arena."[16]

Chicago Tribune writer Bob Greene, who has covered many concerts as a reporter, advises parents not to allow their kids to attend a "festival seating" concert. He says that the risk of a tragedy occurring is too great—"do everything you can to keep your children from going," he warns parents.[17] This is good advice, but we can add: that includes going to see groups that portray violent themes.

In these music forms, overtly anti-Judeo-Christian and satanic themes are also common—themes that justifiably outrage those in the Christian community, just as music from Eastern Europe with anti-Semitic themes is criticized by the Jewish community.

Rolling Stones leader Mick Jagger, a rock-and-roll performer and not a heavy-metal singer, was one of the first to glorify Satan in his song "Sympathy for the Devil." But the three kinds of heavy metal—speed metal, thrash metal, and death metal—first openly scorned women and the Christian faith. Two such groups were Slayer and Venom. Here is a sampling of their lyrics:

Slayer, "Necrophiliac"[18]
I feel the urge,
The growing need,
To f—— this sinful corpse;
My task's complete,
The bitch's soul
Lies raped in demonic lust.

Venom, "Sacrifice"[19]
Sacrifice,
Oh so nice . . .
Sacrifice to Lucifer, my master.
Bring the chalice,
Raise the knife,
Welcome to my sacrifice;
Plunge the dagger in her breast,
I insist.
S-a-c-r-i-f-i-c-e . . .
Demons rejoice,
Sacrifice, sacrifice,
Name your price.

These lines appear on the jacket cover for Venom's album *Welcome to Hell*:

We're possessed by all that is evil
The death of you, God, we demand
We spit at the virgin you worship
And sit at Lord Satan's left hand.[20]

The following photos of album cover graphics provide a sampling of the kind of artwork typical of much heavy-metal music:

11.1. Note the themes of death in this illustration.

11.2. A demon figure grips a likeness of Christ used as a slingshot.

11.3. This illustration depicts the threat that many youths feel in their own homes. Note what appears to be an open Bible, a crystal ball, and the "horned hand" sign, which youths identify with Satan.

In one heavy-metal magazine, a well-known singer who was satirizing Christian music spoke of his new "born-again" act that would feature the decapitation of John the Baptist. Is it surprising that the first voices opposing this influence on youth were from the church at large—from Catholic to Baptist to Episcopalian?

There is little disagreement that music such as this is potentially harmful to those on the isolated emotional fringe. Numerous youths I have interviewed, who either witnessed acts of violence or were the object of that violence, said that they were convinced the violent lyrics of the music they and their friends listened to inspired the violence. *Not one youth said that these lyrics were a deterrent to violence.*

Tragic Case Histories
In December 1987, a tragic event occurred in Joplin, Missouri. According to one participant, as well as several experts who studied the case, preoccupation with heavy-metal music was a factor.

Theron "Pete" Roland, Ron Clements, and Jim Hardy were teenagers in a self-styled satanic group. They ritually sacrificed animals and listened obsessively to heavy-metal music with satanic lyrics. This preoccupation with violence led to the "sacrifice" of classmate Steven Newberry, during which the three bludgeoned him to death with baseball bats and then dumped his body down "the well of hell."

The factor of heavy-metal music showed up in another violent incident, which occurred in 1985. Two days before Christmas, Raymond Belknap, eighteen, and James Vance, twenty, smoked marijuana and drank beer while listening to the heavy-metal group Judas Priest. Then they shot themselves with a 12-gauge shotgun.

Belknap died immediately. Vance, after several excruciating surgeries, later succumbed from the blast to his face, embracing the Christian faith before he died.

THE EFFORT TO COUNTER DEGENERATING LYRICS

Tipper Gore's book *Raising PG Kids in an X-Rated World* in part chronicles the downward trend of entertainment marketed for youths. Different branches of the arts now frequently debase Christians, Jews, minorities, and women. One of the worst of the recent offenders is the group Guns 'N' Roses, which puts down blacks.

Although not a musician, one nightclub comedian, Andrew Dice Clay, set a tone for angry and irrational lewdness that was so offensive members of NBC's *Saturday Night Live* troupe refused to appear on a TV broadcast Clay was to host on May 12, 1990. Identifying this trend toward baseless vulgarity, *Time*'s May 7, 1990 cover story was entitled, "Dirty Words—America's Foul-Mouthed Pop Culture." It begins:

He struts onstage, and 17,000 New Yorkers start to cheer.
Andrew Dice Clay tells jokes for a living—dirty jokes, stag party jokes, jokes designed to singe a churchgoer's soul and turn a

feminist's stomach—but he attracts crowds whose size and ardor would thrill a rock star. . . . He is America's rajah of comic raunch. . . . "I know you know the old s---," he slurs between drags on a cigarette. "But it's a new decade, and I got new filth for ya." And he does too. Again the crowd roars.[21]

Juxtaposed to the lead of *Time's* write-up was a shot of the heavy-metal band Mötley Crüe. Each member defiantly extended his middle finger toward the lens of the camera; red and silver satanic pentagrams adorned their leather-covered fists and one member's forehead.

The lie sold by many of these performers is that they believe in their material. Clay admitted, however, on a nationally broadcast, late-night talk show, "I don't like this stuff. Everybody else does. I just deliver it."

Other groups, such as 2 Live Crew, feature grotesquely raunchy music that isn't so much an expression of anger—as found in heavy metal—but more like school kids learning their first cuss words. Like Andrew Dice Clay, 2 Live Crew band leader Luther Campbell appears to know that his licentious antics inflict harm. He told reporters that he wouldn't let his seven-year-old child listen to his albums that contained sexually explicit language. "She's not ready for it," he said. "She's not an adult."[22]

Degenerating comedy routines and musical lyrics have not gone unchallenged. One music critic wrote, "In popular culture's market system, it is up to listeners to repudiate messages they dislike, passively or actively—and to disabuse bigots of any claim to the mainstream."[23]

Fortunately, some local communities have taken action. This has resulted in numerous obscenity arrests of reckless bands and indictments of record-store managers for selling albums with explicit lyrics to those who are underage. In addition, music distributors and retail chains have responded to public pressure by pulling a number of recordings from their catalogs and stores.

The familiar cry of "censorship" by these offending groups is the flimsy cloak they try to hide behind. In 1973 the U.S. Supreme Court ruled that for speech to be considered obscene, it must fail the following three-part test: "if it is patently offensive to community standards, if an average person would find that it appeals primarily to prurient interest, and if it lacks serious artistic, political, or scientific merit."[24]

Even members of the press who champion freedom of speech and expression have denounced the offensive lyrics these bands spew forth. One editorial expressed,

> Suggestive lyrics have given way to explicit ones. Some of what these groups sing, you wouldn't want to see on a public restroom wall, let alone on an album played by a teenager. Among the messages are: (1) Women are sex objects to be abused; (2) violence is a good way to resolve conflicts; and (3) it is okay to hate people who are different.[25]

One expert on civil liberties wrote, "The First Amendment does not shield speech from criticism. We must continue to defend their right to be offensive, but we must also condemn comedy [or music] that offends for the sake of offending."[26] While we must not move toward censorship, we must vigorously protest and support organizations that effectively lobby for change.

The Parents' Music Resource Center has made a difference. Run by Tipper Gore (wife of U.S. Senator Albert Gore) and Susan Baker (wife of Secretary of State James Baker), the Center effectively lobbied Congress for several years, resulting in the warning labels now placed on musical recordings that contain explicit lyrics.

Even if your child doesn't listen to this kind of music, he or she probably has schoolmates who do. Facing up to this trend as part of mainstream pop culture is disquieting, but at least you won't be blindsided if your youth tells you about it. Also, these lyrics seem to appeal to those who are more prone to violent acts and who come from dysfunctional homes. It's helpful to point this out to kids so they can understand what makes some of their friends tick.

In some cases, this understanding can be helpful when well-adjusted kids carefully reach out to offer help to troubled kids. Our family has had several experiences in which our kids, tipped off by the music their friends played, were able to find an adult to help that child who was in familial or other kinds of trouble.

MUSIC AS ENHANCER AND ENERGY METER

For all of us, music can be a wonderful vehicle to mirror our feelings, soothe hurts, or provide a vehicle for reflection. Upbeat songs can help pull us out of the doldrums. Music is an enhancer of what we feel, and often reflects our energy level.

Heavy-metal, punk, and hard-core music are, in a way, like a two-way magnifying glass. In one direction these styles of music magnify for adults what is going on inside some youths; in the other direction the music intensifies and focuses youths' attention on their pain. It is important, however, to distinguish between the *sound* of heavy metal and the *lyrics* of heavy metal or other jarring forms of music.

Not all heavy-metal, punk, and hard-core songs have demeaning lyrics. For example, some Christian bands use the heavy-metal *sound* to communicate a Christian message to disenfranchised kids, who would normally never listen to a Grammy-award-winning Christian singer like Michael W. Smith or Sandy Patti. Here's an example of lyrics by one Christian heavy-metal band, Bloodgood (the group's name was taken from the band leader's name, Michael Bloodgood), from their song "Out of the Darkness":

I am the witness of disaster
It seemed the only way was down
I saw the wicked in his scheming
I heard his victims crying out
Why do the evil prosper, his victims crushed
I see the shadows growing, I've had enough.

(Refrain:)
Out of the darkness into the light
I heard ten thousand cry
Out of the darkness into the light
Turn or you will die.

My God how long will you forget me
O Lord I need to see your face
The enemy has come against me
He laughs at me, prepared to slay
Yet I will trust in You, Lord, my heart will sing
I'll wait to hear your voice God, you'll hear me scream
(Repeat refrain)

You are the helper of the helpless
The adversary has no might
I hear your voice of thunder,
The lightning strikes

The night will flee before you,
You'll win the fight![27]

The themes in Christian heavy metal are the same as in traditional hymns: salvation, discipleship, resisting temptation, grace, and so on—but the lyrics are often far more intense. Most adults may not like the discordant and loud sounds of this style, but these Christian bands have brought kids who are already listening to heavy metal back to better values.

Why are kids attracted to this sound? One producer characterized the average age of heavy-metal listeners as thirteen to sixteen. They are usually high-energy kids. Some have family problems and others don't. What they do have in common is that they're intense, so they listen to a music style that's intense—its high-energy level matches their own.

Especially during periods of cultural intensity, kids will want to listen to music that is at a higher energy level than their parents' music. Kids who listen to heavy metal usually don't listen to any other styles of music, which is why Christian heavy metal is sometimes the only musical vehicle that can reach them with a positive message. When they get older, though, they usually move on to other styles of music as their energy level and focus in life changes.

Some Christian kids who don't come from troubled homes, but who do feel pressured by schoolmates who do drugs, for example, are provoked by what is around them, and so they react intensely. The intensity of Christian heavy metal reflects what these kids feel.

Producers of Christian heavy metal don't recommend it for all kids, but for some it provides a positive, usually temporary, bridge. They also don't recommend a listening volume that will impair hearing, but encourage kids to lower the sound enough to benefit from the words.

What's most important to note here is that it has not been observed that the *sound* of heavy metal inspires disenfranchised youths to commit crimes or become involved with satanism. Rather, it is the *lyrics* that inspire horrific acts of violence.

SPECIFIC AREAS OF CONCERN

Now let's look at three particular areas in today's music trends that many parents are concerned about: "backmasking" or subliminal messages, sexual themes, and music videos.

The Question of Backmasking and Subliminal Messages

For the past several years, much has been made of what is called "backmasking"—words that can be heard in a rock song when a record or tape is played backward. I'm including the following section in this chapter because there have been so many questions about the alleged impact of backmasking.

Currently, there are two types of backmasking: (1) When the audible lyrics of certain songs are played backward, a covert message is revealed; and (2) an unintelligible sound byte is deliberately laid in one of the tracks of music, so that when the song is played backward, a message is revealed.

The most heralded example of the first type of backmasking was noted in the song "Stairway to Heaven," recorded in the late sixties by the group Led Zeppelin. According to Rev. Eric Holmberg, founder of Reel to Real Ministries and an expert on contemporary rock music, this song and virtually every other example of this first genre of backmasking are the product of chance, not deliberate intent. He says that if you recorded all the church hymns ever written in different styles, you might even hear the word *Satan* in one of the hymns played backward.

One group, Venom, deliberately used the second technique, a garbled sound byte that revealed a message when the song was played backward. Here are the words that can be heard when "In League with the Devil" is played backward:

Satan, Satan
Raised in hell, raised in hell
I'm going to crush your bones
Steal your soul
You're gonna bleed
You're gonna bleed from me.[28]

This second type of backmasking is uncommon but easy to spot because of what experts describe as an unusual "phase" sound.

Even if these kinds of messages were deliberate, testing shows that a message heard backward cannot be understood, nor can it influence behavior. In a controlled experiment, psychologists John R. Vokey and J. Don Read at the University of Lethbridge found that backmasked messages did not influence the behavior of their test groups. They concluded that the brain cannot unconsciously reverse words played in a forward mode and "hear" a message.[29]

Some groups, however, such as Christian Death (not a Christian group), have included lyrics with individual words reversed. Christian Death used this technique in their song "Stairs." As they are sung, the lyrics read as follows:

> This is the city of God
> Ereht si on ytic fo dog
> Nmad eht eman fo dog[30]

If you play this song backwards, it remains garbled. But if each individual word in the last two lines is reversed and then *read,* the lyrics become:

> This is the city of God
> There is no city of God
> Damn the name of God

These lyrics refer to the city of Jerusalem, often called the City of David or the City of God. Anti-Christian themes are common when this kind of reversal is present. This technique is similar to some satanic rituals, in which the cross is inverted or Christian liturgy is read backward as a symbol of rebellion.

Some speculate that these lyric reversals are created to communicate a blasphemous message. A more likely reason for the technique is to create a gimmick that will get kids talking, consequently selling more records. Thus the blasphemy is just a byproduct of greed and childish rebellion.

Another sales gimmick is to record a "subliminal" message at such a low level that it can't be heard unless the volume is raised or the track is isolated and listened to separately from the loud instrumentals or voices. In their song "You're Not the One," Blue Oyster Cult implanted, "Furthermore, our father who art in heaven—Satan"!

Even if these subliminal messages could be heard, which most can't, they would have little influence on behavior because the words that *can* be heard are as severe, or even *more* severe, than subliminally planted phrases.

To summarize, the influence of backmasking and subliminal messages has been greatly exaggerated. First, there are very few examples relative to the number of songs produced. Second, most of these messages can't be understood. And third, ideas suggested by straightforward lyrics are already degrading and potentially destructive in their influence.

Sexual Themes

By far the most influential and easily understood of the destructive music trends are performers whose recordings, live performances, and videos are designed to sexually titillate. The promotion of sexual themes has come a long way since Elvis Presley's appearance in 1957 on the *Ed Sullivan Show*—but only from the waist up, to censor his gyrating hips. In 1962 John Lennon appeared in concert with a toilet ring around his neck, signifying his sexual encounter backstage. In 1973, rocker Alice Cooper dismembered baby dolls in his concerts as he simulated sex with a snake. In 1975, Mick Jagger unveiled a forty-foot-long balloon—representative of a male phallus. In 1981, Prince stripped to his bikini underwear during a concert and simulated sexual antics on a brass bed positioned center-stage.

Currently, one of the most visible of these performers is Madonna, who last year grossed over $60 million. Her music video *Justify My Love* alone sold over 500,000 copies. Here is how one music critic chronicled Madonna's exploits:

> July 1985: *Playboy* and *Penthouse* publish nude photo-
> graphs. . . .
> April 1989: Fundamentalist groups pressure Pepsi-Cola into
> dropping a commercial using Madonna's "Like a Prayer." The
> video of the song includes images of interracial love, stigmata,
> and burning [Christian] crosses.
> June 1990: During the "Blond Ambition" tour, the Toronto
> police are summoned to Skydome Stadium after complaints
> about Madonna's erotic antics in "Like a Virgin" [in which she
> simulated numerous sexual acts].
> October 1990: Dressed in lingerie and draped in an Ameri-
> can flag, Madonna exhorts MTV viewers to vote or face a
> "spankie." The Veterans of Foreign Wars complains that the use
> of the flag "borders on desecration." [Madonna's line was: Dr.
> King, Malcolm X, freedom of speech is as good as sex.]
> November 1990: MTV refuses to run the video of "Justify
> My Love," which depicts voyeurism, bisexuality, and mild
> sadomasochism. In December, *Nightline* broadcasts the video,
> earning the ABC program its second-highest ratings.[31]

Another music critic wrote of her movie *Truth or Dare,* a pseudo-documentary of one of her tours: "Madonna bares her breasts, but not her soul. . . . But Dare's revealing material does humanize the B---- Goddess. She cavorts in bed with gay dancers. . . . She pushes the envelope on stage (simulating masturbation in *Like a Virgin*) and off (simulating oral sex with a water bottle)."[32]

The director of *Truth or Dare,* which played in theaters across the United States in 1991, observed of Madonna's troupe: "This world was very Feliniesque. The dancers were accessible and flamboyant, and Madonna was like the matriarch in a circus. There was an odd connection among the people because almost everybody came from a broken home or from an unusual family."[33]

It is not uncommon that many performers who exploit youths with explicitly sexual themes are themselves from broken or dysfunctional homes. In a sense, their exploitation of youths is in some instances a twisted form of revenge for the victimization they suffered—a form of control. It's somewhat analogous to the troubled male whose sexual conquests are wrapped up in a warped sense of self-esteem or the female who gives of herself sexually to control men—whom she identifies with an abusive or neglectful father. This is a tragedy in itself, and the exploitation of youths from stable and unstable homes is predictable.

As we'll explore in chapter 12, family instability is one primary factor fueling a youthful desire for teen sexual activity. That artists exploit this vulnerability in our culture is inappropriate. As with unwanted TV programming, parents should lodge their protest with sponsors. (Pressure by the Catholic church in Rome in May 1990 forced Madonna to play to a greatly reduced crowd and the cancellation of a second anticipated concert.)

In 1991, the use of sexual themes even slipped into a pop video released by a critically acclaimed Christian artist. The song itself, which became a hit on the pop charts, contained no sexual themes, but the music video of the song featured a suggestive sequence in which a teen coyly played with the buttons of her shirt, as if teasing her boyfriend that she might undress. The video was an instant success on most secular charts.

As Christian music increasingly moves to the mainstream and more artists "cross over" into the secular charts, so will the pressure increase, subtly and not so subtly, to incorporate sexual themes in order to "reach a bigger audience with your message." I personally became acquainted with the artist associated with the above video, and I have always been impressed by this person's integrity. I hope that this video reflects a temporary lapse of judgment and not a fundamental change of philosophy when communicating with youths.

Music Videos and MTV

In 1981, MTV entered the cable market and changed the very appearance of television, from commercials to movies to news shows. Lightning fast edits, jerky pans and zooms, and exotic lighting are part of the style. The result is a visual overload that can transform even inept singers into stars overnight.

The demand for this jarring style was birthed because kids like things snap-popping, and not always with a clear sense of meaning. It's a feelings-oriented way of communicating that downplays thinking: you don't evaluate, you just feel. If only for this reason, MTV is a problem. Kids need to be challenged to think things through and sort out what they feel, rather than just indulge their emotions without understanding what's driving them.

The idea behind music videos was initially as free airtime to promote performers. Then some music videos earned a place as a form of artful expression. Michael W. Smith's video "I Missed the Way" is one elegant example. Solid with content, this piece urges kids who have gone the way of the prodigal son to return. Bebe and Cece Wynan are another example of a top-forty success whose music videos, such as "It's Time," are positive reinforcements for kids.

Music videos, like television, should be watched in moderate doses because of the heavy reliance on visual imagery. In many cases, listening to a song while imagining what it means is far better for stretching young minds than having the lyrics spelled out pictorially. Some songs, however, such as Michael W. Smith's "Secret Ambition," which is about the passion of Christ, can be more powerfully imparted through a music video.

The medium of music videos itself can be a positive experience. MTV and similar ventures that exploit violent and sexual themes, however, should be excluded altogether. Violence and sex are easy to portray visually, and MTV serves up quantum doses of this twenty-four hours a day. If you want to get a peek of teenage hell, turn on the "Headbanger" show on the weekend. I encourage all parents to do so just for the education—and to note the name-brand sponsors. Many kids I have interviewed who involved themselves in satanism repeatedly spoke of watching these shows and feeling inspired by what they saw and heard.

Just consider one visual sequence: "the commanding macho musicians point contemptuously to a woman in her underwear crawling on hands and knees to eat out of a dog dish."[34] In another video two young children watch a young couple involved graphically in the sex act.

Who sponsors MTV? Advertisers from Mars candy to Samsonite luggage. Paige Miller, director of marketing services at Samsonite, in an MTV advertisement in the business section of the *New York Times,* said, "MTV targets young adults with exactly the cutting edge we were looking for. Sammies are designed for young active people and that's what we're looking for. MTV is a part of virtually every young adult's life. If you advertise to that age group, MTV definitely needs to be one of your choices."[35]

Many network news programs, such as CBS' *48 Hours,* now emulate MTV techniques through slicker and faster presentation of stories with reduced content. This trend reflects a deliberate marketing strategy for increased revenue through reaching the lucrative eighteen-to-thirty-four age group, which has been taught to get what they want fast, without thinking about it. In response to these industry tactics, wise parents will keep MTV out of the home and music videos to a minimum.

CONCLUSION

For most kids who listen to destructive music, the music itself is usually not the root of the problem. Some kids will listen to outrageous music forms simply to test their parents or out of basic rebellion, but most do so because of other problems: troubles at home, lack of friends, despair brought on by geographical moves, and so on. Music and drugs are often only the gasoline poured on an already raging fire.

This audible distress signal can have a lifesaving consequence when it lets others know that these kids are in trouble and need help.

For kids who are simply rebelling, a plan of action might involve a stern "no"; pointing out the ill-effect on others in confronting the lie behind such statements as "it can't change how you think"; and most importantly, directing kids to other music forms or artists who might have a similar sound without the offensive lyrics. Remember, *kids want to know where the limits are,* even when they don't show it.

Finally, even though destructive trends are accelerating, there are still many artists to choose from whose music is acceptable. Learning who those artists are requires a little bit of homework: listening to the local radio stations, inquiring of your kids and others besides your own, taking a trip to the music store. This homework is essential even if your kids aren't preoccupied with or frequently confronted by debasing music, because their friends are.

CHAPTER TWELVE

Sex and Teens, Part One:
A Threatening Firestorm

◆

*Seventy-two percent of all high school students have had
sexual intercourse by the twelfth grade.*
1991 Report by the Center for Disease Control

Two teenagers and two adults I interviewed . . . each with his or her
own unique horror story.

Two young teenage girls were raped.

The first was raped on a date by a teen she knew. As I talked to
her, she was blankly passive. Her lips moved, but her staring eyes were
dead, her emotions buried deep. She wasn't ready to let the horror of
that date overwhelm her again.

On another day, a second young woman turned away in shame. Her
hands shielded her hot, tear-streaked face from me. Through sobbing
screams she described what they did to her. Boys she knew. A group
of them. The shame shouldn't have been hers, but it was.

On another day, a man now in his twenties spoke of a different kind
of shame. Although he had not been raped and had not participated in
a similar act of violence, he talked about the time it took to overcome
his shame.

Before he married, he had slept with another. He loves his wife,
but he regrets that their bedroom intimacy, shared in love, had been
compromised years before. He knows there are other happily married men and women who share the same shame, and he knows he

165

is forgiven; but still, his regret remains.

I interviewed the fourth man, skyscraper tall Earvin "Magic" Johnson, star forward of the Los Angeles Lakers, in the fall of 1989 in Salt Lake City, Utah. I interviewed Johnson because I had heard that firewalker and infomercial king Tony Robbins had invited him to a seminar when they both were in Hawaii. Magic said that he declined the invitation because "it was a little too far out for me."

It's unfortunate that Johnson didn't use the same kind of wisdom in his private sexual life. On November 7, 1991, he announced to the world that he was infected with the HIV virus—which leads to AIDS—from heterosexual relations. Less than two months earlier, he had married his longtime girlfriend in a small Baptist church in Michigan. Most of the press praised him as a hero for his decision to come forward publicly. Former Lakers coach Pat Riley led his New York Knicks team in the Lord's prayer on the court prior to their game that night.

At his press conference, Johnson could have seized the moment and urged kids to embrace the virtue of abstinence unashamedly, because premarital sexual contact can have devastating consequences. But he didn't. Instead, he chillingly said, "I will now become a spokesman for the HIV virus because I want young people to realize they should practice safe sex. I want them to understand that safe sex is the way to go."

Safe sex? Ron Ralston, a popular speaker on university campuses, commented, "People confused Magic's openness and sincerity with the truth." How can you have safe sex when condoms fail in over 14 percent of heterosexual relations and 18 percent of homosexual relations?[1] And the rate is certain to be even higher for young, inept teens, because condoms can slip and break. (Additionally, New York City alone experienced a recall in November of 1990 of 750,000 defective condoms, and there is no scientific evidence to date that the HIV virus cannot penetrate latex.) Did Johnson really mean that safe sex was acceptable for kids, or did he just say this in the heat of the moment—the star still needing to feel that he could do something for his fans and remain in the limelight?

A day later, on the *Arsenio Hall Show,* Johnson made his intentions clear: "Please get your thinking caps on and put that cap on down there," he said, pointing down at his lap, "and everything will be all right."

Dave Anderson, sportswriter for the *New York Times,* ran a story on November 14, 1991, bannered, "Sorry, But Magic Johnson Isn't a Hero." Of the basketball star who dropped out of college and fathered a child out of wedlock, he wrote: "Say a prayer for him. But since his disclosure a week ago, too many people sound as if they're praying to him."[2]

In a *Sports Illustrated* article earlier that week, Johnson wrote that he didn't know whom he got the HIV virus from, indicating that he had used his celebrity status as a platform for engaging in rampant promiscuity. Anderson (as well as another of the *Times* writers, Robert Lipsyte) was correct in not labeling Johnson a hero. While expressing compassion toward the suffering that will inevitably be Johnson's final companion, he called him to the carpet for claiming that "God" was leading him. Here is the conclusion to Anderson's article:

> Magic Johnson writes [in *Sports Illustrated*] that having contracted the HIV virus is "God's way" of directing him "to become a teacher, to carry the message about the dangers of AIDS to everyone" after he educates himself about the disease.
>
> "Everything I've done," he writes, "He's directed me."
> Not quite everything, as Magic Johnson knows too well now.[3]

12.1. TV personality, Linda Ellerbee, demonstrates for kids how to use a condom.

12.2. Johnson consoles a small child who has AIDS while he talks with kids about "safe sex."

On March 25, 1992, the children's cable show *Nickelodeon* aired a television special with Johnson and Linda Ellerbee about AIDS. Sponsored by the Nestle Chocolate and Confection Company, Nickelodeon took out full-page ads in newspapers across the United States encouraging kids and families to watch. Graphically, Ellerbee explained and demonstrated how to use a condom to *grade school children* on the set who hadn't even reached puberty. From Johnson, only one brief comment was made about abstaining from sex until marriage; the rest of the time he talked about AIDS and safe sex if one doesn't abstain. Johnson and Ellerbee may be sincere, but downplaying the necessity of abstinence in the face of a life-threatening disease is misguided and irresponsible.

Many kids were shocked and overwhelmed by Johnson's disclosure: Their basketball hero faces an almost certain early death unless a cure is found. But perhaps an even greater tragedy is that many kids thought that their $12-million-a-year hero was right in urging safe sex. As a parent, one can only wonder how many kids will die needlessly because of Magic's misguided advice.

THE PRESSURE IS ON

The trends of date rape, gang rape, premarital sex, and the spread of AIDS are all swiftly accelerating. Before we look at what the proven and good options are in the next chapter, we must first take a look at what's happening to stoke the flames of the impending firestorm among teens.

The statistics are plainly depressing. Studies indicate that about 80 percent of unmarried teenage males and 75 percent of teenage females in the United States have had sex.[4] Here is the latest breakdown of those statistics by grade level:

- ◆ Twelfth grade: 72 percent are sexually active.
- ◆ Eleventh grade: 57 percent.
- ◆ Tenth grade: 48 percent.
- ◆ Ninth grade: 40 percent.[5]

For these teens, the opportunity to set aside that special relationship for a future spouse is lost. Researchers warn that teen sexual activity has escalated dramatically over the past twenty years, and that current rates *increase significantly every year a student is in school.*

When kids are confronted by friends and media messages that taunt, "What, are you afraid of losing your virginity?" they need to know that this is the wrong question. They need to be able to shoot back, "What's the matter, are you so weak that you can't give that gift to the one you will live with the rest of your life?" But the pressure that media messages spew at them is unrelenting. The example I'm about to cite should make any thinking parent in America angry enough to turn off the electronic spigot and weld it shut.

Another Public Example

In 1991, ABC's series *Doogie Howser,* watched by millions of preteens and teens, fired a brutal volley at its viewing audience. In the 1991 season premiere, the character Doogie—a child genius who is a doctor and is looked up to by kids as a positive role model—turns eighteen and laments, "Being a virgin is driving me nuts." One of his pals, Vinnie, informs him that thirty-seven girls lost their virginity over the summer, and then delivers a chilling line: "Peer pressure, it's a beautiful thing."

Before the half-hour show ends, Doogie ceases to be a virgin by bedding his girlfriend, Wanda, and then tells the countless numbers of teens and preteens watching the show, "I felt happy, worried, proud, scared, a little nauseous."

Ed Bark, TV critic for the *Dallas Morning News,* said that his kids, ages seven and nine, weren't going to watch. But what about the hundreds of thousands of families who didn't have the chance to preview the show as Bark did? Millions of preteens and teens tuned in every week, including our own. From the bits and pieces of the series I had previously seen, it seemed like clean, wholesome entertainment. Then executive producers Vic Rauseo and Linda Morris decided to turn to the dark side.

When questioned by Bark about the insanity of broadcasting this show in light of a million teen pregnancies and the spread of sexually transmitted diseases, Rauseo and Morris replied:

> "All we tried to do was be honest," explained executive producer Vic Rauseo. "And Doogie is a doctor. He has a very sophisticated job; he's a very sophisticated kid. He's been in love with this girl for two years. And it seemed it would be dishonest, it would make him kind of weird if nothing happened."
>
> Says executive producer Linda Morris: "We have researched many organizations, and most of the statistics show that teenagers are having sex. And that at the age of eighteen, approximately three-quarters of all teenage boys have had sexual relations. So I don't think we're breaking any new ground here."[6]

These producers clearly believe that kids who don't have sex are "weird" and are not "sophisticated" like Doogie. ABC is so committed to this insidious message—so they wouldn't be "dishonest"—that they blasted it to preteen kids whom they know watch the show every week. *New York Times* critic John J. O'Connor (not to be confused with New York's Cardinal O'Connor) wrote, "Society may frown on children having more babies at earlier ages, especially in urban slums, but the children are only taking their cues from the multi-million dollar image factories plucking recklessly at their daily lives."[7]

O'Connor then detailed a survey of a fourth-grade class in Brooklyn. The survey revealed that their favorite program was *True Colors,* in which one episode featured a nineteen-year-old who admitted that he was a virgin and that he had to rectify the situation as quickly as possible.

The only thing the producers of "Doogie" almost got right were some of the statistics. Critic Ed Bark wrote,

> It's also true that many of the first [sexual] encounters result in unwanted pregnancies and other serious consequences. Doogie is a boy genius who loses his virginity with an uncommon nobleness. He's also a role model whose conduct in a television series isn't inconsequential. *But Mom, Doogie did it!*[8]

Why should parents react and take preventive measures against these kinds of damning messages? A major reason is that, alarmingly, the age of a teen's first sexual intercourse is dropping fast:

◆ By the age of fifteen, 29 percent of girls and 35 percent of boys are sexually active.[9]

◆ In 1982, about 30 percent of fifteen- to seventeen-year-old women were sexually active. In 1988, the number had jumped to 40 percent—an increase of about one third.[10]

◆ In 1988 in the Baltimore-Washington area, one study revealed that "6 percent of the ten-to-twelve-year-olds . . . had sexual intercourse in the four weeks before the interviews."[11]

◆ In 1989, 75 percent of eighteen- to nineteen-year-old white women had sexual intercourse during that year, up from 64 percent in 1982.[12] (A study released by the Alan Guttmacher Institute further noted that there was only a small increase in non-Hispanic black teenage women who were sexually active, but there was an 18 percent increase among non-Hispanic whites.)

THE CONSEQUENCES: PREGNANCY AND DISEASE

What do these statistics tell us? First, *more kids are sexually active than ever before, and at an earlier age.* Second, *more sexually active teens usually means more teen pregnancies.* Third, *the spread of sexually transmitted diseases threatens to destroy our culture.*

In 1990, approximately one million teenagers became pregnant out of wedlock. Thirty-one thousand of them were younger than fifteen.[13] Precise figures are difficult, if not impossible, to determine because some states do not require clinics to report abortions.

Additionally, 20 percent of all sexually active teens don't use contraceptives.[14] Some communities, such as New York City, dispense condoms in the schools without parental consent to abort the spread of AIDS. According to estimates, however, approximately 14 percent of these contraceptive measures fail. (One of the only positive statistics is that there has been a drop in the teenage pregnancy rate per person because more teens use contraceptives. This doesn't mean the overall *number* of pregnancies has dropped, just the pregnancy per person rate.)

As the number of sexually active teenagers has skyrocketed, along with a steep drop in age of first sexual contact, researchers have discovered that the *younger* a youth, the *more* sexual partners he or she has per year.[15] This means that the spread of the killer HIV virus among young people is a certainty. Timothy C. Brock and Laura A. Brannon, professors at Ohio State University, point out that every time one has sex with a partner, one comes in contact not only with the biochemicals of that person, but possibly with the biochemicals of *all their previous partners*. This means that if a person has only one new sexual partner a year between the ages of fifteen and twenty-three—and assuming that each partner has done the same—by the time that person reaches twenty-three, mathematically he or she could be carrying "the bacterial fellow travelers from no fewer than 522 [persons]."[16]

For people with AIDS, which attacks the immune system, the disease is usually fatal. In a sinister twist of bacterial life, the human immunodeficiency (HIV) virus can remain dormant in a person for a period of up to ten years *after* it has been contracted before it balloons into AIDS. How many teens have the HIV virus is difficult to assess, because blood tests require parental approval—a significant obstacle. Nationally, in 1990, only about six hundred teen cases of AIDS were reported to the Center for Disease Control in Atlanta, Georgia. This estimate however, is appallingly low. By May 1992 in just one city, Fort Meyers, Florida, school officials suspected over 100 cases. (According to the World Health Organization's April 1992 forecast, *50 million* will be infected in Asia alone by the year 2000, with 165,000 expected to die in Thailand—a country that has 750,000 prostitutes.)

Nationally in 1992, over *1.5 million people* are believed to be carrying the HIV virus—and that's a *conservative* estimate. Some experts predict that there will be over *five million* carriers in just a few years. One of the only positive fallouts from Magic Johnson's disclosure is that the Center for Disease Control (CDC) proposed changing how they report the numbers of those in whom the HIV virus had manifested itself in the AIDS disease. In 1991, the CDC reported that 195,718 people have AIDS, but that another 160,000 should be added to this number. This means that over *a quarter of a million people* have AIDS and will probably die in the next few years. But that number could easily be many times higher, because the CDC's previous estimates have been seriously flawed by an inability to fully account for all carriers.

Seventeen-year-old Jerrel Dean Martin didn't care about statistics. He never thought he would contract AIDS. But tightness in his chest and swollen glands prompted the Dallas-Ft. Worth Metroplex resident to go to the Tarrant County Health Department, where he tested positive for syphilis and the HIV virus.

"I was so young," he told a reporter. "I cried for three days. I thought, 'Oh, my God. I'm going to die tomorrow.'"[17]

One pediatrician, who is not a moralizer, said, "It is terrifying to think that a number of the kids I see may be dead in the next ten to fifteen years due to AIDS. I have never been one to preach, but I now lecture every family about sexual activity. I don't want to see a holocaust of kids dying because of a lack of restraint."

And this doesn't include the growing numbers of other sexually transmitted diseases (STD), such as herpes, syphilis, chlamydia, genital warts, or a new strain of gonorrhea that is resistant to antibiotics.

Why people continue to allow TV programs and music with sexually provocative messages to be piped into their homes is sheer cultural insanity. The motives of people who churn out these materials are easy to understand: They're driven by greed and lack the creative integrity to find other ways to entertain.

This rising teenage sexual activity coupled with sexually inciting messages, is not, however, isolated to the United States. In the former Soviet Union, the premarital sex rate for youths under twenty-one has climbed to 66 percent as a glut of pornography is plaguing that region. Additionally, one-fifth of the 6.8 million abortions in the now-dismantled Soviet Union involved teenagers.[18] (In 1990, ABC devoted an entire special, "Sex in the Soviet Union," to this changing morality.) No wonder many Russian parents are uneasy about embracing all that the West has to offer.

On December 15, 1989, *Playboy,* one source of these dehumanizing messages, proudly boasted in a full-page ad in the *New York Times*:

> On November 29th, Hungarians came one step closer to something they've been fighting for since 1956. Freedom.
>
> Not just political freedom but freedom of the press. And the first American consumer magazine published in Hungarian was PLAYBOY. No surprise, since we're the magazine that led a social revolution in America by standing for personal, political and economic freedom.
>
> That's the power of PLAYBOY. A power that reaches 15,000,000 readers worldwide.[19]

Editorials in local newspapers often warn of the increasing numbers of teen pregnancies, imploring their readerships to "educate" kids to postpone sexual activity until they're older. Why? Because it's a financial drain, not because it's the morally right thing to do (that it is a virtue to refrain from sexual activity until marriage). The state of Maryland, for example, estimates that the cost of "unwanted pregnancies" in 1990 was "$454 million a year in prenatal care, welfare, and other services."[20]

Increased teen sexual activity at ever younger ages, out-of-wedlock pregnancies, and the increased spread of sexually transmitted diseases should motivate any mature parent—even those who don't subscribe to Judeo-Christian beliefs—to turn off sexually stimulating media that can reach their children, while simultaneously encouraging the virtue of abstaining. For many parents this has been the case, but others may need to take heed of the following violent trends to be motivated.

TRENDS IN SEXUAL VIOLENCE

As the family fabric has broken down, acts of violence committed by teens have escalated during the last ten years. One of those acts is rape committed against women. Alarmingly, a U.S. government survey revealed that *one* out of *eight* women have been raped and *61 percent were raped when minors.*[21] Incoming freshmen at many colleges, such as Bard College in Annondale-on-Hudson, New York, are now going through orientation classes that include information on "date rape," an increasing phenomenon.

"Date rape" is when a woman is violated by an acquaintance—someone she knows—on a date. At the University of Louisville in 1989, eleven cases of date rape were reported. After freshman orientation in 1990, sixty cases were reported during the course of the school year. The increased number of reports was in part due to the fact that these women felt that they would be believed. Awareness of date rape is relatively recent, and although no statistics are available, the general consensus on college campuses and in law enforcement is that it, like other violent crimes, is on the rise.

Rape is a savage act of violence—an acting out of rage that usually has to do with dominating and defiling a woman. Sexual pleasure is usually the smallest motivating factor. Predictably, rapists often come from troubled homes. This fact doesn't excuse their crime, but simply identifies the environment in which they were raised.

What makes date rape particularly vicious is that it's perpetrated by someone familiar to the victim: "In one survey of women on thirty-two college campuses, 15 percent had experienced at least one rape, and 89 percent of the time it was by men the women knew. Half the rapes occurred during a date."[22] To date, no reliable statistics are available for high school students, but increased reports from law enforcement seem to indicate that date rape for high school students is also on the rise.

In one study, only seventeen of 1,152 male college students admitted that they used force to have sex. However, Dr. Neil Malamuth, a psychologist at UCLA, said, "When men are asked if there is any likelihood they would force a woman to have sex against her will if they could get away with it, about half say they would. But if you ask them if they would rape a woman if they could get away with it, only about 15 percent say they would."[23]

A 1979 California study found that 43 percent of male high school and college students considered it "acceptable" to force sex on a woman by the fifth date. Thirty-nine percent said it was acceptable to force sex on a woman if a man had "spent a lot of money on her."[24]

Unless we see a reversal in troubled families and a change in media messages that encourage sexual activity, it's realistic to expect that number of incidents of date rape will only continue to mushroom.

Although not as common as date rape, gang rape is another form of acquaintance rape that "occurs disproportionately on college campuses" and usually goes unreported.[25] Dr. Chris O'Sullivan, a psychologist at Bucknell University, says that in a study of twenty-three cases of gang rape, most of the men thought that it was "okay" to participate because the woman was promiscuous. (Note that these men didn't consider chastity a virtue apart from whatever a particular woman's sexual mores were, nor did they consider this particular kind of rape a crime.) Additionally, Dr. O'Sullivan observes that the women raped in these cases knew one or more of their attackers, and most of the rapes "involved fraternities, or football or basketball teams."[26] (Please don't become paranoid about campus men's groups. These are isolated cases.)

The idea of a gang rape usually has to do with regarding the "sexual humiliation of women as a positive value," says Dr. O'Sullivan:

> In many fraternities, these values are expressed in a variety of practices, from having ugly-date contests (won by the man who takes the most unattractive woman to bed) to arrangements for observing sexual encounters, including peepholes into bedrooms and videotaping setups. These settings are the ones in which the majority of group sexual offenses on campus occur.[27]

Dr. O'Sullivan said that women who avoid going upstairs to use a bathroom in a fraternity house unless accompanied by another female and who realize that getting drunk can be interpreted as being "available" are less likely to be victims of a gang rape because of increased "respectability."

Psychologist Dr. Charlene Muhlenhard advises that to avoid all forms of date rape, a woman should give a clear indication that sex is not a part of the date. If she is accosted, "physical resistance, screaming, claiming to have a venereal disease" and the most powerful statement, "This is rape and I'm calling the cops," are all effective deterrents.[28] The American College Health Association adds that *alcohol and drugs can increase the likelihood of rape,* because communication is impaired and inhibitions removed. Also, they suggest:

◆ A woman should believe in her right to set limits and communicate these limits clearly, firmly, and early.

◆ Men should be aware of social pressures. It's okay not to "score."

◆ Be assertive with someone who is sexually pressuring you. Some men interpret passivity as permission.

◆ Women should consider their attire, because some men assume sexy dress and a flirtatious manner mean a desire for sex.

◆ Both men and women should pay attention to what is happening around them and refrain from putting themselves in vulnerable situations.

Individuals who don't avoid potentially compromising situations are needlessly asking for trouble. Yet one woman wrote,

> I have flirted with men in bars. Men have flirted with me in bars. I know a lot of men and women who flirt with each other in bars. Is flirting sexually suggestive? Of course. But all I know is, if I flirt with a man in a bar, I don't deserve to get raped.[29]

True, she doesn't "deserve" to get raped for flirting in a bar. But she is disregarding the fact that not every man plays by the rules—and drinking and flirting are clearly not *deterrents* to rape. Similarly, young men should stay away from environments in which liquor and sex are encouraged hand-in-hand.

SUMMARY

Ten years ago, discussions about premarital sex among teens centered around moral issues and the devastating consequences of unwed pregnancies. But the effort to avoid consequences by teaching youths to use birth-control aids has failed—evidenced by the one million out-of-wedlock pregnancies occurring each year.

Today, teen sex issues center around the increasing frequency of acts of sexual violence and the potentially fatal consequences of sex. Many people falsely believe that AIDS is only a homosexual problem. To explode this myth all you have to do is look at Africa, which has the greatest number of AIDS cases: 75 percent of those afflicted are heterosexual. In this country, as the age of first sexual contact continues to plummet and teens have more sexual partners per year than *any other age group*, it's only a matter of time before the HIV virus goes on a death march among the young and threatens our blood supply.

When I started writing this book in 1990, only about 600 cases of teenagers with AIDS had been reported. When I submitted my manuscript to the publisher in the fall of 1991, the total number of HIV-infected persons jumped from estimates in the tens of thousands in 1990 to the hundreds of thousands. By early 1992, estimates had risen to 1.5 million, and by May 1992 some experts were citing figures in multiple millions. Exactly how many kids have the HIV virus hasn't been established, but the fact that there could be hundreds of thousands of kids infected in the near future isn't a wild estimate in light of the reports from local communities.

Unless kids are motivated to abstain from sex, there is no guarantee of protection. Nearly one out of six condoms fails, which means that 15 percent or more of those sexual contacts are potential transmitters of the AIDS virus. Attempting to curb the spread of AIDS through social education alone is just a dream: kids who are hot and heavy in the back seat of a car are not going to think through the "issues" methodically. Kids believe they're invincible until they see their friends die, and the AIDS virus can hide for up to ten years.

Kids need much more than simply education. They need nurturing parents. As we'll see in the next chapter, teens who wait are not fluky exceptions to an inevitable reality. Many teens and single adults have adopted a morally sound and non-life-threatening approach to sexual activity. *Kids need to know that it's possible—although at times challenging—to lead a healthy and fulfilling life without premarital sex.* Although it's important to sound this message in churches and schools, the priority environment is the home: this is where children can be nurtured and guided effectively.

Up to this point we have only looked at the harrowing problems searing the lives of youths in the path of the advancing firestorm. In the second half of our exploration of sex and teens, we'll look at some powerful preemptive measures that parents can take to promote a healthy attitude in their kids toward sex and dating. Parents ultimately cannot make decisions about sex for their children; the choice is left to the child. But parents can take responsibility, to the best of their abilities, to nurture and guide their kids by teaching them what *is* the right path to follow.

CHAPTER THIRTEEN

Sex and Teens, Part Two: Joyfully Preparing the Way

In the last chapter, we took a hard look at the harm premarital sex can visit upon a teenager. In this chapter we'll look at how to help young people embrace the virtue of abstinence—joyfully preparing the way.

Prior to the eighties, the worst a youth might experience from premarital contact was emotional trauma, a venereal disease, or pregnancy. Today, it can cost their lives as AIDS spreads out of control. Lost in the publicity over these harmful trends is the fact that there really *is* joy in remaining celibate until married.

Cal Thomas, a noted syndicated columnist, wrote the following after Magic Johnson revealed that he had AIDS:

> Sex is more than the physical act. It is thoughtfulness, tenderness, selflessness, and commitment. It is caring, sharing, learning about another, giving of one's self fully to another and knowing a person in the deepest possible way.[1]

Thomas' description is in stark contrast to Magic Johnson's experience, which has reinforced the prevalent attitude that casual sex is fine as long as you use protective measures. But expressing our sexuality doesn't have to be this way. The story that follows is about another basketball star. I finished writing it up two months before Johnson's disclosure.

A TRULY MAGICAL MOMENT

Shan Ferch: an excellent student, a leader on his campus at Pepperdine University in Malibu, and a stand-out guard on his 1990 basketball team.

Jennifer Crowell: an operatic voice, former Miss Teen Washington, and a student at Biola College outside Los Angeles.

The two were in love. Shan wanted to propose, and he had a plan. First, he wrote and composed a love song to Jennifer, although he had never played an instrument. Then he invested two years teaching himself how to play the song on a keyboard he kept hidden from Jennifer. When he thought that he could play and sing well enough to please her musically critical ear, he invited her to a basketball banquet—actually, a ruse for the big event he'd been planning for two years.

Before the "banquet," Shan arranged for his buddies to haul a piano to a nearby beach and set it a few feet from the breaking surf. Shan instructed them to place on top of the piano a simple wicker basket filled with six dozen white roses, a bottle of sparkling apple cider, and two long-stemmed wineglasses. In this setting Shan would propose to Jennifer, all videotaped by his friends hiding on the cliff above.

When Shan picked up Jennifer, he said, "Look, we're a little early. Let's take a walk along the beach."

As they strolled along the sandy shore colored by the stunning sunset, Jennifer pointed to a distant object. "What's that out there?" she asked.

"I don't know," Shan shrugged.

As the piano came into focus against the backdrop of the jagged cliffs, Jennifer knew Shan was going to propose. But she assumed that Shan was going to ask her to play for him. When she reached the piano, she was overwhelmed by the roses. Nervously she sat down at the piano bench, quickly trying to figure out what she should play.

Shan sat down next to her, and he asked her to slide over. Then, looking intently at his love, Shan—who often wrote poetry—recited a new poem. Jennifer sat, her playful smile softened, and her clear blue eyes misted. When he finished the verses—the words to the song he had composed—he sang it to her, accompanying himself on the piano.

"We Live as One"
Our love is strength and truth,
It is not from me nor because of you.
It's clear to me that selfless flame will burn,
In the fortress not bound by Time.

The path we trod upon our knees
Through knives of pain and suffering,
Has shown us how Christ tore through an iron sky
Just that you and I could live as one.

So now my plea, my cry to you,
Is to write with me on a selfless page
Your hand in my own, clothed in Christ our Lord,
No more to die as two, we live as one.

Then Shan, on one knee, framed by the orange sun setting into the shimmering ocean, proposed to Jennifer.

At their wedding, Shan again sang the song he wrote to the woman he cherished, who was soon to be his lover. Their wedding night was another expression of their love, which they joyfully reserved for one another.

Today, Shan is doing graduate work in the field of psychology at Pepperdine while Jennifer completes her undergraduate degree in music at Biola. This couple is poised to have a wonderful influence on the lives of many others throughout their lifetime together.

WHAT PARENTS CAN DO TO PREPARE THE WAY

Is there a loving parent who doesn't hope his or her child will resist the temptation of premarital sex and marry a truly remarkable man or woman, if marriage is to be a part of his or her life? (I have several close friends whose joy it is to be chastely single.) It's not impossible to see this dream come true.

Good looks and popularity often bring young couples together, rather than character qualities. But Shan and Jennifer sought the latter, rather than temporal qualities that fade like images in yellowed scrapbooks.

Parents can help their kids learn to choose the best by being aware of the pressures they face and responding preemptively with good alternatives.

What Some Families Have Done
Jennifer's and Shan's parents took action ahead of time. Their experiences provide helpful practical examples of what parents can do to prepare the way for their kids' decisions about sexuality.

Jennifer's parents are Fred and Susie Crowell, the couple we met in chapter 8 who have devoted their lives to helping young people, especially through the sport of basketball. The Crowells have seen what works and what doesn't when it comes to raising kids, especially regarding the issue of sex. The way they have raised Jennifer and her fourteen-year-old brother, Jay, confirms the validity of their approach.

Shan's parents had a tougher road. They divorced when he was nine. But nine months later, the entire family embraced the Christian faith and his parents remarried. Shan experienced firsthand the truths and values taught in the Scriptures as evidenced by the restoration of his family. And one of those values was to be chaste until marriage—not as a call to martyrdom, but as a virtue.

"Promise" jewelry. The Crowells started to prepare the way for Jennifer to make the right choices about sexuality and marriage with some simple steps. When she turned thirteen they gave her a heart-shaped locket as a symbol of her promise to remain pure until she married. (My wife and I gave our daughter a heart-shaped "promise" ring. My sons will receive a masculine-looking ring when they are of age.)

A "promise" locket or ring, which a youth wears without ever taking it off until his or her wedding day, provides a tangible reminder of the promise to remain chaste. Receiving this object can be a very special moment, because it's rare that kids receive jewelry that is a symbol of virtue. This is an ideal time for parents to explain why remaining pure is a precious commitment. The occasion will most likely lead into an even more intimate parent-child relationship by saying, "The door is open for us to talk."

I'm convinced that when promise jewelry is given and shared in love, maybe during a special dinner out, it provides a powerful reinforcement for strengthening youths to get through heated moments of temptation. Few other simple acts can have such a profound effect in helping kids practice an important virtue.

Written assignments. When Jennifer approached dating age—which in the Crowells' house was fifteen—her parents helped her develop a healthy sense of awareness about dating with an unusual assignment. Fred and Susie asked her to write down a description of what she would and wouldn't do on a date, the type of person she would go out with, what the Bible says about dating, and her long-term goals in dating.

I heartily recommend this thoughtful process and time of reflection for all families. Here are a few examples of how these questions can be posed:

1. *What you will and won't do on a date.* Would you get in a car with a drunken driver? Would you let a date put his or her hand under your clothing? Would you go to or stay at a party where there is drinking or drugs? Would you go to a movie that was sexually provocative or in which unduly coarse language was used?

As Fred Crowell points out, being specific is important, "because if you don't predetermine what you're going to do, you'll be a victim of on-the-spot decision-making."

There will, of course, be differences in how guys or girls express themselves, but the subjects addressed should be the same. For example, a teenage boy would write that he wouldn't make advances toward a girl other than hugging and kissing, or that he wouldn't take a girl to a party where drugs and drinking are present.

An equal emphasis here should be placed on the *positive* things that a youth *will* do, such as: show respect for my date, be courteous, and suggest positive party environments, music, and movies.

Before giving such an "assignment" to your youth, be certain that you and your spouse discuss some of your expectations, items that you feel should be off-limits, and a healthy list of positive alternatives. Providing positive ideas lets kids know that we're not just trying to shut them down.

2. *What type of person you will date.* What are the character qualities you'd like to see in the individuals you date?

Some of the qualities that Jennifer listed as important to her were: doesn't drink or do drugs, kind, treats his mother respectfully, respects the virtue of abstinence, a Christian, and honest.

3. *What the Bible says about dating.* What does the Bible teach about how you are to conduct yourself on a date? What does it have to say about what your attitudes should be toward dating?

This area will be tough because there are no specific passages about dating, since it was not a cultural practice in biblical times. Be prepared for your child to point this out to you after consulting a Bible concordance on the subject.

Susie Crowell says that she directed Jennifer toward passages that address the qualities of virtue, sex, honesty, and purity. Fred also recommends that youths read the story of how Amnon raped Tamar in 2 Samuel 13, pointing out that one of the reasons Amnon hated Tamar afterward is that people always hate their weakness, and sex was Amnon's weakness—as it is for many men. Therefore, men will tend to value women who don't just give in to them.

4. *Long-term goals in dating.* What are your goals in dating? Why do you go out on dates?

Among the goals parents can point youths toward are: making friends, learning about how the opposite sex thinks, and having a good time in a wholesome setting. Susie warns against "looking for your mate" as a goal, because people who fall in love don't necessarily have to meet on a date. It can put too much pressure on dating itself. At some point, dating will become a part of most courtships, but it isn't necessarily the point of contact.

My wife, Sandy, and I, for example, met in a Sunday school class shortly after I became a Christian. We were both college students in New Orleans, and we got to know each other while attending retreats with the college department at the church. We soon became best friends, but we didn't date until two years later. Mutual respect and admiration drew us together, rather than physical attraction.

I believe that this foundation for our marriage is why our nineteen-year journey has only grown stronger when faced with adversity while our love for each other has deepened. Although I didn't see this in my family as a youngster, it didn't stop me or Sandy from purposefully choosing to lean toward the good.

Some simple rules. The Crowells had only a few rules about dating:

◆ Going steady or having just one boyfriend is allowed at age fifteen, not before.
◆ Double dating is allowed at age fifteen, not before.
◆ Single dating is allowed at age sixteen.

Parents can expect some resistance to these first two rules, even from non-rebellious kids. But studies have shown that kids who postpone dating are less likely to become sexually active. We worked through these rules with our own daughter, and although she resisted as expected, she later thanked us for caring. The Crowells also set these guidelines:

◆ Curfews are rigidly enforced.
◆ Being in a room alone with a date is not allowed.
◆ Kissing is limited to ten minutes.
◆ No petting.
◆ Limit sitting in a parked car with a date to five minutes.
◆ Whoever asked Jennifer out had to come over for dinner or
  dessert sometime before her date. (A number of times Jennifer
  chose not to go out with a guy after she saw how he interacted
  with the family. She commented, "After seeing them with
  my family, I realized that they weren't the type of person I
  wanted to date. My parents didn't have to say anything, I just
  knew.")

This last rule obviously relates to a teenage girl, but it can be
adapted for a teenage boy. He can request that he pay a courtesy call
to meet her parents. This may seem awkward for the girl, since most
kids don't do this, but it's easily overcome if he says something like,
"Our family has a tradition that I meet my date's folks. It's our way of
showing respect for you and your family." Of course, if a girl comes
from a troubled home, meeting the parents may be difficult if not
impossible, so a parent must be flexible; in this case, he might bring
her to his home to meet his parents. Regardless, a good message is
sent that family values are an important priority.

Fred says that he had only two rules for a fellow who took out
Jennifer. After he met the family, Fred would talk with the teen alone
for a few minutes, sharing with him these thoughts:

One of my philosophies in life is that I don't have a whole lot
of rules, because if you have a whole lot of rules you probably
won't keep them. And you won't remember them. So I'm only
going to give you two, and I think you can remember two,
don't you? One, Jennifer knows exactly how far she can go
on a date. Don't try to take her beyond that. She can explain
to you clearly what her limits are. Second, treat her in such a
way that you will never have to come and apologize to me for
the way you treated her. Because the one thing you don't ever
want to happen is for me to get between you and Jennifer. My
family is the most important thing in my life in terms of my
earthly relationships. And so those are the only two rules. Do
you have any questions?

The ideas of integrity, fear, respect, and family love for Jennifer, Fred says, were made clear from the beginning. The two "rules" also made the young man think through who he was taking out and why. The fear factor was clearly a deterrent when a gray area was broached, but it forced the young man to make a responsible decision or ask Fred or his own parents about what would be acceptable.

What's most appealing about this approach is the idea of encouraging youths to make the right decision.

If you have a son, the best approach might be to have him tell his date's parents that there are two rules he always follows about dating, explain to them the two rules, and assure them that they can trust him to keep those two rules. If your son can't meet with his date's parents, then he should tell this directly to the girl. Naturally, some kids will laugh at this and won't want to go out with your son or daughter, but it will attract teens who do respect the wisdom of these rules—or at least accept them—and families who live by them.

"But what if no one will go out with me?" is a question that some youths will ask. Or worse, they really *are* in a school or social environment in which boys won't ask them out or girls will refuse their requests. Hank Harmon, a friend of mine, has handled this issue.

CHARTING THE PATH

Hank was formerly a football coach in Branson, Missouri. Gifted with a high IQ and wisdom for living, he was often sought out by students for help with their problems. One day two young women, Sherry and Loretta, came up to him during study hall and complained, "No one will ask us out. The only girls who are getting dates are the ones who will put out. We weren't raised that way, but how else can we get a date? We're ready to chuck it and go with the flow. There doesn't seem to be any point to not giving in. We just don't like sitting at home when everyone else is having fun."

"I want you girls to do something for me," Hank responded gently. "Take a sheet of paper and draw a line down the middle. On the left side of the page I want you to write down all the ideal qualities in a man that a woman would like to marry. Then bring it up here and we'll take a look."

About twenty minutes later they brought him their lists. They had written down qualities like faithful, will talk to you, hardworking, God-fearing, and gentle.

"Now what I want you to do," Hank went on, "is to make a list on the right side of the page of all the qualities in the kind of woman you think this man would like to marry."

After another twenty minutes of intense effort, they came back to his desk.

"Would you like to marry a man like the one you've written down?" he asked them.

"Sure," they said peevishly.

"Well then, quit worrying about finding that man, and start working on being that woman." Sherry and Loretta didn't expect Coach Harmon to say that, but they did take his advice to heart.

Hank talked to Sherry and Loretta ten years later at a class reunion. He reports that each is happily married with a couple of kids, and both thanked him for his sage advice given in a study hall—probably one of the most important classes they ever attended.

PROMOTING HEALTHY SEXUAL VALUES

There are many sex education programs which are ineffective and actually promote promiscuity. One organization, the Sex Information and Education Council of the United States, released new guidelines for kindergarten through twelfth grade including concepts such as, "homosexual love relationships can be as fulfilling as heterosexual relationships." Endorsed by Dr. M. Roy Schwarz, the American Medical Association's senior vice president for medical education and science, these kind of educational programs send the wrong message. But there *are* other programs that don't.

Project Self-Respect, a recommended sex education course for public schools, teaches abstinence. Through role-playing exercises, youths think through their response when pressured to have sex. Here is one sample dialogue:

> *Taunt:* What's the big deal? It's like breathing and eating. It's just natural.
> *Response:* Hardly. People die if they don't eat or breathe. No one has ever died from not having sex. A lot of people are dying *because* of sex. I'll keep eating and breathing. But NO, okay?

The ideas communicated in this program and others are excellent. But sex education in schools by itself won't reverse nearly three decades of society's attacks on the sanctity of sexual relationships being reserved for marriage. To counter this entrenched trend will require consistent moral teaching at home and in churches, and, when appropriate, setting a moral tone in schools and other institutions.

Tim Stafford, an expert on youth trends, offers this advice for helping youths develop healthy sexual values:[2]

1. Kids need a philosophy of sex affirming that sex is only wonderfully expressed in marriage, and that teaching should come from a parent and church youth leaders.

2. The threat of disease should not be relied on as the primary deterrent to sexual involvement. It might be effective with some kids in some situations, but most kids don't think anything will hurt them. However, the disease factor should be a strong motivator for parents to pay attention.

3. Don't give the impression that sex is unpleasant or dirty, or that premarital sex always brings overwhelming guilt. A 1980s study by Robert Coles and Geoffrey Stokes, "Sex and the American Teenager," found that kids who say their parents taught that sex is "not healthy and normal" were more likely than others to engage in premarital sex.

4. "Sexual experimentation" is not even an option. Surveys show that couples who have sex usually cannot stop. And the ghosts of those memories usually haunt individuals long into adulthood. Also, kids often hear the lie that "experimenting" before getting married helps people make a better marital decision. In other words, test the waters first, as if sex is the primary component of a marriage.

But statistics explode this myth. A University of Wisconsin study revealed that among physically healthy couples, those who live together first are 30 percent more likely to be divorced within ten years than couples who go straight to the altar.[3]

Kids don't think about the fact that their spouse could be maimed or stricken with a disease, rendering sex in some marriages impossible. Then what would you do? Discard your husband or wife because he or she is now physically flawed? In marriage, the emphasis should be on unconditional love, with sex as an extended expression of that love—not as the focal point.

5. The test of "true love" is if a couple is willing to get married and declare their commitment before family, friends, and God. Weddings aren't guarantees of healthy marriages, but they do provide the best test ever designed for separating big talkers from the truly committed.

6. Parents should emphasize that sexual purity is tremendously

important to them. They shouldn't be embarrassed about sensitively planting the seeds of a healthy perspective regarding the overall issue when children are in their preteens.

If your child has already had sexual relations, there is still hope. All is not ended. Some of the finest Sunday school teachers I have met, for example, unwisely chose to have premarital relations but were later reconciled to themselves, those they hurt, and the God who freely forgives us. Jesus told those who broke His laws, "You are forgiven," and "Go and sin no more." He knows our need to be forgiven, and also our need to be commanded to obey the rules.

Significantly, studies—such as the 1986 Lou Harris Poll and the Coles Stokes survey—show that *the more importance youths place on spiritual values, the less likely they are to engage in sex.* Each survey reveals the same thing, and the message is clear: Teach kids the good, and they will respond. Participation in a youth group, accepting the truths of the Scriptures, and attending church are not perfect deterrents, but they are more effective than anything else. Even those who grow up in a wholesome environment can fall into sexual sin—but overall, experience shows that they are less likely than youths outside that environment.

When we told our daughter she couldn't date or go with someone until she was fifteen, there were a couple of times that she came to us and complained because her friends could have boyfriends, and she felt left out. The first time she complained she was thirteen. "Going with someone" at that age didn't mean going steady, it just meant that a boy and a girl agreed to "like" only one person—the junior high version of going steady. I'm sure that in the coming years another expression will take the place of "going with someone."

But we, like many other parents, didn't prohibit our daughter from getting together with her friends. We had chaperoned parties at the house, which her friends said were their favorite parties. Simply playing music and sitting around, which bore most kids, were replaced by contests, creative treasure hunts, and other structured activities. We also encouraged both her male and female friends to come over to the house even when there wasn't a party.

We made sure that our daughter and her friends had fun and that they knew they could talk to us—that we were not out of touch. We also encouraged groups of kids to go on an occasional outing, such as a show or a skating party. This wasn't classified as dating because these outings were always chaperoned, even if the parent was in the background.

We have also tried to ensure that our daughter had plenty of enjoyable extracurricular activities and hobbies, so she was never forced to sit around idly. Piano, all-region choir, church activities, and arts-and-crafts projects filled much of her free time.

The key point was that we wanted our house to be a place where our daughter could have fun—either by herself or with her friends—within the rules we established. Added to this we gave her plenty of personal quality and quantity time. For us, rules and discipline without creative outlets and activities are unacceptable.

If you feel you lack a creative spark to fuel kids' activities, find someone who can help you plan for them. Ask around at your church, your neighborhood, or your workplace. You'll find someone to help—even your own son or daughter!

CONCLUSION

I believe that the pressure on kids to engage in sex is the second most significant trend affecting their lives today, after the disintegration of the family. Skin-flicks at drive-ins have given way to home videos that can be screened in private; the sexual themes in the music of the seventies are now visually played out in music videos. It's not that temptations haven't always been there—what's different today is the intensity of the media messages encouraging kids to have sex at younger ages, the catastrophic number of teen pregnancies, the rising incidence of violent rape, and now life-threatening diseases.

Even if youths come from stable homes, there is great pressure from their friends to have sex, because sex can become the replacement for feeling secure in one's home. Overwhelming numbers of homes are torn apart, and this means that more kids will look for sex instead of a warm hug at home. Many students have told me that it's the "holding" they like best from sex, not the physical pleasure itself. In the extreme, males who harbor anger from a troubled home are venting that rage in sexual violence.

Kids from troubled homes need help from those who care: a youth minister, a teacher, a school counselor, a crime prevention officer. But there's no quick fix for these youths. As their numbers increase, kids from stable homes need to understand what might be driving their classmates in record numbers to catastrophic sexual relationships. This will help them make better choices about whom they will date, how to get help to a friend in trouble, and the need to ask questions before dating a person from a troubled home. This doesn't mean that kids from stable homes shouldn't date kids from unstable homes, just that they should be more observant and ask more questions before committing to a date.

Simply saying "don't" to kids about sex is almost irrelevant without firm teaching and options rooted in love. The guidelines for teaching kids to make good decisions (chapter 8) apply here: teach by example, communicate expectations clearly, and discipline when necessary. But most importantly, parents must start early to communicate and reinforce healthy values about sexuality so that kids will believe in and develop an earnest desire to practice the virtue of abstinence until marriage.

Abstaining is not outdated. It is the only option that even makes sense. And it is the only choice that offers a joyful path for a youth's journey to maturity.

CHAPTER FOURTEEN

The Drug Menace

◆

For some people the phrase "drug menace" solely conjures up images of crack houses and the approximately 300,000 babies, predominantly from inner-city communities, who are born with traces of illegal drugs in their systems.[1] They falsely assume that our national drug problem boils over principally in the inner city, and simmers elsewhere. The fact, however, is that more white youths abuse drugs than any inner-city ethnic group.

In November of 1989, the following notice was sent home with our kids, who attend school in the suburbs:

Drug Bulletin
The following information came to our attention through the Narcotics Division of the Dallas Police Department:

A form of Tattoo called the "Blue Star" is being sold to school children. It is a small sheet of paper containing blue stars the size of a pencil eraser. Each star is soaked with LSD. Each star can be removed and placed in the mouth. The LSD can be absorbed through the skin simply by handling the paper.

There are also brightly colored paper tabs resembling postage stamps that have pictures of Superman, butterflies, clowns, Mickey Mouse, and other Disney characters on them. These stamps are packed in a red cardboard box wrapped in foil. This is a new way of selling acid by appealing to young people.

A young child could happen upon these and have a fatal "trip." It is also learned that little children could be given a free Tattoo by other children who want to have some fun or by others cultivating new customers (without the child's knowledge). . . .

If you or your child get any of the above, DO NOT HANDLE THEM BAREHANDED! Contact your local police department. These are known to react very quickly, and some are laced with STRYCHNINE.

Symptoms: hallucinations, severe vomiting, uncontrolled laughter, mood changes, and change in body temperature.

Drugs can be threatening weapons, and those driven by greed will take aim at the unsuspecting. An estimated $40 billion in drugs is illegally consumed in this country each year—more than the federal government spent on all criminal-justice programs in 1990.[2] On average, over 65 percent of all criminal offenders test positive for drugs.[3]

But another drug that is illegal for minors can be just as deadly.

"Whatever you write," I was urged by Lee Dogoloff, executive director for the American Council for Drug Education, "be sure to let parents know that *alcohol* is the number-one drug abused today. Not cocaine, not marijuana, not LSD—but alcohol, a drug that's illegal for minors."[4]

Recent statistical studies confirm this warning. The "Partnership Attitude Tracking Study" of nearly nine thousand children, teens, and adults revealed that alcohol outstrips other drugs in teen use (see table 14.1).[5]

Another study revealed that 38 percent of all high school students drink at least once a week; 32 percent said they had ingested five or more drinks in a row (binge drinking) within two weeks of the survey; and 33 percent said they didn't think it was bad. On college campuses, 41 percent said they had been on a binge within two weeks of the survey, and the same percentage didn't think it was harmful.[6] At one Ivy League school where I lectured in 1988, over 40 percent of the students said that they had "a problem with alcohol consumption."

Startlingly, most youths' first contact with drugs and alcohol is *in the home,* not on the street.

TABLE 14.1—DRUG USE AMONG TEENS AND ADULTS

Drug	Percentages of Teens 13-17 Who Have Used	Percentages of Teens 13-17 Who Said They Are Hooked	Percentages of Adults Who Said They Are Hooked
Marijuana	27	5	16
Cocaine	8	1	16
Crack Cocaine	4	1	none
Alcohol (more than just a sip of beer, wine, or hard liquor)	69	11	16
Cigarettes	53	22	90

Note: Cigarette smoking has been declining steadily among all ages to a new low of 28 percent (Centers for Disease Control, 1991).

Most drug agencies confirm that while illegal drug use among youths appears to have peaked—although the problem is still acute and in some areas, such as on the West Coast, is on the rise—alcohol-related problems have remained dangerously chronic.

On today's streets, the drugs of choice are marijuana, cocaine, stimulants such as amphetamines, and in some communities the hallucinogen phencyclidine (PCP, or "Angel Dust"). Other drugs can, like a fad, become popular in a particular city or neighborhood; for example, LSD, a hallucinogenic drug from the sixties, has been observed making a comeback in some upper-class neighborhoods.

A STREETWISE PRIMER ON DRUG USE

The primary purpose of this chapter is to provide an introduction to the most prominent drugs currently used by youths today: their street names, effects, purchase price, and what they actually *look* like. Many parents aren't familiar with which drugs are most likely to be bought by youths, how they're ingested, and other basic information that's necessary for a working knowledge of illicit drugs.

We'll start our streetwise primer on drug use by taking a look at a mistaken stereotype of drug abuse.

Who Uses and How Much

Prejudicially, many Americans think that substance abuse rates are highest among minorities. However, as evidenced by the landmark study of seventy thousand high school seniors by the University of Michigan's Institute for Social Research, minority consumption of illegal drugs—excluding alcohol—is far lower than that of whites (see table 14.2).[7] This important study (further addressed in chapter 21) revealed that religious values appear to be the most important deterrent to drug use; additionally, a much higher percentage of African-American youths than white youths responded that religious values were important. (Again, the spiritual factor is found to be significant against a harmful youth trend.)

Because drug education programs have been implemented in schools nationwide, the substance usage rate seems to have peaked. This doesn't mean that there's no longer a problem in urgent need of our attention. A quick trip to any hospital, detoxification center, or counseling clinic is a reminder that the situation remains critical. A 1990 Congressional report concluded, for example, that there are 2.2 million "hard-core" cocaine addicts in the United States.[8]

An Overview of Illicit Drugs
Five different types of drugs can be abused and illegally ingested: narcotics, depressants, stimulants, hallucinogens, and cannabis (see table 14.3).

The following definitions are adapted from the U.S. Department of Justice's booklet *Drugs of Abuse* (1989). Not included here are "inhalants," such as fumes from glue, aerosol cans, spray paint, typewriter correction fluid, shoe polish, and even water repellents. If you need information about inhalants, which have become a chronic problem in many communities—in 1989, 25 percent of 7500 students surveyed in Texas had abused inhalants—please contact one of the agencies listed in the appendix, a local drug program, or a juvenile officer.

Narcotics. Medically, the term *narcotic* refers to opium and opium derivatives, such as heroin, or synthetic substitutes. Narcotics are essential in the practice of medicine: they are the most effective agents known for relieving intense pain. They are also used in cough suppressants, as well as in a centuries-old remedy for diarrhea. Under medical supervision, they're administered orally or by intramuscular injection. As drugs of abuse, however, they also are sniffed, smoked, or self-administered by the more direct routes of subcutaneous ("skin-popping") and intravenous ("mainlining") injection.

TABLE 14.2—COMPARATIVE DRUG USE BY SEX AND RACE

TYPES OF DRUGS	PERCENT WHO USED IN LAST TWELVE MONTHS											
	White Male	Black Male	MexAm Male	PR&LA Male	Asian Male	NatAm Male	White Female	Black Female	MexAm Female	PR&LA Female	Asian Female	NatAm Female
Minimum N =	(28056)	(3688)	(1518)	(680)	(982)	(537)	(29808)	(4499)	(1599)	(712)	(917)	(531)
Marijuana/Hashish	40.2	29.8	37.3	30.6	19.6	42.0	36.0	18.4	26.0	21.3	17.1	44.0
Inhalants[a]	8.8	2.6	6.0	5.1	4.8	9.6	5.2	2.2	4.3	2.9	3.2	4.4
Hallucinogens	8.3	1.9	5.9	6.5	3.0	10.0	5.0	0.6	2.2	2.1	2.2	9.0
LSD	7.0	1.3	5.2	3.4	2.5	7.8	3.9	0.3	1.6	1.1	1.9	7.2
Cocaine	11.9	6.1	14.7	15.6	5.8	14.2	9.3	2.6	7.6	8.2	5.7	15.5
Heroin	0.7	0.7	0.9	1.2	0.4	1.5	0.3	0.4	0.4	0.4	0.2	1.0
Other Opiates[b]	6.5	1.9	3.2	3.0	3.1	7.4	5.3	1.2	2.1	1.6	2.1	5.7
Stimulants[b]	13.6	4.6	11.3	8.0	5.6	17.0	14.7	3.1	10.1	5.9	7.0	19.4
Sedatives[b]	5.3	2.2	4.7	4.6	3.4	8.8	4.4	1.2	2.7	2.6	2.6	6.4
Barbiturates[b]	4.4	1.9	4.1	4.0	2.6	7.2	3.8	1.1	2.4	2.5	2.3	6.2
Methaqualone[b]	2.5	0.9	1.2	2.3	1.5	4.8	1.4	0.3	0.5	0.5	0.9	2.2
Tranquilizers[b]	5.8	1.7	2.6	3.1	3.2	6.9	5.9	1.4	2.1	4.1	1.8	8.7
Alcohol	88.3	72.5	82.4	80.6	69.3	82.0	88.6	63.9	73.6	77.2	67.5	81.3

[a]Date based on four questionnaire forms. N is four-fifths of N indicated.
[b]Only drug use that was not under doctor's orders in included here.

(*American Journal of Public Health*, vol. 81, no. 3, March 1991.)

TABLE 14.3—CONTROLLED SUBSTANCES, USES AND EFFECTS

	DRUGS/CSA SCHEDULES	TRADE OR OTHER NAMES	MEDICAL USES	DEPENDENCE Physical	DEPENDENCE Psychological
NARCOTICS	Opium II III V	Dover's Powder, Paregoric Parepectolin	Analgesic, antidiarrheal	High	High
	Morphine II III	Morphine, MS-Contin, Roxanol, Roxanol-SR	Analgesic, antitussive	High	High
	Codeine II III V	Tylenol w/Codeine, Empirin w/ Codeine, Robitussan A-C, Fiorinal w/Codeine	Analgesic, antitussive	Moderate	Moderate
	Heroin I	Diacetylmorphine, Horse, Smack	None	High	High
	Hydromorphone II	Dilaudid	Analgesic	High	High
	Meperidine (Pethidine) II	Demerol, Mepergan	Analgesic	High	High
	Methadone II	Dolophine, Methadone, Methadose	Analgesic	High	High-Low
	Other Narcotics I II III IV V	Numorphan, Percodan, Percocet, Tylox, Tussionex, Fentanyl, Darvon, Lomotil, Talwin[2]	Analgesic, antidiarrheal, antitussive	High-Low	High-Low
DEPRESSANTS	Chloral Hydrate IV	Noctec	Hypnotic	Moderate	Moderate
	Barbiturates II III IV	Amytal, Butisol, Fiorinal, Lotusate, Nembutal, Seconal, Tuinal, Phenobarbital	Anesthetic, anticonvulsant, sedative, hypnotic, veterinary euthanasia agent	High-Mod.	High-Mod.
	Benzodiazepines IV	Ativan, Dalmane, Diazepam, Libruim, Xanax, Serax, Valium, Tranxexe, Verstran, Versed, Halcion, Paxipam, Restoril	Antianxiety, anticonvulsant, sedative, hypnotic	Low	Low
	Methaqualone I	Quaalude	Sedative, hypnotic	High	High
	Glutethimide III	Doriden	Sedative, hypnotic	High	Moderate
	Other Depressants III IV	Equanil, Miltown, Noludar, Placidyl, Valmid	Antianxiety, sedative, hypnotic	Moderate	Moderate
STIMULANTS	Cocaine[1] II	Coke, Flake, Snow, Crack	Local anesthetic	Possible	High
	Amphetamines II	Biphetamine, Delcobese, Desoxyn, Dexedrine, Obetrol	Attention deficit disorders, narcolepsy, weight control	Possible	High
	Phenmetrazine II	Preludin	Weight control	Possible	High
	Methylphenidate II	Ritalin	Attention deficit disorders, narcolepsy	Possible	Moderate
	Other Stimulants III IV	Adipex, Cylert, Didrex, Ionamin, Melfiat, Plegine, Sanorex, Tenuate, Tepanil, Prelu-2	Weight control	Possible	High
HALLUCINOGENS	LSD I	Acid, Microdot	None	None	Unknown
	Mescaline and Peyote I	Mexc, Buttons, Cactus	None	None	Unknown
	Amphetamine Variants I	2.5-DMA, PMA, STP, MDA, MDMA, TMA, DOM, DOB	None	Unknown	Unknown
	Phencyclidine II	PCP, Angel Dust, Hog	None	Unknown	High
	Phencyclidine Analogues I	PCE, PCPy, TCP	None	Unknown	High
	Other Hallucinogens I	Bufotenine, Ibogaine, DMT, DET, Psilocybin, Psilocyn	None	None	Unknown
CANNABIS	Marijuana I	Pot, Acapulco Gold, Grass Reefer, Sinsemilla, Thai Sticks	None	Unknown	Moderate
	Tetrahydrocannabinol I II	THC, Marinol	Cancer chemotherapy anti-nauseant	Unknown	Moderate
	Hashish I	Hash	None	Unknown	Moderate
	Hashish Oil I	Hash Oil	None	Unknown	Moderate

1. Designated a narcotic under the Controlled Substances Act (CSA).
2. Not designated a narcotic under the CSA.

TABLE 14.3 *(Continued)*

	TOLER-ANCE	DURATION (Hours)	USUAL METHODS OF ADMINIS-TRATION	POSSIBLE EFFECTS	EFFECTS OF OVERDOSE	WITHDRAWAL SYNDROME
NARCOTICS	Yes	3-6	Oral, smoked			
	Yes	3-6	Oral, smoked, injected			Watery eyes, runny nose, yawning, loss of appetite, irritability, tremors, panic, cramps, nausea, chills and sweating
	Yes	3-6	Oral, injected	Euphoria, drowsiness, respiratory depression, constricted pupils, nausea	Slow and shallow breathing, clammy skin, convulsions, coma, possible death	
	Yes	3-6	Injected, sniffed, smoked			
	Yes	3-6	Oral, injected			
	Yes	3-6	Oral, injected			
	Yes	12-24	Oral, injected			
	Yes	Variable	Oral, injected			
DEPRESSANTS	Yes	5-8	Oral			
	Yes	1-16	Oral			
	Yes	4-8	Oral	Slurred speech, disorientation, drunken behavior without odor of alcohol	Shallow respiration, clammy skin, dilated pupils, weak and rapid pulse, coma, possible death	Anxiety, insomnia, tremors, delirium, convulsions, possible death
	Yes	4-8	Oral			
	Yes	4-8	Oral			
	Yes	4-8	Oral			
STIMULANTS	Yes	1-2	Sniffed, smoked, injected			
	Yes	2-4	Oral, injected	Increased alertness, excitation, euphoria, increased pulse rate and blood pressure, insomnia, loss of appetite	Agitation, increase in body temperature, hallucinations, convulsions, possible death	Apathy, long periods of sleep, irritability, depression, disorientation
	Yes	2-4	Oral, injected			
	Yes	2-4	Oral, injected			
	Yes	2-4	Oral, injected			
HALLUCINOGENS	Yes	8-12	Oral			
	Yes	8-12	Oral			
	Yes	Variable	Oral, injected	Illusions and hallucinations, poor perception of time and distance	Longer, more intense "trip" episodes, psychosis, possible death	Withdrawal syndrome not reported
	Yes	Days	Smoked, oral, injected			
	Yes	Days	Smoked, oral, injected			
	Possible	Variable	Smoked, oral, injected, sniffed			
CANNABIS	Yes	2-4	Smoked, oral	Euphoria, relaxed inhibitions, increased appetite, disoriented behavior	Fatigue, paranoia, possible psychosis	Insomnia, hyperactivity, decreased appetite occasionally reported
	Yes	2-4	Smoked, oral			
	Yes	2-4	Smoked, oral			
	Yes	2-4	Smoked, oral			

Depressants. Substances regulated under the CSA (Controlled Substances Act) as depressants have a potential for abuse associated with both physical and psychological dependence. Taken as prescribed by a physician, depressants may be beneficial for the relief of anxiety, irritability, and tension, and for the symptomatic treatment of insomnia. In excessive amounts, however, they produce a state of intoxication that is remarkably similar to alcohol.

Stimulants. The two most prevalent stimulants are nicotine in tobacco products and caffeine, the active ingredient of coffee, tea, and some bottled beverages that are sold in every supermarket. When used in moderation, these stimulants tend to relieve fatigue and increase alertness.

There are, however, more potent stimulants (such as cocaine, which is the strongest). Because of their dependence-producing potential they are under the regulatory control of the CSA. These controlled stimulants (including cocaine) are available by prescription for medical purposes; they are also clandestinely manufactured for distribution on the illicit market.

Hallucinogens. Hallucinogenic drugs, both natural and synthetic, are substances that distort the perception of objective reality. They induce a state of excitation of the central nervous system, manifested by alterations of mood—usually euphoric, but sometimes severely depressive. Under the influence of hallucinogens, perceptions of direction, distance, and time become distorted. A user may speak of "seeing" sounds and "hearing" colors. If taken in a large enough dose, the drug produces delusions and visual hallucinations. Occasionally, depersonalization and depression are so severe that suicide is possible, but the most common danger is impaired judgment, leading to rash decisions and accidents.

Cannabis. Cannabis sativa L., the hemp plant, or marijuana, grows wild throughout the world and has been used as a drug for centuries. In 1839, it entered the annals of Western medicine as an analgesic and anticonvulsant agent. By 1941 it had been deleted from the *U.S. Pharmacopoeia* and *National Formularly,* the official compendia of drugs. Cannabis products are usually smoked in the form of loosely rolled cigarettes, commonly called "joints." They may be used alone or in combination with other substances. Low doses tend to induce restlessness and an increasing sense of well-being, followed by a dreamy state of relaxation and frequently hunger, especially a craving for sweets. High doses may result in image distortion, a loss of personal identity, and fantasies and hallucination. Very high doses may result in a toxic psychosis. (Note: Hashish and hashish oil are derivatives obtained from the secretions of the cannabis.)

Because cocaine and marijuana are the two most common illegal drugs used by youths today, we will look at them in detail. This doesn't mean that there aren't numerous others being consumed by youths, but space in this text won't permit even a short examination of those drugs. The purpose for the inclusion of the "Controlled Substances" chart (table 14.3) is to help you gain an appreciation of the relationship between those drugs and their basic characteristics.

To get a rundown on what is in vogue in your immediate neighborhood, check with your local juvenile officer, police narcotics squad, drug rehabilitation centers, school personnel, or other community authorities. Sometimes drugs that are no longer popular resurface for a later generation of kids looking for something "new." As already noted, this recently occurred with LSD in some communities.

TABLE 14.4—"CRACK" COCAINE: EFFECTS ON THE BODY

Crack reaches the brain within ten seconds after smoke is inhaled. The drug's impact begins immediately. The average high per $10 buy is five to seven minutes.

BRAIN The biochemical state is altered. Addiction takes place faster than with any other drug—including heroin.	EYES Pupils may dilate, becoming more sensitive to light. This may cause user to think he sees "halos" surrounding objects on which he attempts to focus. The halo effect is often called "snowlights" by users.
HEART Heartbeat becomes more rapid, increasing by 30 to 50 percent, and may become irregular. In rare instances, may cause heart attack.	LUNGS Chronic crack smoking may lead to hoarseness and bronchitis, similar to the effects of marijuana or tobacco smoking. Cocaine snorting does not produce the same effect.
LIMBS May convulse as muscles involuntarily contract.	ARTERIES Blood pressure increases from 10 to 15 percent. Blood coursing through the vessels at a more rapid speed may cause, in rare cases, brain hemorrhage.
CENTRAL NERVOUS SYSTEM Stimulation of the system produces euphoria, talkativeness, hallucinations, irritability, and suspicion.	WEIGHT Cocaine use can lead to severe and rapid weight loss.

NOTE: There are indications that the paranoia and violent temper outburst often accompanying cocaine abuse are increased in intensity among those who "freebase."

FACTS ABOUT MARIJUANA

You should know that ...
- Marijuana contains more cancer causing chemicals than regular cigarette smoke. Smoking one marijuana cigarette, known as a "joint," is the same as smoking one pack of tobacco cigarettes (twenty cigarettes).

- Marijuana contains over 400 chemicals that are harmful to the heart, lungs, and brain functions. When a joint is lit, these 400 chemicals combine to form over 2000 chemicals that go into the smoker's lungs.

- Smoking marijuana speeds up the heart's pumping and increases blood pressure. It affects the lungs as tobacco smoke does, only to a greater degree.

- Today's marijuana is about twenty times stronger than it was in the 1960s, because marijuana growers have discovered new ways of producing stronger crops.

- Marijuana reduces the body's ability to fight diseases. White blood cells, which defend the body against disease germs, are reduced by smoking marijuana.

- The chemical that produces the "high" feeling, called THC, or tetrahydro-cannabinol, is fat soluble. This means that it is stored in the fatty tissues of the body, such as in the brain and reproductive organs, for at least three weeks after a person has smoked only one joint.

- Women who smoke marijuana during pregnancy have babies with higher rates of birth defects and lower birth weights than babies of women who do not smoke marijuana.

- Smoking marijuana can prevent the physical body from growing properly (especially in young smokers) and can slow down a person's emotional growth.

- Marijuana makes is much harder to learn and retain information, because it interferes with thinking, understanding, and reading ability. Marijuana makes it hard for a student to remember things a teacher has said. Sometimes loss of memory can be permanent.

- People who smoke marijuana lose some of their driving skill. A person's reaction time, such as being able to stop properly at a red light, slows down. The ability to see clearly and accurately is affected, and the sense of time is altered.

- Smoking marijuana and taking other drugs at the same time, such as alcohol, is even more dangerous. This is called "poly-drug" abuse.

People who smoke marijuana ...
- May develop a dependence on it, which means that they feel a need for it in order to feel good or cope with problems. They may also develop a "tolerance" for it, which means that their bodies need more marijuana to get the same high feeling.

- Often lack motivation, not wanting to do anything. Schoolwork, sports, and chores are often neglected.

- Often change their behavior, becoming moody and irritable with friends and family.

- Often have red eyes and feel tired, having no energy.

- Often do not dress neatly or keep up their appearance.

STREETWISE GUIDE TO DRUG USER'S SLANG
(Local slang varies, so check with authorities
in your area for accuracy.)

AMPING—Accelerated heartbeat after using drugs

BASE—Filler mixed with or removed from cocaine

BASED OUT—To have lost control over basing

BASEHEAD—Person who bases. See BASING

BASING—Smoking cocaine through a pipe

BATT—Needle for IV drug use

BOLLO—See ROCK

BONG—Water pipe, used for smoking drugs

BOY—Street name for heroin

BREAKDOWNS—$20 rock that can be broken down into two $20 rocks. See ROCK

BUMP—Fake rock cocaine

COCTAIL—Cigarette laced with crack. See LACE

COKE—Cocaine

COME UP—Person who sells drugs; to increase a small amount of money

CRACK—Cocaine in ready-to-smoke rock form

CRANK—Speed

CUT—Filler used to increase amount of cocaine

DOPE FIEND—Person who is dependent on crack

DOUBLE UPS—See BREAKDOWNS

EIGHT (8) BALL—Eighth of an ounce of cocaine

FREEBASE—Cocaine that is free of base. See BASE

FREEBASING—See BASING

FRY DADDY—Marijuana joint laced with crack

GONE—Person who has lost everything to crack

GRIMMIE—See FRY DADDY

HIGHBEAMS—Wide-eyed appearance of a person on crack

HIT—Crack or joint that is being smoked

HOLDING—To have crack in hand

HORN—Crack pipe. See PIPE

HUBBAS—See CRACK

JOINT—Marijuana cigarette

LACE—To add drugs to another substance, other drugs or food

MAINLINE—Injecting drugs directly into the bloodstream

MIX—Cocaine environment; whatever is happening to a person or persons in the cocaine environment

OZ—Ounce of cocaine

PCP—Phencyclidine, a hallucinogen

PEBBLES—See CRACK

PIPE—Numerous types used to smoke cocaine, crack, or marijuana

PREMO SQUARE—See FRY DADDY

QUARTER OZ—Quarter ounce of cocaine

RES—Potent residue left in pipe that is scraped and smoked. See PIPE

ROCK—Cocaine in ready-to-smoke rock form

ROCK STAR—Person who uses rock cocaine

ROLLERS—Police

RUNNERS—People who sell or deliver drugs for other people

SET—Place where drugs are sold, mainly street corners

SHOT—Amount of cocaine (i.e., 10-shot, 20-shot)

SHOT TO THE CURB—See GONE

SKINPOPPING—Injecting drugs in any part of the body without hitting a vein

SNITCH—Informant who tells police about drug actions

SPACEBASE—Crack mixed with PCP. See PCP

SPEEDBALL—Mixture of cocaine and heroine

SPEEDBALLING—Injecting or smoking mixture of cocaine and heroine

TOSSUP—Woman who engages in sex for crack

TWEAK MISSION—When a person goes all out for crack

TWEAKING—To be in a state of drug induced paranoia

UZI—See PIPE

WHITE—Cocaine

WIGGING—Behavior resulting from past use of mind-altering drugs

Adapted from "Texans' War on Drugs," Houston, Texas. Refer also to table 14.3, "Controlled Substances, Uses and Effects," on pages 198–199, for other street names for specific drugs.

Cocaine

Powdered cocaine is often sold in vials (a two-ounce vial sells for about $200), in small capsules (a capsule the size of a cold-medicine capsule sells for about $10), in foil papers (usually at least a tenth of a gram for $10), and in any other creative container available. According to narcotic law enforcement agents, capsules and papers are currently the most common methods. (On the West Coast, cocaine is sold in gram "bindles," which are often pieces of Zig-Zag [tradename] cigarette papers or magazine pages folded into squares or rectangles.)

The average high per $10 buy is about ten minutes. Crack cocaine (also called rock cocaine), which is smoked—called freebasing—has a greater immediate impact than powder cocaine, which is snorted, because it reaches the brain faster (table 14.4). Although injecting cocaine—which is rare among teens—has about the same effect as crack.

Cocaine triggers the release of the stored supply of dopamine in a user's brain, which induces the "high." Once the brain's supply of dopamine is depleted, however, the user "crashes" and experiences profound depression. The following photographs show the various ways cocaine is sold and related paraphernalia, with explanations of how each is ingested.

14.1. Cocaine in powdered form. A tenth of a gram sells for approximately $10. This dosage gives a "high" for about ten minutes. It can be snorted, smoked, or injected.

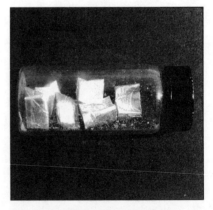

14.2. Powdered cocaine sold in "$10 papers," similar to the foil used in chewing gum wrappers.

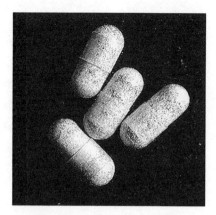

14.3. Powdered cocaine sold in capsules. Market value: $10 each.

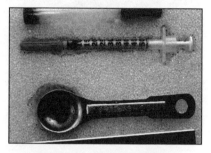

14.4. "Cook spoon" and needle used for injecting cocaine. The user takes an amount of powdered cocaine and places it in the spoon, which is filled with liquid—water, beer, etc. A lighted match is held beneath the spoon so that the heat mixes the drug into the liquid. The mixture is then injected into a vein ("mainlining") or just beneath the skin ("skin-popping").

14.5. A fancy "cut kit," sold in head shops, that is used to snort cocaine. The round, flat object in the center is a piece of slick petrified wood, on which the powdered cocaine (in the vial, lower left corner) is poured. A mirror, glass top, or any other slick surface can also be used. The little spoon on the right is used to scoop the cocaine out of the vial. The razor blade is used to "cut" the cocaine into thin "lines." The small tube on the right is used to snort these lines into the nose.

14.6. A popular brand of powdered vitamin B used to "cut," or thin, powdered cocaine so that a "buy" will last longer. There's no clear reason why this particular brand is so popular. (Powdered vitamin B is not illegal.) Another commonly used "cut" substance is lactose, which is milk sugar.

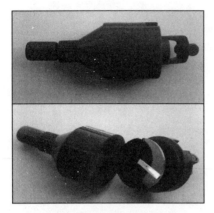

14.7. A small "sifter" used to fluff up a quantity of cocaine. This equipment sells for about $5.

14.8. Rock cocaine sold in a small, self-sealing bag. Market value: $10-20 each.

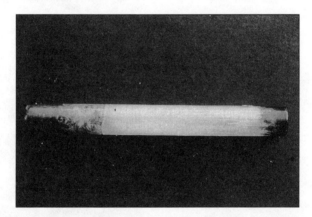

14.9. Crack pipe, homemade from a glass tube the size of a cigarette. A small amount of steel wool is put in one end and a "rock" is put inside the steel wool. The user then takes a match and heats the end of the rock, turning the rock into fumes, which are simultaneously smoked.

Officers say that finding rolled-up dollar bills or short, cut-off straws may indicate drug use, since most people don't carry such items—particularly rolled-up dollar bills. They are used because most people carry money.

Marijuana

Marijuana, also called weed, buds, grass, blow, sess, pot, reefer, Thai stick, and a host of other names, is second to alcohol as the illegal drug most used by youths. (Approximately 15 percent of all juveniles arrested for any type of crime test positive for marijuana.[9]) Experts suggest that this is because marijuana is not perceived to be as harmful as other drugs, and also because it's relatively inexpensive.

Marijuana is smoked and sometimes even ingested orally. Hand-rolled "joints" in cigarette papers are the favorite method for smoking.

Some parents who used marijuana years ago think that it isn't a very potent substance today. They're wrong. The active ingredient in marijuana, tetrahydrocannabinol (THC), can be up to twenty times more potent today because it's possible to grow a more potent plant.

The reason marijuana is often combined with drinking is because pot suppresses nausea, allowing greater consumption of alcohol. But the extreme danger here is that vomiting is the body's way of expelling toxic poisons. Therefore, if youths drink and smoke a joint, it is possible that they can die from toxic poisoning because their body won't expel the lethal alcohol. As one expert put it, "Our body is smarter than we are."

The accompanying box, "Facts about Marijuana," provides important information about marijuana (see page 202). While the following photos provide a brief visual representation of marijuana use:

14.10. Finely ground marijuana sells for about $100 per ounce, which will yield fifteen to twenty "joints." Depending on size, one tightly rolled joint can cost from $1 to $10. Users sometimes mix rock cocaine or other substances with marijuana.

14.11. A cheaper and coarser grade of marijuana.

14.12. Two different types of "roach" clips used to smoke a "joint." The lion figurine separates, concealing the clip inside. Almost any object that can hold a hand-rolled cigarette can be used, although the user can simply hold the joint in the hand to smoke. The purpose for the clip is to enable the user to smoke all of the joint. Also, the longer the active ingredient THC is smoked, the stronger it gets. Some youths save the butts, because of the concentration of THC, and then roll the butts into a joint.

Signs of Possible Abuse

There's no surefire way to know if a youth is using drugs, because unless a person is severely impaired by drug use, he or she may look, talk, and act like anyone else. The following signs provide at best an imperfect gauge for determining whether or not to investigate the possibility that a youth may be using drugs.

Behavioral Changes
- ◆ Numerous unexcused absences at school
- ◆ Frequent illnesses
- ◆ Excessive secretive phone calls
- ◆ Long visits to the restroom
- ◆ Behavioral problems with family, friends, etc.
- ◆ Frequent violation of family or school rules.
- ◆ Poor attention to detail
- ◆ Declining work performance
- ◆ Accident prone
- ◆ Lethargic behavior

Physiological Changes
- ◆ Bloodshot eyes
- ◆ Incessant talking
- ◆ Excessive perspiration

◆ Hyperactivity
◆ Tendencies toward violence
◆ Slurred speech
◆ Problems with coordination
◆ Chronic nasal problems
◆ Excessive weight loss
◆ Unusual craving for sweets or dramatically increased appetite

Drug Paraphernalia
◆ Hand-rolled cigarettes
◆ Cigarette papers
◆ Roach clips
◆ Plastic baggies
◆ Glassine envelopes
◆ Bent spoons
◆ Razor blades in unusual places
◆ Short straws
◆ Rolled dollar bills

As with all the descriptions of the various trends in this book, be careful before making a snap decision that your son or daughter is a drug user based upon these potential indicators. Bleary or bloodshot eyes might simply indicate an unexpected allergy or sleeping difficulties due to a concealed problem. A rolled dollar bill, however improbable, could be a part of some new fad or a product of some idle time in class.

The box on page 203 lists some of the common names and terms for illegal drug activity in use among youths today. Awareness of these expressions can also help you spot possible drug use.

If you suspect that your child is using drugs, please follow the recommended outline in chapter 19, "A Framework for Getting Help," for devising a strategy to respond to the problem.

THE ALCOHOL FACTOR

Recent news accounts have reported stories of high school football teams releasing players for drinking beer. At one high school, eight players were dismissed. Each player had signed a statement that he wouldn't drink any alcoholic beverages, under penalty of removal from the team.

The reason these stories received coverage in the press, however, was because *parents* were irate that their sons were removed. Never mind that the activity was illegal, or that the players had given their word and then broken it.

For many young people, the alcohol problem is worsened because their parents don't have a good handle on the issue.

Clearly, as indicated by the statistics quoted earlier in this chapter, alcohol has been and continues to be the number-one nemesis of young people. More young people die due to alcohol-related incidents than any other cause. Most juvenile officers will tell you that alcohol is a factor in 50 to 90 percent of their juvenile arrests. (Additionally, according to a 1991 Surgeon General's study, nearly three million youths drink alone, and over four million drink when upset, indicating that many are prone to become alcoholics.)

Still, parents think, "Yeah, but I had a few beers every now and then when I was a kid, and it never hurt me." This may be true, but look at how many kids are in chronic emotional pain—pain they seek to numb with alcohol.

Billy Graham points out, in his book *The Holy Spirit*, that the biblical guidelines on this subject indicate that although there is no specific *commandment* against drinking, there is a biblical *principle* not to drink for purposes of intoxication. In his epistle to Timothy, the apostle Paul condemns "indulging in much wine" along with "pursuing dishonest gain" as behaviors that should be shunned by church deacons (1 Timothy 3:8). But Paul condoned a medicinal use for drinking: "a little wine" for Timothy's stomach problems (1 Timothy 5:23). And wine has always been used in the Jewish Passover, which Jesus endorsed by using it as the representation of His blood in His last meal with His apostles—now ritualized as the Lord's Supper or Holy Communion. Additionally, the writer of Proverbs provides a clear guideline in his counsel for responsible leadership: "It is not for kings, O Lemuel— not for kings to drink wine, not for rulers to crave beer, lest they drink and forget what the law decrees, and deprive all the oppressed of their rights" (31:4-5).

Current medical studies seem to indicate that wine taken in moderation significantly reduces the risk of heart disease. Yet alcohol is one of the leading killers of young people. What message should we communicate, then? If we point out that wine in moderation can be beneficial, will this encourage more youths to begin consuming alcohol, and thereby increase the numbers of alcoholics? I don't think that there's one pat answer. Here is how our family has worked through this dilemma.

First, our kids are not allowed to drink while they're minors, because it's illegal and any medical benefits they might receive at their young age would be marginal at best. It's far better for them not to drink, and thus avoid any indirect encouragement of drinking with other youths.

Second, I was not brought up to be a teetotaler, but I personally chose not to drink several years ago because six people I knew died of alcohol abuse within two years of each other. I didn't want my drinking in moderation to affect a recovering alcoholic.

When I started talking to friends about this, I discovered other acquaintances who were closet alcoholics. Only once, at a party several years ago, did I take a drink of wine. I then offered some to another acquaintance. It turned out that this person, who attended a local church, was a recovering alcoholic. That's when I said, "No more." If I change my mind about personally consuming wine in moderation as a health benefit, I will do so only in my own home so as not to be a stumbling block, however inadvertently, to someone else.

———————◆———————

Despite the dangers of alcohol abuse, and the prevalence of kids in pain, advertisers continue to be grossly irresponsible in promoting alcohol consumption to young people. Millions of dollars are pumped into beer advertising during sporting events on television to make drinking alcohol seem appealing and youthful. While beer companies in particular have made a gratuitous statement against drinking and driving, there is virtually no emphasis on waiting until reaching legal age.

During spring break at Daytona Beach in Florida, which draws hundreds of thousands of young people (many of them underage), the breweries are out in full force with all kinds of advertising gimmicks to sell their wares, from artificial ski slopes to bikini contests. With all the pressure on kids to drink illegally, parental influence can still be a more powerful force.

But as Lee Dogoloff warns, "Until parents get their heads screwed on straight, there's no hope for our kids." He recounted a dialogue with parents during a recent visit to an upper-class high school in Washington, D.C.:

You don't get the question anymore, "Why can't I do pot if my parents drink?" Education has answered that question. Parents are clear about that and so it's reinforced in the home. But parents aren't clear about drinking under the age of twenty-one.

When I suggested to the parents that drinking is illegal, half the audience thought I walked on water and the other half thought I was from outer space.

One parent asked me, "You mean if my nineteen-year-old son comes home from college at Thanksgiving, he can't have a sip of wine?"

I replied, "Let's say your son comes home from break and brings a girl with him, and wants to sleep with her."

"Oh no," the father responded quickly, "we wouldn't allow that."

"Why, then," I asked, "are you clear about this but not about something which is illegal and the leading cause of death for people your son's age? Don't you realize that the death rate for every other age group is going down, *except* for those your son's age? This is because of accidents and suicide driven by drugs and alcohol."[10]

THE FAMILY FACTOR

Schools Reinforcing Family Influence

At our kids' elementary school, the yearly "Red Ribbon Campaign" was again kicked off this fall. It was first launched when Drug Enforcement Administration Agent Enrique Camarena was murdered by drug traffickers in Mexico in 1985. Kids are encouraged to wear a red ribbon as a symbol of the need to reduce the demand for drugs and in order to create positive peer pressure.

In the "Red Ribbon Campaign" flyer sent home with our kids, the American Council for Drug Education urged parents to:

- ◆ Start drug prevention early.
- ◆ Don't be an enabler.
- ◆ Remember that you are a role model for your child.
- ◆ Take advantage of every teachable moment.
- ◆ Reinforce the information and rules you teach.
- ◆ Know what goes on in your child's life at home, at school, and with friends.
- ◆ Don't be afraid to set limits.
- ◆ Learn the telltale signs of drug and alcohol use.
- ◆ If you think your child is trying drugs or alcohol, do something about it.

◆ Keep in touch with the parents of your child's friends.
◆ Remember: PARENT POWER IS STRONGER THAN PEER
PRESSURE!!

If needed, the appendix lists national clearinghouses that can provide everything from recommendations for drug education, to catalogs of free materials on substance abuse, to ways to get help for youths with alcohol or drug problems.

The Need to Take a Stand
The most important deterrent to youths illegally using drugs, as already cited, is the importance they place on their religious values; and studies indicate that the next most important deterrent is stability in the home.

I contacted approximately two dozen government and private agencies for information in putting together this chapter. When I pointed out that the statistical data indicate that family stability is one of the two most important factors, every agency representative agreed. They all said that the number of divorced and dysfunctional homes must be reversed. They all recognized that families with problems must make living together in a healthy mental state their first priority. To a person, each affirmed that if the destruction of the American family were reversed, the youth drug and alcohol problems would virtually disappear.

However, *not one public or private officials would go on record and allow me to quote him or her about the importance of the family factor.* They were each afraid to do so. Why? Why not go on record if they thought restoring family stability could wipe out this menace?

As I stated in chapter 7, politicians are afraid of voter backlash. Those in government agencies are afraid of rocking the political boat and losing their jobs, while private agencies fear losing donations from those who live in a troubled home environment. In addition, many in Congress and the media have themselves been divorced or have severe marital problems, adversely affecting their kids. For many of these professionals, the pain of acknowledgment often inhibits them from stating the truth publicly.

Currently, some of the only organizations or institutions willing take a clear stand on this issue are religious groups, such as Focus on the Family. Why? Because there is a clear mandate in Scripture that marriage is a sacred commitment.

Perhaps the time has come, though, because of the pain in our society and the overwhelming evidence, that even a secular institution could herald this call to protect the sanctity of the family and people would respond. It isn't bad that religious groups continue to be the most vocal advocates for the family, for their actions have helped preserve our society. The problem, though, is that the message from these groups is inappropriately dismissed by the non-religious as simply "religious."

In the early days of the war on drugs, it was the church and religious organizations that beat the drum for restraint and treatment. Today, we have effective secular organizations, such as the Partnership for a Drug Free America. Perhaps the time is right for secular organizations—maybe the Partnership for a Divorce Free America or Partnership for Healthy Homes?

If we put as much concentrated effort into restoring the family as we do for the drug problem, our country would unquestionably start to recover. I'm not suggesting that we elevate family to a god-like status, only that the family must be preserved. Perhaps, because of the pain in our culture, even those without a religious faith would be willing to respond to such a call to preserve the family if it were eloquently stated.

SUMMARY

In addition to pointing out the dangers and saying no, the following factors provide the best defense against the use of illegal drugs: Teach kids how to be discerning and make good judgments; help them learn how to handle stressful situations—particularly involving friends; and do everything possible to strengthen the family.

All parents should educate themselves on the basic types of drugs and the signs of potential involvement. Even if their own children aren't at risk, there are most likely kids in the neighborhood who are, and these kids can be helped by concerned families. According to Detective Pat DeGregorio of New York City—whose own sixteen-year-old daughter became a user—only honesty, forceful action, and effective therapy can help restore a young life.[11] Government and private agencies enforce the law, educate, and treat those who seek treatment, but only the American family can weed out the root of this evil.

Special thanks to the Dallas Police Department's Narcotic Squad, Chief Rick Hatler, Detective Stan Griffis, and Detective Warren W. Wilson for their assistance in helping me shoot the photographs used in this chapter.

CHAPTER FIFTEEN

Gangs: From the Inner City
to the Suburbs

15.1. In response to increased suburban gang activity, even the local convenience store gets involved.

In cities such as Los Angeles, "drive-by" shootings by gangs such as the Crips and the Bloods are the nightly terror. Teens and kids as young as ten hop into cars with everything from cheap handguns to Uzi semi-automatic machine guns for random killing.

Years ago, it used to be that gang crimes, such as heavy drug trafficking, were just an inner-city phenomenon. No more. The 1980s saw a major shift as gang activity emerged even in the suburbs. Four distinct types of gang activity now affect youths: inner-city gangs such as those I just mentioned; suburban gangs that are more affluent; hate-oriented gangs, such as skinheads; and occult gangs (which will be addressed in chapter 16). Of the four types, the last three classifications are now found in middle-class and upper-middle-class neighborhoods.

In this chapter I'll give you a basic overview of what propels kids into gang activity, what they seek as the payoff, common types of gangs, why they disengage, and how to discourage gang activity in your neighborhood. This basic primer is essential no matter what community you live in, because the social conditions necessary for the proliferation of gangs are now present in most communities.

WHY KIDS JOIN GANGS:
THE PREDICTABLE PROFILE AND PAYOFFS

When asked, most gang members can't articulate the underlying reasons why they started "gang banging"—street lingo for gang activity. But with patient dialogue, the predictable reasons eventually come out.

In most cases, the desire to belong to a gang is the result of trouble at home. Does this profile sound familiar? (*Profile* is used in a generic, not a clinical, sense.) Virtually every gang member I have interviewed came from a family with one or more of the following factors: divorce, separation, physical and/or sexual abuse, and dysfunctional parents. (This profile also fits youths involved in most occultic and cultic groups.)

These conditions are further exacerbated by joblessness, poverty, lack of education, language barriers, academic deficiencies, and destructive elements from pop culture, such as violent themes in music and film (for example, the 1989 movie about gangs, *Colors*).

But most experts cite family breakdown as the primary motivation for gang involvement. This is true in the inner city as well as in middle-class and upper-middle-class neighborhoods. Kids are in pain from families torn apart.

What kids knowingly or unknowingly seek as the *payoff* from gang participation is a *mask* to hide their pain, a *distraction* from their pain, or a *power* device over their pain.

The Mask
Gang activity, distinctive garb, and lingo can act as the mask a youth hides behind, concealing how he or she really feels inside. If Dad is abusing you—verbally or physically—you can pretend you're tougher in the gang. If you're feeling insecure because no one's home, the gang provides the facade—the illusion—that you're safe.

An example of the mask in another context is the person who

drinks at a party in order to put up a brave front. He wants to create the illusion that he's something he isn't.

The Distraction

For some youths, gangs are the distraction, or escape, that diverts their attention from what's really bothering them. This is particularly true for youths who have a lot of idle time—they need something to fill the void so they don't have to think. Some kids turn up the volume on their stereo or boom box to drown out their problems; others watch TV non-stop for hours. Gang members spend time with the gang.

The Power Device

Many kids I've interviewed over the years have been hurt both physically and mentally by those in their family, and some of them think that gang involvement will give them power over their external and internal hurts. Externally, a gang provides a shield against those who might hurt them. In some inner-city neighborhoods, if you aren't a member of a gang, you're exposed to the whim of the streets, seemingly without protection. The gang promises protection from the streets—and even from abusive families. Additionally, some gangs offer sex, money from illegal activities, etc.

In middle- and upper-middle-class neighborhoods, the focus in a gang is usually the promise of power over internal pain, originating from family problems, a problem with a girlfriend or boyfriend, or simply personal insecurities.

Gang members are often from single-parent families with financial problems—although the money factor isn't as significant in middle-class neighborhoods. Universally, however, family troubles are the underlying problem. Regardless of payoffs or behavioral factors, most kids never make the connection that knowingly or unknowingly their gang is usually exploiting their condition.

COMMON GANG BEHAVIOR

Common to most gang members is that they often have too much time and too little to do. This is why gang-related crimes tend to peak during the hot summer months, when school is out. Spurred by a combination of family problems, isolation, free time, and often economic problems, gang activity typically expresses itself in four different types of behavior. Often, more than one type is found in each gang.

The first type is *social.* According to gang expert Cookie Rodriguez, who twenty years ago was a gang member in New York City and now runs the Street Church Academy in Dallas, the dominating factor kids seek from gang involvement is a sense of identity. They want to belong to something that makes them feel important and gives them attention—even negative attention is better for some kids than none at all at home. Some are also seeking protection, excitement, and fun: what could be referred to as *social gang members,* who seek to "achieve their individual social goals as a part of the group."[1] Unique gang attire and customs—hats, coats, insignias, bandannas, handshakes, hairstyles, graffiti, lingo—help create this identity.

Another type of behavior can be found in *delinquent gang members,* who "are concerned primarily with material gain through delinquent activity."[2] Such activity can include drug peddling, robbery, extortion, and even murder. This type of gang member is essentially a juvenile delinquent, who simply commits crimes in a group context.

A third type of behavior is found in *violent gang members,* who "seek emotional gratification by way of violent behavior."[3] This type of behavior differs from delinquent gang members in that the focus is on violence rather than on other crimes such as robbery or drug peddling. It's not uncommon for this type of gang member to commit random as well as planned acts of violence—assaults, shootings, and rape are standard fare. In this classification are gangs that commit racially motivated crimes against different cultural or ethnic groups and neo-Nazi hate gangs that vent toward minorities.

The fourth type of gang behavior is *thrill-seeking.* Here, youths are just out for mischievous "fun," but this type of behavior can be found in any of the other three listed. In the last couple of years this form of gratification appears to be growing faster than any other. It's common, however, for more than one type of behavior to be active in a youth's involvement in a gang.

WHERE GANGS FORM AND THE TYPES OF GANGS THAT ARE PRODUCED

Currently, different types of gang activity form in the inner-city neighborhoods than in the suburbs. Typically, the suburban gang is a tame copycat of inner-city gangs, usually expressing itself with a thrill orientation. The types of gangs that are now present in the United States and their associated activities are covered in the overview that follows. I have chosen to address the hate gang separately, because of its unique qualities.

Inner-City Gangs

Inner-city gangs, sometimes led by adults, are more common than suburban gangs and have received the most amount of press. These gangs are usually driven by turf or racial boundaries. In *turf gangs,* territorial boundaries are established and outside gangs are forbidden to cross established streets, parks, etc. *Racial* or *ethnic gangs* form around one's skin color or ethnic background. Some gangs combine both factors.

The more obscure gangs often form from a bunch of kids who are just hanging out, while established gangs that branch out are better organized. The smaller gangs may or may not commit crimes or do drugs, but most gangs have members who are involved in illicit drug trafficking.

Membership in these gangs is usually limited to males, but some gangs do recruit females, and some are all female. (In one incident, three girls, ages fourteen to sixteen, were arrested for "initiating" another girl in what's called "crossing the line"—a new member crosses the line and submits to a beating by other gang members to prove her worth.)

Recruiting is done by personal contact at school, malls, parks, and other gathering places. While most gangs are confined to middle and high schools, some even set up "junior" gangs to begin the recruitment process in elementary schools. The more notorious gangs, such as the Crips and the Bloods, who originated in Los Angeles, have branches across the United States in other metropolitan cities. This spread is usually driven by a franchising of drug trafficking. As of this writing there is significant evidence that some of these inner-city gangs are spreading to middle-class and upper-middle-class communities.

Suburban Gangs

"In Tucson, Arizona, a white middle-class teenager dressed in gang colors died a victim of a drive-by shooting, as he stood with black and Hispanic members of the Bloods gang."[4] The spread of inner-city gangs to affluent communities occurs but, as of this writing, not frequently. What *has* become more common, though, are suburban rip-offs of inner-city gangs. These kids and young adults join existing gangs or form their own with the glamorized notion that they now have a novel way to be defiant and rebel.

One member of the South Bay Family gang in Hermosa Beach,

California, who goes by the name of Road Dog and whose family owns a chain of pharmacies, said: "This is the nineties, man. We're the type of people who don't take no for an answer. If your mom says no to a kid in the nineties, the kid's just going to laugh." His friends shouted their support, as another gang member lifted his long hair to reveal a tattoo on a bare shoulder that read: "Mama tried."[5]

The smallest percentage of kids in suburban gangs come from stable homes and are just seeking a new way to rebel. Most come from problem homes just like those in the inner city. The difference is that these kids often have money. One social worker commented, "They play the part. They vandalize. They do graffiti. They do all kinds of stuff. But when it comes down to the big stuff, it's: Wait a minute. That's enough for me. I want to change the rules. And then they realize it's a little bit too late."[6]

These kids often don't realize that bad finds bad, until they come across hardened gangs that mean business. One girl I interviewed, who tagged along with a gang-member friend to an isolated location to do some drugs, was gang-raped by members of several gangs who were there. Another threat is from dangerous drug dealers, who are always on the lookout for new gangs to turn into quick new profit centers and from which to recruit sellers.

It's disturbing that although economic conditions are much better outside the inner city, family relationships are only marginally better. When families are torn apart, kids in the suburbs feel just as much pain as kids in the inner city. One difference is that kids in the suburbs have more money to spend on non-gang distractions to bury their pain. Surburban youths in gangs have tended to be less violent, because their affluence gives them more choices to vent and express their discontent. This doesn't mean that these gangs pose no threat: increased gang activity always raises the juvenile crime rate.

If family problems are not reversed, we can expect that suburban gangs will continue to grow. In Dallas County, for example, the number of gangs in both inner-city areas and suburbs jumped from approximately 70 in 1989 to 143 in 1990, with an average of six crimes committed a day.[7] In affluent Plano, the fourth fastest-growing suburb in the U.S., gang membership was up 37 percent from 1990; an estimated 330 youths were identified as gang members, and another 500 came into Plano from other communities to pursue gang activity.[8] This trend is indicative of most metropolitan areas.

If the current trend of troubled families continues to persist, one can expect to see suburban gangs continue to grow in numbers. Additionally, if the United States experiences a severe economic downturn, expect the numbers of suburban gangs to skyrocket as youth lose the mobility and the money they currently use to drown out their familial pain. Also, expect acts of violence to increase. We have already seen this trend emerge as tens of thousands of European youths have joined hate gangs, unleashing their anger with a vengeance.

Hate Gangs

Hate gangs have surfaced in the United States largely during the last ten years. Fueled by irrational hatred, they are some of the most terrifying and worrisome. Skinheads are the best known type of hate gang, and their behavioral mode is usually violence against anyone they choose to hate. Most skinheads express their wrath through racial and anti-Semitic hatred, and they are found in every type of community except ethnic inner-city neighborhoods. Most, however, are found in middle-class and lower-middle-class communities, although some members come from the upper-middle-class. Predominantly white, skinhead gangs typically have a neo-Nazi bent and are found throughout the United States and Western and Eastern Europe.

Some experts speculate that inspiration for the skinhead hatred directed at Jewish people in the U.S. and Europe has been fueled by adult neo-Nazi hate groups, the fortieth commemorative anniversary of the Holocaust (1985), and the fiftieth anniversary of *Kristallnacht* (1988), when the Nazis unleashed their terror on the German Jews by burning Torahs, smashing shop windows and furniture in homes, and killing many people.

Danny Welch of Klan Watch Intelligence, a watchdog of the Southern Poverty Center, says that the roots of the skinhead movement can be traced to England in the sixties, among young toughs who worked in factories and wore heavy steel-toed boots and braces (suspenders, in this country). By the seventies, extremist factions took on an ideological bent, and by the mid-eighties the skinhead movement had taken root in the United States—possibly spurred on by the Aryan Nations, a neo-Nazi group based in Idaho. In the fall of 1989, skinheads provided protection during a rally sponsored by Aryan Nations in Polaski, Tennessee; but the skinhead ideology for the most part has been unsophisticated and inarticulate.

Today, skinheads sport various hairstyles, from spikes—a shaved head with a center Mohawk teased erect—to tightly cropped cuts. Army fatigues and black boots are common. What is especially frightening is that these youths hate on impulse, inspired and sometimes directed by adult neo-Nazi fanatics such as Tom Metzger, whose group the White Aryan Resistance (WAR) was found liable in the November 1988 beating death of an Ethiopian immigrant. A Portland, Oregon, state court leveled a $12.5 million wrongful-death verdict against Metzger and WAR, effectively shutting down his cable talk show *Race and Reason,* his publications, and telephone message lines.

15.2. Example of skinhead hate literature confiscated in North Dallas suburban junior high school.

15.3. Another example of skinhead hate literature.

The rise of skinhead groups in the United States closely parallels the reemergence of similar youth groups in Austria and Germany. In what was formerly East Germany, for example, it's estimated that over thirty thousand youths are involved in this activity.[9] As detailed in chapter 5, over one hundred video games have been distributed in Germany and Austria that include "graphics of swastikas, Hitler, and of gassed and tortured prisoners."[10]

Similar to the U.S., this region has experienced a general moral decline and a reduced status of the family. In 1992, I interviewed a number of experts on this activity in Hungary and Austria. Each said the profile I compiled of a U.S. gang member matched their youths. A similar decline in the family also occurred prior to Hitler's ascent into power (although divorce wasn't as common because it wasn't culturally accepted). When this was linked with the economic depression of the 1930s it fueled the rise of the Third Reich.

The lesson seems clear: When there is a moral breakdown followed by a time of great economic stress, people may direct their pent-up anger at a scapegoat.

In Germany in the thirties and forties, this rage was methodically vented on the Jews, Slavs, and Gypsies. In Dresden, Germany (formerly East Germany), in June of 1991, skinheads vented their anger by burning down a bordello and decrying pornography. The over 45,000 skinheads in the now united Germany regularly target racial violence at Arab and Asian immigrants. In the United States, hate-oriented gangs unleash their fury on anyone who is different from their group. One skinhead gang called the SHARPS, SkinHeads Against Racial Prejudice, has even carried out acts of aggression against other skinhead gangs that are racially biased.

In the United States there are an estimated 2,500 individual skinheads. Actions by these gangs account for the smallest number of crimes committed by gangs. This isn't because these gangs aren't violent, but rather because their numbers are smaller than other gangs. Anti-Semitic skinhead attacks, for example, accounted for 8 percent of the 1,432 anti-Semitic attacks in the U.S. in 1989, but few of the acts were related to another in an organized fashion—which makes them all the more dangerous, because they're unpredictable.[11] One reason this type of gang activity must be watched carefully is that if it continues to grow, it may swell into a rising desire for fascist or anarchist control, similar to what occurred prior to World War II.

Because of our societal conditions, many at-risk youths are easily manipulated by shrewd adult leaders such as Metzger, who can quickly develop a following through a multitude of media—phones, TV, publications, etc.—and use such tools to exploit and dominate the fear and pain of these youths in a frightfully cohesive way.

In the adult population, there are rumblings of this same discontent, following a similar pattern around a charismatic leader. Disturbingly, in the fall of 1991, ex-Klansman David Duke captured 40 percent of the white vote in his bid for the governor's office in economically depressed Louisiana. We can hope that this is not a foreshadowing of things to come. However, because of the large white population in the United States, if this country hits a sustained period of economic decline, I believe that hate gangs will top other gang types in posing the greatest potential threat for explosive growth. If this is true, it's critical that we don't dismiss such activity now as insignificant.

In the summer of 1991, I explained to the Des Moines, Iowa, chapter of the Young President's Organization that because of current family conditions, gang activity would likely emerge in communities that on the surface seemed unlikely candidates. Some skepticism was raised. Just a few weeks later, however, the normally tranquil community of Dubuque, Iowa, headlined the news with hate gang disturbances. White youths, who had formed the National Association for the Advancement of White People, were terrorizing blacks. Until such activity directly confronted them in their own usually placid state—the same would be true for most of us—it was hard for the business leaders of Des Moines to accept the reality that gang activity could affect their community.

SIGNS OF GANG INVOLVEMENT

Except in the case of occult gangs, addressed in the next chapter, it isn't difficult in most situations to identify youths involved in gangs. If you're uncertain about a group you see in your neighborhood, check with your child, cops, teachers, youth pastors, and social workers—they're often the first to pick up on new gangs and their characteristics and can usually tell you if there's cause for alarm. Here are some of the more typical indicators:

- ◆ Common attire.
- ◆ Handshakes and language that are unique to the group.
- ◆ A territorial meeting hangout—this can be anything from a pharmacy, to a mall, to a car wash.
- ◆ Alienation from family.
- ◆ Withdrawal.
- ◆ Obsessive desire to stay with the group in which the above characteristics are evident.

If the number of gangs continues to increase, as many experts predict, there will probably be an increase in the number of gangs that *don't* break the law. Kids in a law-abiding social gang will probably be drawn together because of the need for a place to belong, which they consider safe—a place to be accepted and have fun in.

Therefore, just because some of the above indicators of gangs are present in a group of kids doesn't necessarily mean that the group poses a threat to society. In fact, some of these gangs—which more appropriately should be called groups or even clubs, since they don't commit crimes—might actually be a temporary help to some kids, until they can be channeled into more productive activities in school, sports, church, and community activities. It's even foreseeable that anti-gang gangs, such as the Guardian Angels, might be formed by kids who are tired of being intimidated by the streets. I'm not advocating this kind of activity, but rather trying to heighten awareness of what might be spawned in the future. Although the inner needs of these kids will be the same as those in other gangs, approaches to channeling their aspirations and addressing their fears will of course have to be different.

WHY YOUTHS DISENGAGE FROM GANG ACTIVITY

To this point, we have learned that the following things are predictable about gang activity: the profile of a gang member, the payoffs they seek to deal with their problems, the kinds of behavior exhibited, and the types of groups that form. Also predictable are the reasons—there are eight—why youths disengage.

The most expedient way to disengage the majority of youths from a gang is to first discover the reason(s) for the youth's involvement, the payoff(s) he or she seeks, and the specifics of that youth's environment and personality. Then, after carefully considering these factors, the most likely reasons for disengagement are used as a foundation for building a strategy for permanently separating a youth from the gang.

Law enforcement officers in the United States and Europe have told me that when implemented by a qualified juvenile officer, youth pastor, social worker, or caring adult, this strategy for disengagement is one of the best they have encountered. In fact, for the increasing skinhead problem, they believe this strategy cuts through the political rhetoric and can more quickly isolate a youth from a manipulative adult leader who hides behind a political agenda.

Here are the eight reasons for disengagement:

1. Youths simply lose interest as they get older. (Most gang members don't exceed the early twenties.)
2. The gang activity doesn't satisfy their expectations for a mask, distraction, or give them power over their pain; and they realize that what the gang promises is an illusion—a lie.
3. They become frightened by the *gang's* activities.
4. They become frightened by some *associated* activity. For example, youths who join a gang to have a caring "family," sometimes get out if they become terrified of an external danger, such as drug dealers who threaten the gang.

5. It is successfully pointed out that their pain and their fear of pain is being exploited by the gang leaders. Gang members don't like to believe that *anyone* or *anything* can manipulate or have control over them.

6. They realize that they fit a predictable profile—that is, gang members come from a certain type of family, have certain expectations, behavior, etc. The *secretiveness* surrounding a gang is what lures some to became involved—exemplified by secret hand signs, clothing, etc. I have helped youths disengage after pointing out that while they think they are a mystery to their friends, they aren't to those who understand gangs. However, this must also be accompanied by compassionately talking to them about their pain and what they can do to deal with it honestly.

7. Family relationships are restored and their familial problems are addressed.

8. Someone helps them find a solution to successfully deal with the source of their pain or problem.

Here are two sample scenarios for matching the reason(s) for involvement and the payoff(s) a youth seeks with the most likely reason(s) why he or she will disengage.

Scenario one. An inner-city youth from a single-parent home is a latchkey child—no one is ever home when school lets out. He is afraid: his apartment has been vandalized, and bullies extort money from him. He wants power over those who threaten him, so he joins a gang, although he is also frightened by some of the gang's activities.

Likely reasons for disengagement: numbers 3 and 8.

Strategy for disengagement: Communicate with the youth that he is trading the threat of being harmed by bullies with the threat of being harmed by the gang activity; find a person with authority who can address the threat from the bullies; develop a relationship with a crime prevention officer and patrol officer who can reassure the youth that his apartment will be more carefully watched.

Scenario two. An affluent suburban youth, who is angry over his parents' divorce, joins a secretive skinhead gang in order to rebel. This provides the youth with a distraction from his pain.

Likely reasons for disengagement: numbers 2, 6, and 7.

Strategy for disengagement: First, someone must see if reconciliation between the youth's parents is possible. If it isn't, then ask the parents if one or both of them will devote themselves to strengthening their relationship with their son. (In many cases neither of these first two actions will occur.) Next, an adult, who can gain the trust of the youth, gets the youth to acknowledge that the divorce is what thrust him into the gang and that his pain still remains—that the distraction of gang activity will do nothing to address and heal the pain. Finally, if none of the above work, the secretive factor indicates another strategy: a person the youth trusts points out that he fits a predictable profile—there is nothing secretive about why he is involved or how he is expressing his rage.

Of course, many variables can come into play. The purposes of these scenarios are: (1) to stimulate a suitable person (which may or not be the parent) for establishing a strategy that will help a youth; and (2) to help parents understand what will help a youth disengage. Sometimes a youth will disengage after just a few days of discussion and action, while for some it may take months or, in extreme examples, even years. Please see chapter 19, "A Framework for Getting Help," for additional thoughts on establishing a strategy and chapter 20, "Community Action Can Make a Difference," for some ideas on how one suburban community successfully addressed its gang problem.

If a gang problem is threatening your family, here is a quick list of who to call for help:

◆ Juvenile or gang squad officer.
◆ Local community services (the chamber of commerce can usually direct you).
◆ Church or ministry that specializes in ministering to gangs.
◆ Social workers and mental health care professionals who work with gangs.

THE FAMILY AND CHURCH FACTOR

Across the board you hear the same response from teachers, community officials, law-enforcement officers, and social workers: *Get families to stay together and stay healthy.* Sick families produce sick societies. Programs and task forces are helpful, but they can only do so much. Establishing longer hours for safe gyms, stepped up patrols in parks, encouraging local businesses to hire more youths, church- and community-sponsored social activities, summer camp experiences, and dialogue between cops and kids are all essential ingredients for turning this problem around. But these measures don't get to the root cause.

The first place to push back on the gang problem is in the home. Newspaper editorials frequently mirror this observation in our paper, the *Dallas Morning News*: "No amount of effort by the police and business community can take the place of parental involvement and responsibility."[12]

When it's impossible to repair the damage in the family, one of the next best places for a youth to gain stability, counsel, and direction is in a balanced local church.

Cookie Rodriguez, whose Dallas gang ministry is one of the most highly regarded in the country, makes it clear that the programs she has initiated are only secondary to God's power and love in a youth's life.

Those in local churches must individually and corporately reach out to kids who are at potential risk for gang involvement. For Christians, helping kids at risk is a responsibility, not an option. Captain Melvin Fetchner, who served in the 1991 Persian Gulf War, took his responsibility seriously by setting a positive example and seizing opportunities as they opened up.

One man in Captain Fetchner's squad (I'll call him John) was a former skinhead. Sporting a small gremlin tattooed on his shaved head, John lacked self-esteem. But he wanted to finish his tour to "make my mother proud of me." John had great respect for his captain's quiet example of personal dignity and morality.

15.4. John (on left, with two of the men in his unit in the Kuwaiti desert), a former skinhead whose life changed under the influence of a caring commander.

When confronted with the possibility of his own death—his squad was a part of the west pincer movement across Saddam Hussein's army in Kuwait—John went to Captain Fetchner with questions about being right with God, and asked him to explain what he was reading in the Bible. John even asked for a verse each day to contemplate. Isolated in the desert, John considered for the first time what was really important in life.

John's life began to change because Captain Fetchner took the time to care, sharing the Word of God as well as his own life—something all of us can do in our own neighborhoods, for even hardened gang members are not out of reach of the grace of God, mediated through human kindness.

SUMMARY

When in Salzburg, Austria, in 1992 my wife and I took a stroll in the huge Platz in front of the Dom of Saint Rupert, one of Europe's oldest churches. It was drizzling, and we were the only tourists in the square. As we walked, I noticed an extraordinary amount of graffiti on the walls surrounding the Platz, similar to graffiti used by hate gangs in the United States: a swastika, the name of an American heavy-metal band, and a large red circle with an "A" filling its circumference, which stands for "Anarchy."

As I examined the dark, arch-shaped, covered passageways around the church, I noticed a group of youths with spiked hairdos and black leather jackets about a hundred feet from us. Unprompted, one girl, who said her name was Raija, walked over to us. Dressed in a simple, black wool coat and a round black hat with gold trim, she asked me, "Do you like punks?" (They called their small gang a "punk gang.")

"Some I do, and some I don't," I said, surprised by her question. No student in the U.S. has ever asked me such a question unprompted.

"Well, I believe in God," she said, gesturing to the massive domed church, "but my friends don't."

A lengthy discussion ensued about her beliefs and her home life. She was astonished that I knew what drove her and her friends into their gang and that she was not different from youths in U.S. gangs. Within minutes, she sought our counsel about her personal family problems, how to approach them, and practical things she might be able to do.

Before we left, we agreed with her assessment that believing in God and Jesus Christ was a good thing, but we added that she must *love the truth more than she feared the pain from her family.* The warmth that radiated from her face when she accepted this was for my wife and me one of the great unexpected joys of our trip.

As confirmed by Raija and a number of European experts, what I had compiled—the profile of a gang member, what they hope to get, and the reasons they get out—is consistent worldwide. Why gang activity is growing is not a mystery. Nor is it surprising that when caring adults put the focus back on the home and honestly confront problems, kids no longer want to participate in a gang.

If gangs are forming in your community, some ideas detailed in chapters 19 and 20 may be helpful. Local church ministries can also be a crucial deterrent—through ministries to at-risk kids as well as to kids already in gangs. It's best to start with at-risk kids while they're still in elementary school.

Some foundational material in the first section of this book is especially important here. Chapter 3, "Secrets, Lies, and the Truth," is helpful for teaching kids when keeping secrets is harmful—especially secrets related to gang activity, such as extortion of money at school or secretive initiation rites. Kids should be encouraged to dialogue with local law enforcement, who can provide protection.

The lessons in chapter 4, "Illusion and Reality: Checking Out the Facts," can help youths understand that what gangs promise are illusions. A trip to the local jail or talking to former gang members is one way to check out the facts. Juvenile officers and gang ministry workers can also help.

Although increasing gang activity is a formidable problem, the battle can be won when families, communitites, and those who care about biblical principles reach out to these kids.

CHAPTER SIXTEEN

Cults and the Occult, Part One: A Parent's Primer

◆

Since the mid-sixties, occult and cult involvement among youths has steadily risen. At any given time, 1 to 2 percent of all youth become involved in cult activity.[1] This spreads across an array of activity, from teens involved in what they believe are ancient satanic rituals, to cultic skinhead groups who covertly plan random acts of violence, to a host of cults influenced by some Eastern religions.

Many of these cults express themselves violently, which is not surprising since criminal acts of violence by youths are on the rise. Estimates by experts put the total number of cults in the United States at over five thousand, with about half or more affecting youths, and the number of youth participants in the tens of thousands. The total number of youths involved in occult and/or cult activity, however, is in the hundreds of thousands, if not higher, when the estimate includes those who dabble with Ouija boards, healing crystals, etc. A simple survey conducted in a representative sampling of schools multiplied by the number of schools in the United States would show that this is a conservative estimate. And this trend shows no sign of reversing itself.

The issues surrounding potential youth involvement in cults and the occult can be complicated even for professionals. I will limit my treatment to an overview of this activity to provide a base from which you will be able to: (1) grasp the nature of and the differences between cults and the occult, because they can be significantly different; (2) understand why kids are drawn into each; and (3) learn how to seek help if a youth is in trouble (chapter 19 will also provide advice here). In chapter 17 I'll suggest some basic preventive measures for foolproofing kids against the influence of cults.

UNDERSTANDING CULTS AND THE OCCULT

Let's start out by establishing some working definitions for *cult, occult,* and related terms. These explanations are for adults; in the next chapter, I will provide some simple definitions that can be used to explain to kids what cults and the occult are all about.

Cult: An isolated and/or anti-social group of persons who give their allegiance to a leader or leaders, whose purpose and/or goal it is to attain manipulative power through unquestioned loyalty to a system of beliefs.

Occult: The attempt to attain alternative supernatural powers, which may be real or imagined, apart from the powers of the Judeo-Christian concept of God.

Occultic cult: An isolated and/or anti-social group of persons who give their allegiance to a leader or leaders, whose purpose and/or goal it is to attain both manipulative and occultic power through unquestioned loyalty to a system of beliefs.

Satanism: When people, either singly or in a group, profess occult allegiance to Satan and express that faith through any or all of the following activities: prayers, chants, spells, sacrifices, and related actions. These behaviors may be formalized or created spontaneously by the person or group; additionally, it is not necessary that the participant believe in Satan or the associated practices.

Occultic ritual: A sequence of actions performed to attain occultic powers.

These terms are frequently used interchangeably, but it's important that we understand the differences between them. When their meanings are not clearly established, confusion often arises when trying to help kids at risk.

Cults
The word *cult,* from the Latin *cultus,* originally referred to a ritual, ceremony, or liturgy. In recent times, however, it has been used to

designate a group that controls and manipulates its members through certain mechanisms of recruitment and indoctrination, some of which are: (1) isolation or "involvement" of members to the point that the group controls all incoming information; (2) economic exploitation or an enslaving organizational structure; (3) esotericism, or what has been referred to as "the segmentation of the joining process."[2] This last mechanism refers to withholding information from members regarding exactly what is expected of them and where the group is going, so that they're always kept in the dark. This makes it easier for the leader to control members by claiming to have secret knowledge and, more importantly, enables the leader to deviously shift his or her plans without those plans being contested.

The word *cult* by itself, however, does not necessarily refer to a group that looks for supernatural powers. It can simply refer to a manipulative and/or anti-social group, which may or may not be criminally destructive. A cult can believe or disbelieve in the supernatural, or it can promote or reject criminal activities. Its key feature is a leader or leaders who control members through beliefs or ideas in an isolated context.

Dr. Margaret Singer, professor of psychology at the University of California at Berkeley and an expert on cult behavior, says that the cult leader seeks to make followers "totally or nearly totally dependent on him or her for almost all major life decisions, and inculcates in these followers a belief that he or she has some special talent, gift, or knowledge."[3] She traces the twentieth-century awareness of cultic archetypes as follows: (1) the Russian purge trials in the 1930s, in which people were manipulated into both falsely confessing and falsely accusing; (2) prisoners of war who were subjected to an indoctrination program, or brainwashing; (3) Charles Manson's diabolical influence and control of a group of middle-class youths in 1969; (4) Jim Jones, the controlling and manipulative religious leader who led over nine hundred followers in mass suicide; and (5) New Age and philosophical cults, along with "pseudo-growth" and "pseudo-therapy" groups, dominant in the nineties.

The Occult
The Latin word *occult(us)* means covered over, concealed, or hidden. In medicine, *occult* is used to specify a disease whose symptoms are hidden. Popularly, *occult* is used to describe everything from psychic research to demon possession and implies secret access to supernatural or paranormal powers.

For our purposes, I'm limiting the definition of the word *occult* to the seeking of supernatural powers. (Alleged psychic powers, as discussed in chapter 6, are not included because these purported *human* powers have never been proven to exist.) The supernatural powers that are sought are not like the biblical concept of God's power to heal, but rather the dark or evil powers of another supernatural being, such as Satan or the Egyptian god, Seth. This definition does not mean that Seth necessarily exists or has powers, but rather that practitioners attempt to receive powers from him, much like the prophets of Baal, who unsuccessfully sought powers from their pagan god. (See 1 Kings 18 for the confrontation between the Israelite prophet Elijah and the prophets of Baal.)

Some researchers state that the word *occult* solely implies powers that are "hidden" or "concealed." Two additional modern definitions of this word are: (1) of or pertaining to magic, astrology, and other alleged sciences claiming use or knowledge of secret, mysterious, or supernatural agencies, and (2) the supernatural, or supernatural agencies and affairs.[4] These definitions seem inadequate because this would imply that any belief in the supernatural would be occultic, even a belief in God. It is for this reason that I have narrowed the use of *occult* to the *kind* of supernatural power one is seeking.

The phrase "alleged sciences claiming use or knowledge" in the above definition is often the reason why the word *psychic* is mentioned along with occult. This has occurred because there aren't enough words currently in use to cleanly articulate these kinds of concepts without a confusing overlap. But psychic and supernatural powers are entirely different concepts and should not be used interchangeably. As we learned in chapter 6, claims to psychic brain power such as telekinesis, telepathy, and precognition have never been proven to exist. People who are seeking powers, however, usually don't care if the power they are seeking is of a supernatural or supposed psychic origin. They simply want power. (For an in-depth discussion on psychic versus supernatural powers, see *Powers: Testing the Psychic and Supernatural,* listed in the appendix.)

Here is a list of common occult practices that appeal to kids:

◆ Ouija boards.
◆ Tarot cards—used for fortunetelling.
◆ Pendulum—participants hold in their hand a chain to which a ball or amulet is attached. Supposedly, powers influence

which way the ball swings. Actually, participants cause the ball to move via minute muscle movements.

◆ Seances.
◆ Spirit channeling (see "New Age" section later in this chapter).
◆ Satanism.
◆ Automatic writing—participants believe that a spirit can communicate with them and enable them to write out its messages.
◆ Firewalking—accomplished because coals are poor heat conductors, although many adherents teach that it is done by tapping into an occult power.

Occultic Cults

The term *occultic cult* defines a group that not only is isolated and/or anti-social but also tries to tap into occult powers. A cult that believes in killing to gain favor from its leader would not be an occult cult, but if its followers believed that killing would give them demonic supernatural power, then it would fall under this definition.

As another example of this distinction, a cult that kills in the false belief that God will reward them would simply be a cult, not an occultic cult, because the expectation of power is from God and not Satan.

Two examples of an occultic cult are:

◆ Satanic cults.
◆ Charles Manson's cult (Manson used tricks to convince his followers that he had powers and that they, too, could have the same powers).

Satanism

Satanism could be considered either a type of an occult practice or a type of an occultic cult. When there is only one person who practices satanism, then this person would be considered an occultist, since he or she is trying to derive supernatural power from an occult source. When a *group* of believers seeks power from Satan, an occult source, this would be considered an occultic cult, because there is usually a leader seeking manipulative control over followers.

Astrology, psychic readings, numerology, and the like are other types of occultic practices, but they are not satanism. However, teens who participate in satanism will often incorporate other occult practices like those just mentioned. (*Note*: Theologically, a Christian might say that all of the above practices are satanic because the participants are pursuing the occult, but for the purposes of properly clarifying these kinds of activities, they should not be labeled as satanism.)

Teen participation in satanism gained momentum around 1985 and has persisted at uncomfortably high rates, primarily in middle-class and upper-middle-class communities. This teen trend represents the first time in U.S. history that youths, without encouragement from adults, have pursued satanism. Most teens who become involved have been observed to do so for one to two years and then cease. During that time, however, rape and drug trafficking are common in such groups. (Conspiratorial adult groups are rare but nevertheless deadly.)

Youths who don't believe in Satan may still be involved in the practice of satanism. It's not uncommon for the leader of a group to disbelieve in the reality of Satan and at the same time use fear of him as a device to control others. Also, one doesn't need to believe in Satan to acknowledge that there are those who do practice satanism. (For more information on this topic, please see the appendix.)

The principal similarity between the terms *cult, occult, occultic cult,* and *satanism* is that each involves some form of control or manipulation. The key differences lie in the *source* from which one hopes to derive power, and *who* is doing the controlling. In a cult, for example, the source and center of power is usually the leader. For a youth using a Ouija board by himself and trying to contact a spirit, the source of the alleged power is the spirit, while the youth is the one who is doing the controlling. See table 16.5 to clarify the relationships between these terms.

New Age

The last term we need to cover is what has become known as the "New Age Movement." The term *New Age* is commonly used to encompass all kinds of practices that prior to 1980 were called occult or metaphysical. Here is a partial list from the hundreds of practices:

◆ Healing crystals.
◆ Psychic readings.
◆ Spirit channeling—participants claim that a spirit can speak through them.
◆ Smell salons—customers smell exotic herbs and spices to cleanse their spirits.
◆ Motivational seminars that use visualization techniques in

which participants are encouraged to empty their minds and chant the names of Hindu gods.

◆ Firewalking.

Boiled down, New Age thought and practices are simply derivatives of Eastern philosophical and religious concepts that have been incorporated with something that either promises people occult powers or a new path to spiritual growth. The loosely knit "movement" that involves millions of participants was popularized by Shirley MacLaine in her book *Out on a Limb,* in which she chronicles her entry into this murky world.

The following thematic Eastern concepts have been identified by researcher Doug Groothuis as common among New Agers:

1. *All Is One.* We are all one and the same: trees, God, airplanes, people, etc. Philosophers call this monism.

2. *All Is God.* Nature is God, material things are God, people are God, etc. This is called pantheism.

3. *Humanity Is God.* We are all Gods unto ourselves.

4. *Change of Consciousness.* The solution to the world's problems lies in changing how we think in order to alter our consciousness. Yoga, Transcendental Meditation, and chanting mantras are some of the suggested avenues.

5. *All Religions Are One.* There is no fundamental difference between Christianity, Hinduism, Taoism, etc. They are all variations on one and the same reality. This is called syncretism.

6. *Cosmic Evolutionary Optimism.* Since it is apparent from history that all of the above have not made humanity better, New Agers believe that we must be forever optimistic in a oneness with the cosmos. When we do this, everything will evolve into a new Utopia.

Acceptance of these ideas in Western culture began to gain momentum in the sixties, paralleling the demise of the American family. Few would have bought into any of these concepts, many of which defy common sense, unless deceivers had first presented demonstrations that appeared to be real supernatural or paranormal powers. Try explaining to a group of third-graders that we are all God, or that everything is God—including their peanut-butter-and-jelly sandwich. They laugh.

New Age philosophy has caught on largely because of three factors. First, increasing numbers of people in our culture are in pain primarily from ruptured families. These people are looking for relief from their pain. Second, thousands of people such as "psychic" James

Hydrick have fooled millions of adults over the last twenty-plus years with deceptions that appeared to be powers. Seductively intrigued, many at-risk adults, after being fooled, asked: How is it done? Can I have the same powers? Enter the farfetched philosophies as the answer to this desire for power, which is how this pop movement commenced. The third factor emerged as another wave of adults, similarly in pain but *not* captivated by power demonstrations, were seduced into buying the "I am me—I am God" philosophy, believing that they were their own gods—capable of taking control over their pain.

UNDERSTANDING KIDS' INVOLVEMENT IN CULTS AND THE OCCULT

Through various media, kids have been bombarded by these same concepts. Some TV talk shows now center around psychics, and even offer 900 numbers to call for instant counsel from psychic gurus—this in addition to constant exposure in many sitcoms. The reason this is significant is because the more youths are exposed to fraudulent claims of powers coupled with bizarre philosophies, the greater the likelihood that they can fall prey to a deceptive practice or group—particularly kids who come from troubled homes.

Why Kids Are Drawn into the Occult

Apart from kids who just dabble for a short time out of curiosity, most who become involved with occult practices do so for the same reasons that youths join gangs: they're in pain from ruptured homes. And like those in gangs, youths who become seriously involved with the occult are looking for a way to mask, distract, or achieve power over their pain.

Here are the four basic ways in which youths are introduced to occult practices:

1. They're just curious.
2. It's something that has been a part of their family, and they don't know any better.
3. They're introduced to it by a friend and participate because of peer pressure.
4. They like the excitement of doing something secretive that has an element of fear, which is like a form of entertainment.

In the case of satanism, every youth I have ever interviewed during a period of five years had the same profile. Each came from a home in which there was physical or sexual abuse, divorce or separation, or one of the parents was addictive or dysfunctional in some way. They expressed the same anger-hate factor as youths in violent and hate gangs.

Why Kids Give Up Occult Involvement

There are essentially eight reasons why kids give up involvement in occult activities, which are similar to those in chapter 15:

1. They simply lose interest, as the activity loses its appeal.
2. The practice doesn't produce what is promised, and/or they realize it is a lie. For many kids, evidence that they have been deceived into believing in a fake power is enough to make them turn their backs on any further involvement.

     These are the most common practices currently deceiving kids with the promise that they have powers:

     ◆ *The Ouija board.* It has been proven that people, not a spirit, push the planchette.

     ◆ *Horoscopes.* All the scientific data conclusively show that astrologers can't predict the future, nor do the planets and stars control or influence human events.

     ◆ *Those who say they can read minds and foretell the future.* They might call themselves: fortunetellers, psychics, sensitives, seers, channelers, readers, etc. While I won't rule out the possibility of supernatural powers, after over twenty years of examining hundreds of cases, I have never found one person who had a power. Most rely on trickery and deception. However, a psychic might *claim* that his power is from God when reading tarot cards, tea leaves, palms, or just looking into someone's eyes.

3. The practice itself frightens them.
4. Fear of unexpected harm. Kids involved in satanism, for example, have disengaged because they were afraid of being harmed by drug dealers who sold to the group.
5. They realize someone's taking advantage of them. Some kids cease when they realize that the practice is just exploiting them—their fears, problems, etc. Many kids don't like *anything* having control over them.
6. They find something that is more effective in helping them solve their personal problems or taking away their pain.

TABLE 16.1—COMPARISON OF TERMS

	LEADERSHIP STYLE (POWER STRUCTURE)	GOAL/PURPOSE	WHAT FOLLOWERS BELIEVE IS THE SOURCE OF POWER	HOW FOLLOWERS BELIEVE THEY CAN OBTAIN POWER	EXAMPLES OF HOW TO EXIT FROM EACH CATEGORY
CULT Ex.—Cult of personality: Hitler used Nazism to develop a cult-like allegiance to himself.	Leader(s) over followers Ex.—Hitler controls Germany	Manipulation and control (leader over group) Ex.—Hitler desires to have political and social control over Germany	1. Leader 2. Leader's ideas, his use of fear, etc. 3. Belief system—doesn't have to include belief in the supernatural. Ex.—Hitler and Hitler's promise of a super race: Aryan and pure	Through unquestioned allegiance to the leader and the belief system. This often entails some form of brainwashing—thought reform. Ex.—Through unquestioned allegiance to Hitler and the Third Reich	1. Reverse thought reform process, if it was used 2. Restore normal ties to family, friends, social fabric, etc. 3. Expose folly of beliefs Ex.—Expose Hitler's intent and overcome instilled fear (applies only to unwilling participants and not to willing war criminals)
OCCULT Ex.—Ouija board used to supposedly contact spirits to divine the future	Individual or group—Some occult practices are practiced by oneself, while others are practiced with one or more persons; in a group context there may or may not be a leader depending upon the type of practice. Ex.—Despondent teen	Individual or group of practitioners want power over life circumstances through manipulating occult power. Ex.—To receive divined information	Whatever is believed to be the occultic source—Ouija board, spirits, psychics, healing crystal, etc. Ex.—Spirits	Occultist obtains power by focusing on supernatural or paranormal powers that are believed to be operative. Ex.—With practice, one can allow the spirits to spell out answers by moving the planchette across the Ouija board	If activity is simply a deception, this must be communicated without alienating believer. (Note: If phenomena is supernatural, such as possession, which is very rare, then it should be dealt with both spiritually and through strategic counseling.) Ex.—Show that it is the person who pushes the planchette to spell words and not a spirit
OCCULTIC CULT Ex.—Spirit channeling group (This is where a phony "channeler" supposedly allows a spirit to speak through him or her.)	Leader over followers Ex.—The "channeler" of the spirit	Manipulation and control—Leader over group while members seek control over life circumstances Ex.—Leader desires to control group while followers want information from "spirit"	1. Leader 2. Whatever is believed to be the occultic source—Ouija board, spirits, psychics, healing crystal, etc. Ex.—The "spirit" contacted and the person "channeling" the spirit	1. By giving unquestioned allegiance to the leader 2. The follower focuses on supernatural or paranormal power that is believed to be operative. Ex.—It is through the leader, who is a "spirit channeler," that followers believe they will be given information	1. Same as 1 and 2 in cult category. 2. Same as occult category. Ex.—Expose that the "channeler" doesn't really contact spirits, but is only interested in manipulating the group for money, ego, etc.
TEEN-SATANISM Note: When a teen-satanic group meets the criteria defined for an occultic cult, it is an occultic cult. If a youth practices by himself, then it qualifies as an occult practice—as does the Ouija board.	Leader over followers when in a group context, but individual is the leader if practiced alone	Manipulation and control—Leader wants to control group while members—or individual in a solo context—want(s) control over life circumstances.	1. Satan 2. Leader of group—this expectation applies only to a group context. 3. Leader's ideas	1. In a group, the followers give unquestioned allegiance to leader who claims to be able to have direct contact with Satan. 2. When practiced by oneself, the participant gives allegiance only to Satan.	1. Identify which of the reason(s) listed in chapter 16 apply to the youth in question and proceed accordingly. 2. If there is a group, one may have to address thought reform (this is rare).

7. For youths deeply involved, some disengage when it is pointed out to them that their profile, their expectations, or their actions are predictable. They don't like someone figuring them out, because secretiveness is often an enticing lure of the occult.

8. Finally, some cease involvement if a parent or peer just says "no more" because it's a bad thing. This is the least common reason for a troubled youth, but it is very common for a youth from a stable home—especially when a youth gets involved in other positive activities instead, filling the void.

How to Help Youths End Their Involvement in the Occult

On the positive side, most kids involved in the occult are fairly easy to disengage. Also, for parents who know of kids involved in cult activity, there are many organizations with good track records who can assist, as well as a lot of good information that is available for the lay and professional community on how to help youths disengage.

When trying to help young people caught up in an occult practice, it is crucial to understand the nature of the practice itself, and whether they're involved individually or in a group context. The reason for clearly defining terms is to eliminate unnecessary confusion and enable those who can take positive action to do so more effectively.

For example, a youth who obsessively uses the Ouija board while alone in her room should not be approached the same as a youth who is enmeshed in a satanic cult. Neither would one use the same approach for a youth who is in a satanic cult as for one who is entrapped in a Jim Jones-type cult that uses thought reform. Each scenario has its own special needs.

To help young people disengage from occult practices, five factors are helpful to understand.

1. When a youth is involved in an occult practice, it's important to distinguish between a passing fancy and long-term involvement. If the interest is superficial, care must be taken not to overplay the issue, which could cause the youth to cling defensively to the practice.

2. One must have an accurate understanding of the particular practice and what kind of deception is operative.

In the case of the Ouija board, for example, it must be pointed out that the youth and not some spirit is pushing the planchette. (This is easily proven by suggesting that the letters be randomly mixed and a covering put over the board so the youth can't see the letters. Now if the planchette is moved around and an intelligible answer is spelled, one can say that it is a supernatural power. It should be noted that all tests like this have failed.)

In the case of spirit channeling, most instances have been traced to the speaker himself or herself talking and providing information, not some spirit as claimed. While it is remotely possible that a person might be possessed, experience shows *this is virtually never the case*. (If one suspects this is the situation and approaching the youth is unsuccessful, seek the help of a mental health care expert and an experienced pastor or layperson to develop a sound and balanced approach. Unfortunately, I know of no resource materials to recommend for this situation. However, since this kind of activity is *extremely* uncommon, it should be the last option considered. *A youth who isn't possessed, but is taken through a process to cast out a nonexistent demon, can be grievously harmed.*)

3. One should determine whether or not other youths are also involved. If they are, it's necessary to distinguish further between a loose-knit group that's been meeting casually or a cult that appears to have formed. If the latter is suspected, steps should be taken for helping a youth disengage from a cult (detailed later in this chapter). If it's just a small loose-knit group, then one might either talk to the youth alone or with all of his or her friends together, depending upon the circumstances.

4. When talking to kids about their participation or interest, parents should be sensitive to which of the reasons listed are the motivating factors for their involvement. If the reason is that the activity is a distraction away from a family problem, then this must be brought into the discussion. If it's simply because of curiosity, then parents should explain the deception involved as well as point out that this interest might lead to something else more harmful. (If you don't feel suited for this discernment process, please read the four steps for helping a youth exit from a cult. Some of these steps, such as selecting a strategist, will be helpful here.)

5. The appeal of the occult is sometimes different than a cult. Pursuit of occult activities doesn't necessarily require participation in a group, which is appealing to some youths. Cult participants, however, are either those who like to be part of a group or have experienced some type of fear or thought-reform—breaking their will—to become part of, and remain in, the cult. For these reasons, disengaging youths from occult practices is usually easier than helping them exit a cult.

In the context of obtaining the above information, one can now apply the framework for assisting a troubled youth, which is detailed in chapter 19.

Why Kids Are Drawn into Cults

What the occult and cults both have in common is that they offer the lie of some special power—which can be occultic, manipulative control, etc.—to participants.

The reasons that youths are drawn into cults are very similar to the reasons why kids are drawn to the occult. I have listed those reasons again with expanded explanations that relate to cult activity.

1. The cult activity is something that has been a part of a youth's family, and he or she doesn't know any better. When practiced in a family context, a youngster usually has no choice but to participate.

This is different from a family that simply practices an occult activity; it's easier for youths to disengage from this kind of situation, because they can reject the practice without rejecting their family. In a cult situation, however, rejecting the cult belief system is equivalent to, and received by the family as, rejecting the family itself.

2. A youth is just curious. This is often the result of something that on the surface looks good and trustworthy. When I was in my early twenties, some followers of Sun Myung Moon—called Moonies—came to my door. They told me how they wanted all churches to become as one. A new Christian, I asked them if they were Christians. They said, "Yes," and invited me to a "strategy planning" meeting to find out how the churches could all become united. I told them I would like to go, although I didn't because I had another commitment that weekend.

A few weeks later, I told a friend about their visit. That's when I learned that they had lied to me—they weren't Christians, but they had been instructed to answer affirmatively when asked.

3. Kids are introduced to a cult by a friend and initially participate because of peer pressure.

4. Kids like belonging to a secretive group.

5. Kids have a problem in their life and, like those in gangs, hope that it will mask, distract from, or overpower their pain/problem. This is the most common reason that kids fall into cults. These pain/problem areas include: desire for attention, distressed family situation, need for identity or a sense of belonging, and a desire for protection.

6. The cult implements some kind of thought-reform (brainwashing) that ensnares a youth. This may occur early on, as a recruitment

mechanism, or later on, in order to undermine a youth's ability to separate from the group and thus ensure continued involvement.

Why Youths Disengage from Cults
The reasons why youths leave cults are essentially the same as those for disengaging from occult activity. But there are a couple of differences. First, it's unlikely, although not impossible, that a youth will disengage simply because a parent says "no" to cult participation. Second, in extreme cases, some youths may need extensive counseling and guidance by those who are skillful in undoing whatever thought-reform process was used by the cult. (See the appendix for organizations that can provide the names of such qualified persons.) One note of caution: a number of non-expert "deprogrammers" are quite inept. It is best if a psychologist with appropriate training in a controlled setting assists someone who has experienced thought-reform.

How to Help Youths Exit from Cults
The prerequisites for helping a youth exit from a cult are trust, good information, sound judgment, and an ability to relate to young people. Specific actions may vary, but basically the process consists of four basic steps:

1. Select a strategist.
2. Develop a preliminary strategy.
3. Implement the strategy.
4. Refine the long-term strategy.

The framework for these four steps is detailed in chapter 19, "A Framework for Getting Help."

The Need for Follow-up Support
When kids exit from a group or cease from behavior that is harmful, they need consistent support and encouragement. The phrase "support group" is not used by health care professionals as an option, but rather as a necessity—especially when applied to youths who have been involved in a cult.

Sending an occasional note or card or making a phone call of encouragement can do much to boost a youth who has just exited from a cult. Genuine outward displays of affection, especially from a parent who has not done so in the past, should be encouraged as soon as possible. Such acts of affection as squeezing an arm or hand, an embrace, an arm around the shoulder, or the words "I love you" said with eye contact can help reaffirm for youths that home is not just a place that represents pain. This may be uncomfortable if family members have not habitually expressed affection for one another—but even modest efforts can reinforce that someone cares.

Support from other parents, kids, relatives, and neighbors is also needed to help youths feel loved and accepted as they realize that they are not dependent upon their former rebellion or old circle of friends.

A savvy youth pastor who is concerned for the spiritual as well as the physical and emotional well-being of a youth can often be a stopgap measure before a treatment center or an effective part of a long-term counseling process. I have seen sensitive youth pastors form the bridge that helped guide a youth back into a healthy circle of friends. Additionally, they can help point kids in a positive direction through youth gatherings and trips, prayer, and Bible studies. Many kids I have interviewed have said that the spiritual growth and awareness experienced by embracing the Christian faith was one of the key factors in their exit and subsequent emotional recovery.

THE SPIRITUAL FACTOR

As with some of the other destructive trends already detailed in this text, the spiritual factor cannot be dismissed. No authoritative studies have been done on the importance of this factor in relationship to disengaging from harmful occult and cult activities; however, I have watched many youths who have disengaged from these activities. I have observed who recovers quickly and who doesn't. I have observed those who disengage from one harmful behavior, such as involvement in a cult, only to take up another, such as substance abuse. I have also observed youths who disengage and whose lives return to a state of normalcy.

Consistently in my observations as a journalist over the last ten years, those who embraced the Christian faith disengaged more quickly and better resisted other harmful activities that fed off the primary reasons propelling them into occult and cult activities. Although restoring family relationships and professional counseling were often crucial elements, the spiritual factor was often the most potent long-term force for effecting a positive change. (In this context, it is also critical that a youth does *not* join a church that is manipulative and controlling. Unfortunately, because of cultural conditions, the number of local churches that have taken on cult-like qualities has increased. For this reason, those who have been involved in a manipulative group or practice must be additionally cautious about the church they join, since they have a greater susceptibility to placing themselves in a similar at-risk environment.)

From a biblical perspective, I believe there are several reasons why the spiritual factor is so important. First, when people get caught up in seeking occultic power or bonding with a harmful surrogate family, spiritual damage inevitably occurs. Embracing the Christian faith is a powerful positive alternative, because it does more than simply replace what had previously been filling the void: it penetrates and heals the hidden parts of the human heart and mind.

A second reason is that the Scriptures are far more than just eloquent or wise words; they are alive—breathing life into dark lives. (Psychiatrist Dr. Paul Meier cautions, however, that appropriate Scriptures should be selected carefully for youths with tendencies to harm themselves. A youth might take literally a verse such as, "If your eye causes you to sin, pluck it out," and harm himself. It is better to give such a youth verses that communicate love, joy, peace, etc.)

One student I interviewed was adamant that embracing the Christian faith was the decisive factor in her disengagement and speedy recovery from an occultic cult. I pressed her hard about her statement, since I avoid accepting someone's personal perspective just because it aligns with mine. In fact, I rarely disclose my personal beliefs until *after* an interview is over so as not to build a certain expectation in the person I am interviewing.

"You've seen a lot of others in treatment centers and have known a lot of kids who were into the occult. Did you ever see somebody just up and stop without becoming a Christian?" I probed.

"No," she responded. "No, I haven't."

"Now are you just saying that?"

"No. Phillip has tried many times, and he has not beaten his addiction. Rick has been into treatment, and Sheila, and Ashley. Jack has been into treatment, and he's the only one who's okay—but he became a Christian."

Because of the profound influence the Christian faith has had on this student and many others, even those who don't embrace faith in

Jesus Christ should consider what benefit this might have in someone's life who is at similarly risk.

SUMMARY

Cults and the occult are different webs of entanglement that both feed off the desire for power—usually power over some kind of pain. A clear understanding of the differences between them and the way they manifest themselves is necessary, however, in order to determine appropriate responses. Don't make the mistake of lumping all these activities together. There are similarities, but there are also significant differences, and that requires varying responses.

Although the spiritual factor is important, it is a mistake to assume that a minister can be a replacement for therapy for a youth who needs assistance from a qualified mental health care professional. Many churches now recognize this need for this and even staff their own qualified professionals. In order to disengage a youth from the occult or a cult one doesn't need to be a Christian, nor does the youth always need to become a Christian. But my experience is that the kind of protection and healing that transcends human ability is available only through a faithful and balanced walk with Christ.

Parents should be cautious of unreliable preachers who talk of spiritual warfare but offer untested and warped solutions. Some of them do this as a smokescreen for their own personal problems, which they aren't willing to address, blaming everything on Satan. Others do so to frighten their followers into sending more money.

Parents must also be careful of some churches, which offer help but themselves exhibit bizarre behavior because of emotional and psychological problems of individual members. In these churches, the sick minister to the sick and nobody gets well.

When you seek Christian counsel related to the occult and cults, don't be afraid to ask questions and talk to people who have been helped by a particular minister or church.

One final note: If you are personally involved in helping a youth separate from one of these activities over an extended period of time, you can avoid becoming obsessed with the task by spending even a small amount of time on positive and uplifting activities. Although there are many intense problems around us, there is always good to be found—even when it isn't obvious. Unless you strike a balance between addressing the bad parts of life and participating in the good parts of life, it won't be long before paranoia and fear set in, skewing your view of the world. Don't feel guilty about backing off for a day and doing something fun and fulfilling. Doing so will actually enrich your efforts to help a youth in trouble.

CHAPTER SEVENTEEN

Cults and the Occult, Part Two: Preventive Measures You Can Take

W hat can parents do to keep kids from getting snared by involvement in cults and the occult? In this chapter we'll review some preventive measures that can make a dramatic difference.

Some of these measures include educating youths about these matters without inspiring unnecessary fear. Additionally, I've included Scripture passages that are relevant to these issues for individual or family use.

At the outset, I want to stress again that the greatest deterrent to involvement in cults and the occult is a healthy family with clear channels of communication. Kids from a secure family environment may dabble briefly with occult practices, but it's unlikely that they will become entrenched.

I mentioned in chapter 6 that virtually all the psychics I have interviewed come from seriously dysfunctional or abusive family backgrounds. After hundreds of interviews with kids and adults involved in cult-like practices, I continue to notice the same pattern predictably emerging: Family breakdown spawns the desire for power to overcome pain. As the problem goes, so goes the solution: Predictably, strengthen the family connections in order to prevent youths from seeking destructive ways to ease their pain.

Here are some specific suggestions for educating kids about cultic and occultic practices.

TEACHING KIDS ABOUT THE OCCULT

Even with kids as young as age five, it's appropriate to begin explaining what the occult and cults are. However, this must be carefully done in a controlled environment, without the distraction of phone calls or blaring radios and TVs. Most importantly, it should be done without inspiring fear, in a context in which kids feel safe and free to ask questions.

Here is a simple explanation of the word *occult* for preteens: *When people do something to try to get supernatural powers that aren't from God.*

You could add to this definition some examples, such as: they might use a Ouija board, go to people who say that they can contact spirits, or use a horoscope to try to predict the future.

(If kids ask about "psychic" mind powers, please refer back to the discussion of this in chapter 6, "Tricks or Powers?" Remember, psychic powers have never been proven to exist. The only time that a discussion of psychic powers should enter into a discussion about the occult—practices that supposedly have a supernatural origin—is when a psychic says that his power is from God or some other supernatural source.)

Although this explanation of the word *occult* is from a Christian worldview, religious beliefs aren't necessary to come to the conclusion that the occult is harmful. History shows that those who participate are more prone to being deceived by other activities in life, since they have already accepted a lie that affects the core essence of what they believe about human existence.

With teens, you may want to use the above explanation combined with some of the definitions in chapter 16. For example, it might be helpful to explain that "occult" originally meant something concealed or hidden. Therefore, those who say that they can give others powers like to do so in a secretive and intrigue-building context, making it easier to manipulate and control people.

Discussing the subject of the occult will usually give rise to questions about Satan's power. For this, go back to chapter 6 to answer these questions. Also, the question usually surfaces about whether occultic claims of powers are real or not. My experience is that most aren't real demonstrations of power, only examples of lying deceptions. These lies might be inspired by people, or they might be inspired from demonic sources. Regardless of the source of inspiration, kids should be encouraged to turn away from lying claims of powers and to love the truth more than they fear their pain. Most kids like this idea, since they hate to be fooled and don't want to accept a lie as the truth.

Sometimes just explaining to kids how they can be fooled by power fakers isn't sufficient to convince them, particularly if they have already been deceived. This is why it can be helpful for some kids to see video footage in which this fakery is revealed. There is something about actually seeing on camera how it's done that can give a person an out—a way to say, "Okay, I was fooled." (Although such footage is rare, an appropriate segment to help youths is in part 4 of the *Kid Tricks* series, *Tricks or Powers?* which is suitable for preteens, and in *Psychic Confession,* which is suitable for teens. Both are listed in the appendix.)

TALKING WITH KIDS ABOUT CULTS

This is one of the harder concepts to describe to youngsters, but the following definition, which I've found helpful for use in elementary school classrooms, seems to do the trick for preteens: *A cult is a group of people who listen to and follow a leader who lies, saying that he or she can give them special knowledge or power.*

To that definition you can add: "Many times people in cults have all kinds of hurts inside them because of bad things in their family and personal life. The person who is the head of the cult tells them that this special knowledge or power will help take away their pain and make them feel better."

I like to give kids this advice after explaining how cult leaders take advantage of people in pain: "If someone tells you that they can give you special powers or knowledge, and they want you to join a group, run. Don't listen to them. Don't argue with them, because they may be really good at lying. What you should do is run from them and tell your parents or someone you trust about those people."

You don't need to go into much more detail than this with preteens, because few cults target them for involvement. The exceptions are teen satanic cults. Most preteens need only to be introduced to the concept of what a cult is.

When a preteen asks for an example, you can talk about some of the many cults that have been spawned during the last twenty years: Jim

Jones, Charles Manson, etc. One unusual example are cults that believe marijuana can give them powers. It's better not to bring up satanic cults as an example when talking with very young children or with kids who are prone to excessive fear.

For teens, try the following definition for a cult: *This is a separate group of people who say that they will follow a leader(s), but what they don't know is that the leader really wants to control them by making them believe in whatever the leader says is true.*

You can add: "The leader is not honest with his group. While he seems to care about his followers, offering them special knowledge or power, he really wants power to control them."

With teens you can be more sophisticated in filling in the basic definition. Explain that cults may or may not promise people supernatural powers. For example, a cult might form around a leader who promises a group that if they live in an isolated commune, they will be safe from nuclear warheads. Most important is that the leader(s) wants unquestioned allegiance to a system of beliefs in order to manipulate the group. What the leader often manipulates is the pain/problem that each member has, claiming that allegiance will give them power over their pain. Offering relief from pain is a powerful motivator that will often elicit the irrational behavior from followers frequently seen in cults.

TRUTH: THE MOST POTENT DETERRENT

Far more potent than describing to youths all the deceptive cultic and occultic activities that can harm them is the fact that most youths want to know the truth. The kinds of specific information offered in this text and the sources listed in the appendix can be invaluable, but a love for truth is the most significant deterrent, especially when information isn't readily available about new deceptive trends and activities. One can't, however, talk about deception without talking about what's real and what isn't, what is true and what is a lie. Such discussions then invoke the question: How do we foundationally know what is the truth?

Experts throughout the United States and Europe have repeatedly told me during the last two years that we must have an absolute moral and ethical base from which to discern the truth. They expressed that unrelenting relativism is destroying Western cultures. Because cults and the occult have to do with the seeking of powers—both human and supernatural—kids need a foundation from which to discern claims and luring promises of power. For youths, no other single factor will provide a better protective hedge against cults and the occult than to embrace the moral and spiritual truths in the Bible and to know why they are true.

Discerning Real and Spiritual Counterfeits

I am often asked how I can spot a con or know when a person is lying, since discernment is often subjective. Infallible scientific devices or processes don't exist that can unravel the unpredictability of human behavior. While I do study the best available techniques and methods, most police officers, investigative journalists, and others in similar occupations make many of their decisions based upon instinct. I sharpen this ability by studying how and why deception works. But more importantly, I intensely study what *is* real and *not* counterfeit so that the moment I get around a counterfeit, invariably I know something is wrong, even if I don't know exactly what it is.

In the same way, many Secret Service agents are able to spot counterfeit money because they have become so familiar with genuine money: the texture of the paper, the density of the ink, the fine details in the engraving. When presented with a counterfeit, they know something is wrong. This is how finely attuned our kids need to become in regard to moral and spiritual truths.

I'm not advocating religious fanaticism or a shallow, unthinking adherence to a religious system. In order to develop a healthy spiritual commitment carried out with integrity, kids should be encouraged to ask questions about their faith. For example:

◆ How do we know that the stories in the Bible are true?
◆ How do we know that Jesus really lived?
◆ How do we know that He really rose from the grave?
◆ How do we know that Jesus is the only way to Heaven?

Authors Josh McDowell and Don Stewart have written many excellent books that give clear and concise answers to these questions (see the appendix). Youths who don't have some head knowledge about why the Christian faith is true will not be able to defend their beliefs or distinguish Christianity from other religions or philosophies. When explaining to youths about cults and the occult, an even greater amount of time should be given to why the Christian faith is true, and therefore is our unshakable source of hope. This emphasis will give priority to dwelling on what is redemptive rather than destructive.

I'm going to suggest some basic concepts, based on scriptural passages, that will help reduce kids' vulnerability while strengthening their faith. They center around these three key themes: *We need to embrace God's truth*; *we must trust in Him regardless of whether or not He manifests supernatural powers in our life to rescue us from our pain*; and *we need not fear what Satan can or cannot do*.

The following lessons work best when the whole family discusses them together. Kids should be encouraged to look up the references for themselves, if possible from their own Bible. For preteens, I recommend *The International Children's Bible,* published by Word, Inc. This translation is easy to read without sacrificing content. Most of the verses that follow are quoted from this translation. For teens, I recommend *The New International Version* in the "Student Bible" format, which has plenty of study guides.

Seek God, Not Powers or Groups

"The thing you should want most is God's kingdom and doing what God wants. Then all these other things you need will be given to you." (Matthew 6:33, ICB)

In this passage from the Sermon on the Mount, Jesus is talking about our daily needs. We don't need to chase after powers or groups to take care of our everyday needs, problems, and pains. If God chooses to do something supernaturally in our lives, fine. And if He doesn't, that too is okay. Our responsibility is to live our lives as Jesus taught and seek Him. Without conditions.

Knowledge and a Sound Faith Help Us Resist Deception

Do not change yourselves to be like the people of this world. But be changed within by a new way of thinking. Then you will be able to decide what God wants for you. And you will be able to know what is good and pleasing to God and what is perfect. (Romans 12:2, ICB)

As you received Christ Jesus the Lord, so continue to live in him. Keep your roots deep in him and have your lives built on him. Be strong in the faith, just as you were taught. And always be thankful. Be sure that no one leads you away with false ideas and words that mean nothing. Those ideas come from men. They are the worthless ideas of this world. They are not from Christ. (Colossians 2:6-8, ICB)

For the Christian, studying and practicing what is eternally true—that is, it doesn't change with the times—provides a reference point and a stability that is hard for cults or deceivers to uproot. True Christian faith involves understanding and clear thinking, not simply "blind faith" that has no undergirding of factual substance.

Jesus taught us how to embrace the Christian faith when He said, "Believe me when I say that I am in the Father and the Father is in me; or at least believe on the evidence of the miracles themselves" (John 14:11). The apostle Paul went on to say,

If you confess with your mouth, "Jesus is Lord," and believe in your heart that God raised him from the dead, you will be saved. For it is with your heart that you believe and are justified, and it is with your mouth that you confess and are saved. . . . "Everyone who calls on the name of the Lord will be saved." (Romans 10:9-10,13)

In addition to making a commitment of faith, Christians are to study the Bible, pray on a daily basis, and demonstrate their faith through concrete actions reflecting that Christ is alive and working in them. This kind of active Christian faith will provide a deterrent to harmful activities, even when the family unit has disintegrated.

Satan—Defeated, Power Limited, Not to Be Feared

Jesus said, "I saw Satan falling like lightning from the sky. . . . I gave you more power than the Enemy has. Nothing will hurt you. You should be happy, but not because the spirits obey you. You should be happy because your names are written in heaven." (Luke 10:18-20, ICB)

God's Spirit, who is in you, is greater than the devil, who is in the world. (1 John 4:4, ICB).

In the first passage, Jesus is teaching the disciples after sending them out for the first time to heal the sick, cast out demons, and proclaim that the Kingdom of God is near. When they came back, they were excited because, "Lord, even the demons obeyed us when we used your name!" Jesus told them not to be excited about the unleashing of power, but rather about knowing that they would live with Him forever in Heaven.

When Jesus said that nothing would hurt them, He wasn't talking about the body, but about the spirit, which will have eternal life through Him. When He was executed on the cross, He absorbed like a sponge human sin/pain, forever separating those who believe in Him from all evil.

Those who are Christians do not need to fear Satan's power, human practitioners of the occult, or cults. We should be knowledgeable of their nature and, when possible, expose them so that others are warned and protected from harm. Although we should have a healthy respect for the destruction they can bring, we are not to fear them.

Do Not Seek Deception

> "Let no one be found among you who sacrifices his son or
> daughter in the fire, who practices divination or sorcery, inter-
> prets omens, engages in witchcraft, or casts spells, or who is
> a medium or spiritist or who consults the dead. Anyone who
> does these things is detestable to the Lord." (Deuteronomy
> 18:10-12)

This passage from the *New International Version* makes it clear that we are to have nothing to do with the occult. Today, some make alluring claims that the source of paranormal or supernatural powers is in each of us, so we don't have to seek outside means such as witchcraft or sorcery. Some say that this power naturally resides in the human brain; others claim that we have a supernatural force in us by which we can take control of life's forces, or even God.

Preventive measures against deception are especially urgent today, since the worship of gods and goddesses is taking hold even in our industrialized, high-tech country. About ten years ago, Brooks Alexander of the Spiritual Counterfeits Project, a think-tank in Berkeley that monitors deceptive trends related to spiritual issues, told me that paganism would again become common. I didn't believe him, nor did I think this was something I would have to warn my kids about. Yet news stories about this "new development in America's spiritual life" are common. Consider this excerpt from a Mother's Day editorial (12 May 1992) from the *New York Times*:

> Some of the people gathered on the Adirondack hillside called the woman a priestess, others a witch. She filled a bowl with water and pondered it for a few moments. Then she passed it to the person on her right, asking the group to concentrate on the water, putting into it prayers for their families.
>
> When the bowl had traveled around the circle, collecting prayers, she rose and carried it to a nearby birch tree. Pouring out the water at the base of the tree, she explained that the tree would carry it up through trunks and branches to leaves. Then the leaves would distribute the prayers on the wind.
>
> Such is the practice of goddess worship, a new development in America's spiritual life, and one worth acknowledging on Mother's Day: it is rooted in reverence for the ultimate mother, for woman as the giver of life. . . .
>
> It still warrants sympathy and respect. For it proceeds from values of nurturing, peace, and harmony with nature—values as profoundly humane as motherhood itself.

In the coming years, I believe that without any trickery, people will simply choose to believe lies. No one tricked this editor into believing in paganism; the editor just decided to accept it as legitimate and worthy of recommendation. If kids are to be foolproof to this kind of deception, they must know *why* what they believe is true and be able to demonstrate Jesus' teachings in their everyday actions.

Additional Verses for Teens

Be certain that you balance any study of occult issues by spending even more time studying Scriptures that teach us how to be more like Christ. Focusing primarily on the negative can create an obsession with the subject of evil. Here are some additional verses related to occultism that you may want to study with your teenager: Exodus 22:18; Leviticus 19:31; 20:6,27; 2 Kings 23:1-25; 2 Chronicles 33; Isaiah 2:6; 8:19-20; 30:8-11; 47:12-15; Jeremiah 27:9-10; Ezekiel 13; Micah 5:12-15; Zechariah 10:2; Ephesians 5:5-16; 2 Thessalonians 2:1-12; Revelation 2:18-29; 9:20-21; 22:12-17.

SUMMARY

Introducing kids to cults and the occult doesn't have to be frightening if care is taken to emphasize positive family living and the trustworthy teachings in the Bible. The key is balance. We can help to foolproof youths by exposing them to what can harm them, and simultaneously letting them know that they are loved and protected by their family and the God who created them.

CHAPTER EIGHTEEN

Public Schools:
Trends that Need Monitoring

◆

NON-TRADITIONAL TIMES—UNCONVENTIONAL METHODS

Let's say you're a public school teacher. You walk into a classroom of twenty-five to thirty students at the beginning of the year. You eventually discover that several of your students have been physically or sexually abused, about one-third to one-half of them have obvious tics in their personality and behavior because of recent divorces and separations, and the kids who don't come from problem situations are agitated because the rest of the class is agitated. What are you going to do?

Since your first responsibility is to teach, you're going to do everything you can to maintain order and keep your students' attention so that you can do your job. After two weeks, though, you feel you're getting nowhere. Teaching in the turbulent environment seems ineffective, and it's no longer a joy—just an aggravation.

Your efforts take place against this backdrop: A 1991 federal government study revealed that only one out of seven students nationally reaches a proficiency in mathematics appropriate for his or her grade level.[1] Many parents won't spend time reading with their kids, which is one of the key predictors of improved academic scores. Instead, they let their kids watch TV—the electronic baby-sitter—without restriction, even though studies show that TV viewing over two hours a day drives down grades.[2]

You, the teacher, have to help prepare kids for college, but these and other factors have driven SAT verbal tests to their lowest scores ever.[3] So where do you turn next?

NEW TRENDS IN CURRICULUM STRATEGY

In response to this kind of chaos, some anxious school systems are using curricula that teach meditation, visualization techniques, chanting of mantras (more on what this is later), trance induction states (also known as hypnosis), misguided self-esteem classes, and even classes on death in which students without parental notification are taken to morgues to see and touch corpses.

If these curricula were taught only in isolated cases, I wouldn't have included this chapter. But they're part of new trends surfacing in elementary through high school curricula in the United States and Canada.

In this chapter we'll look at what some of these trends are, why they're potentially harmful from a clinical perspective, what is driving school districts to use them (often unwittingly), and how to take a balanced approach toward discouraging their use.

Transcendental Meditation
The first call I received about one of these unusual additions to education was in 1986 from a parent in Indiana. In that situation, students were being taught Transcendental Meditation (TM).

TM is a pop Eastern religion that teaches meditation and instructs adherents in how to levitate. (Levitation aspirants were being billed for amounts of up to $20,000 in the 1970s.) But TM levitation has been exposed as a hustle: prospects are shown a photo of a follower seated cross-legged in the Lotus position, apparently hovering in the air. But actually TM practitioners, posed in the Lotus position, were hopping up and down on mats when the pictures were taken. The photo simply shows a person in mid-flight.

The daughter of a friend attended the TM university in Fairfield, Iowa, against my friend's wishes. A few days into her freshman semester, she asked her professors, "If you believe that TM can bring about world peace, why do you charge for it?" When she wasn't given an acceptable answer, she left. She realized that there was more interest in generating revenue than actually saving the world.

Now back to Indiana. At the time of this parent's call I thought the report I was receiving was an isolated case, so I gave the caller the name of an organization with reliable data on TM. I then filed the information she sent, not expecting to get any more calls.

I was wrong. Over the next few years, I received many calls from parents in different geographical regions, detailing exotic curricula being taught in public schools. I decided to find out more.

The Root Cause
As already identified, the driving force behind schools adopting unconventional and potentially harmful programs is the frenzied state in the classroom. This is consistent across the United States where the types of curriculum described have been utilized. Consistently, the agitation students exhibit can usually be traced back to unstable home lives. Many teachers I talk to say that they're being asked to become surrogate parents. They insist, however, that their role should be to reinforce good values, which should first be taught in the home.

What *should* be doesn't match the reality. Large numbers of families are in trouble, values *aren't* being reinforced in many homes, and many kids suffer from latent fears because they don't feel safe coming home to an empty house after school. Therefore, it's now common to find significant percentages of students exhibiting disruptive behavior in the classroom, with low self-esteem, pent-up anger, and unremitting anxieties. These problems have become so acute that teachers are asking for help.

About fifteen years ago, a handful of curricula started to appear that could be used by teachers and school counselors to address the problems of low self-esteem and unrelenting agitation. In October of 1990, a concerned parent from the north Dallas suburb of Carrollton called me about one such program being taught to their elementary school students, *Pumsy in Pursuit of Excellence*.[4]

THE PUMSY PROGRAM

Pumsy is a curriculum that was designed to help raise students' self-esteem and increase positive thinking and coping skills. It was written by Jill Anderson of Eugene, Oregon. Since these kinds of curricula are often updated and rewritten, I have chosen *Pumsy* as an example of what is currently in circulation and because of the number of techniques it employs, although it's not as potentially harmful as other programs. Because of some of these techniques, however, numerous education and health care professionals have warned that it is unacceptable.

The terms I used earlier—visualization, guided imagery, relaxation techniques, and trance induction states—are used in *Pumsy* and a number of other programs. Let's look at what these programs hope to accomplish.

Since many kids are troubled, insecure, and don't like themselves, the idea is to give them the skills they need in order to increase self-esteem and cope with their circumstances. The suggested solution is to change their thinking. This is done by getting kids to imagine that they can have power over their painful situations and become successful. The theory is that if kids can change how they think, they can raise their self-esteem.

On the surface, this sounds okay: help youths to imagine that they can be better, and maybe they will improve. The problem comes in when the use of imagination in these curricula is turned into a magical, escapist kind of thinking that in the long run will actually derail youths.

The bottom-line assertion of these kinds of curricula—and even seminars taught to American business professionals—is this: *If you believe in your head that it's true, then it will become a reality.* As I will detail later, health care professionals warn that these therapeutic techniques should not be used by non-health care professionals because there can be harmful reactions in at-risk students.

Jan Lewellyn and other parents from Carrollton took exception with this kind of thinking as it is communicated in *Pumsy.* Let's take a closer look.

Examining the Flaws in This Curriculum
Pumsy is usually taught by the teacher or a school counselor for up to twenty-four sessions, although many schools only extract certain parts of the program. The central character is Pumsy, a benevolent dragon, reminiscent of the lovable one in the Disney movie *Pete's Dragon.*

I suggested earlier (chapter 5, "Fantasy and Imagination: Where to Draw the Line") that using an imaginary character for story-telling purposes is acceptable provided that a child is not provoked to unnecessary fear, urged to cultivate an obsessive desire for power, or guided into identifying with a negative role model. The problem with *Pumsy* is that it invokes a desire for a magical kind of thinking that could actually be a harmful fantasy to some students, according to psychologist Dr. Margaret Singer.

Here are four of the eight stated themes in the *Pumsy* curriculum (capitalization is in the curriculum materials):

- ◆ "I CAN CHOOSE HOW I FEEL."
- ◆ "I CAN HANDLE IT."
- ◆ "I AM ME AND I AM ENOUGH."
- ◆ "I CAN DO WHAT I NEED TO DO."

Jan Lewellyn described how her son participated in visualization, guided imagery, and psychological techniques that are sometimes clinically used to induce a trance induction state, also referred to as hypnosis. The sessions were led by a counselor who lacked a clinical background—which is the case in most schools.

On pages 42 and 43 in the curriculum, the leader instructs the youngsters to learn how to "paint mind pictures" because the imagination is powerful. Kids are then told to relax, close their eyes, slow their breathing, imagine that they are now at peace in front of a pond, and then to repeat several times in a "clear, strong, voice . . . 'I can choose how I feel.' "

On page 88, kids are taught that they have "COMPLETE CONTROL" and "COMPLETE CHOICE" over what they think, what they feel, and how they handle situations. (Appropriately, in another lesson, youngsters are told that they can't always control what happens to them.) But is it acceptable to tell children that they can have "COMPLETE" control and choice over what they feel?

Trena Brand, a parent in Putnam County, an Oklahoma City suburb, didn't think so. In a presentation to her school board recommending that an alternative to *Pumsy* be found, she wrote:

> My question is: Can we always choose how we feel? Can we choose not to be afraid and helpless when we are tied to a chair [one of the suggested classroom exercises]? Can we choose not to feel sadness when a loved one has died? Can we, by an act of the will, decide to be happy when a child is hurting? This statement is not only untrue, but it is extremely simplistic and sets a child up for failure when they cannot seem to rid their minds of unacceptable thoughts.

Another objection by many parents and health care professionals is the use of chanting phrases while coming out of the relaxation/trance induction state, akin to chanting mantras in some Eastern religions (in which a phrase or the name of a deity is chanted repeatedly in order to "empty" oneself), with the goal that all negative thoughts will vanish. Although the names of deities aren't invoked in *Pumsy*, this chanting as kids return to a normal state is unacceptable to many parents, and for some an infringement on their religious beliefs.

The most bizarre practice, though, is found in the last lesson. Here, kids are encouraged, while in a mild trance induction state, to float out of their bodies. Among occultists, this is called "astral projection," in which a person supposedly wills his spirit to leave his physical body and then return. This practice remains unproven. (While in college, I tested this theory with people who believed they had this power. I placed a number on a table in a different room from where they were lying down. If they had the power, they should have been able to hover over and see the number. None was ever successful, and neither has anyone been successful under scientific conditions anywhere in the world.)

After careful consideration, the Putnam City school district discarded *Pumsy* in 1990. Many other school districts in numerous other states have also come to the same conclusion. In addition, states such as New Mexico and Colorado have passed laws requiring local school boards to adopt policies about the use of psychological or psychiatric methods or procedures in classrooms.

In Carrollton, on November 28, 1990, I participated in a meeting, at Jan's request, with her elementary school principal, a PTA representative, the school counselor, and some parents. The purpose was to consider the viability of *Pumsy*. Here is a summary of what I presented at the meeting:

When a health care professional teaches others to visualize or imagine another environment or how they feel, this can be a good thing. A chronically ill person can be taught how to improve the way she copes with pain. A musician who lacks self-confidence can be encouraged to imagine himself performing up to his capabilities and succeeding. When used in a very limited context, it is simply an added mental boost.

However, unrealistic or escapist thinking, such as, "Whatever the mind of man can conceive he can achieve," is unacceptable. Simply conceiving the idea that I can fly by flapping my arms doesn't give me the ability to do so. There are limitations.

However, let's say a young girl imagines herself becoming a

successful lawyer or nurse, even though her family has no money for an education. In this context, her belief that she can achieve her goal can spur her on to work and put herself through school.

As Dr. Margaret Singer and other noted experts have advised, a school district is asking for trouble when they use the kinds of techniques suggested in *Pumsy* because of the large number of at-risk students in classrooms today. To expect that a non-health care professional such as a teacher or counselor can employ these techniques is like asking parents to use them on their own kids after a night of reading the manual. No thinking parent would take such action. Would you want to teach your child how to alter her state of consciousness, inducing a mild trance induction state that could give her the tools to escape to some place in her head? Unfortunately, this is what is occurring in many classrooms.

The exposed psychic James Hydrick has detailed how when he was locked in a closet by abusive parents, he pretended that an imaginary Chinese mentor taught him how to have powers. He developed this imaginary power mechanism to deal with his stress. Many psychologists I interviewed believe that this escapist mechanism ultimately contributed to Hydrick's formation of a cult-like group.

While most kids aren't abused to this extreme, some are. For a non-professional to teach these kinds of visualization and relaxation techniques without specific knowledge of each child is irresponsible and could actually prove harmful to some children, according to many experts. In fact, a trance induction state (hypnosis) is actually the last form of therapy that should be used, according to conventional wisdom in the mental health care industry. It's simply too easy for a person to create his own personal reality and then accept it as real. Although *Pumsy* is clearly trying to use a mild trance induction state for relaxation purposes, it is being taught by teachers who are unqualified to use such techniques—not to mention the fact that it's often carried out without parental approval.

On a practical level, drilling into a youth such ideas as "I AM ME AND I AM ENOUGH" or "I CAN CHOOSE HOW I FEEL" is flat out untrue. Are kids who are abused self-sufficient when they really need help? Can they perfectly control how they feel? Are they in control of their feelings when they go through puberty?

In actual fact, it's healthy to teach kids that we *aren't* always self-sufficient and that we *won't* always feel good. There is strength in the ability to face pain honestly. What happens to the child who is in trouble and does need help? Can he magically overcome his problem by chanting, "I AM ME AND I AM ENOUGH"?

Carried to its extreme, Dr. Singer says that this kind of false encouragement could influence at-risk youths to become suicidal when they find out that they aren't self-sufficient, as they are overcome with helplessness because they were given the wrong solutions.

The unanimous opinion of those present at the Carrollton meeting in which I participated was that: (1) the visualization, guided imagery, and trance induction techniques shouldn't be used in school curricula; (2) repetitive chanting of phrases without thinking was unacceptable; and (3) acceptable curricula to reinforce self-esteem should be encouraged. However, principal Edie Taylor noted that self-esteem resources were only a Band-Aid approach and wouldn't cure the problem.

Her opinion is clearly mirrored by the statistical data showing that most self-esteem programs don't work. A 1990 California state task force, for example, commented on "how low the associations between self-esteem and its consequences are in research to date."[5] This is not to say that teachers shouldn't encourage kids to be optimistic, to take a positive approach to life, and to recognize their unique importance as individuals. This can only help; and for some kids, it may be just the encouragement they need during a difficult period. But self-esteem curricula isn't the cure-all for problems in the classroom.

As in many other school districts, programs such as *Pumsy* are falling from favor because of the use of therapeutic techniques being employed by those who are not health care professionals. Some parents have also protested the use of *Pumsy* and similar curricula because they espouse a nonChristian view of life. In some aspects this is true, particularly the statement, "I AM ME AND I AM ENOUGH," which clearly flies in the face of a Judeo-Christian world view. However, for practical purposes it's best to stick to the factual issues at hand rather than raising issues of religious belief. Although Jan Lewellyn perceived parts of the *Pumsy* curriculum to be offensive to her Christian beliefs, she focused simply on factual issues in her protest presentation, and the program was removed in just one calm and uneventful meeting.

LONG-TERM CONSEQUENCES
OF THESE CURRICULA TRENDS

There is another reason that these self-realization curricula are harmful. Teaching youngsters these kinds of ideas increases their susceptibility when they're older to far more sophisticated programs and schemes.

Currently, American business professionals are being deluged with expensive and ineffective programs that teach the same kinds of ideas as in *Pumsy*, but on an adult scale. A front-page story in the *New York Times* entitled "Spiritual Concepts Drawing a Different Breed of Adherent" (29 September 1986) noted:

> Representatives of some of the nation's largest corporations, including I.B.M., A.T.& T., and General Motors, met in New Mexico in July to discuss how metaphysics, the occult and Hindu mysticism might help executives compete in the world marketplace.

I have interviewed scores of business leaders who have bought into much of this hokum. They often say, "But I heard that [such-and-such corporation] showed some short-term growth after they implemented their X, Y, Z Mind Dynamics program."

What most aren't familiar with is the phenomenon known as the Hawthorne Effect, so called because of experiments in industrial psychology conducted in 1927–1929 at Western Electric's Hawthorne plant in Chicago.

Western Electric wanted to find out what would increase productivity at its plant. Researchers discovered that when the lighting level in the plant was increased, productivity went up. But it was also observed that productivity went up when the lighting level was turned down so low that it almost resembled twilight. What did this mean? Why did workers outproduce their counterparts who didn't take part in the experiment? The lesson here, which is taught in most business schools, is that if you show your employees *any* attention, even if it doesn't really have any value, productivity will go up for the short-term.

In this context, isolated school districts or teachers will say that some of the more exotic curricula actually work. What works is not the program per se, but rather a teacher who is taking time with students—giving them attention that they should be getting at home but aren't. So in the short term, it appears that the problem of self-esteem is being corrected.

In the long term, however, kids are actually worse off, just like the business professionals, because they have bought into a bogus solution instead of dealing with the root cause. In business, if you don't get down to root issues of product and service quality, cost-efficient production, effective marketing, and on-time delivery dates, you will fail. In school, when youths are troubled, grades are falling, and there is a steady undercurrent of unrest, only addressing the root of those problems will solve them. For troubled youths, these roots include stability in the home, or some kind of outside support system. To counter falling grades, root issues such as increased studying time and better study skills must be addressed. And so on.

OTHER TRENDS TO WATCH

In addition to the trend of self-esteem curriculums, there have also been other disturbing developments in public school agendas in recent years. Their emergence in the educational mainstream requires careful monitoring by streetwise parents.

Hags, Monsters, and Language Skills

In the scramble to raise grades and test scores, some bizarre materials for teaching reading and language skills have been tossed into the melee.

One such series is called *Impressions,* published by Holt, Rinehart and Winston of Canada and distributed by its parent company, Harcourt Brace Jovanovich of Orlando, Florida. These materials use horror and occult stories featuring mutilation and monsters to teach language arts to *grade school kids*.

In one story, "The Foundling," written for sixth-graders, three ugly "hags" hover over an infant as they contemplate what to do with the child they have just found. One hag says, "A sweet morsel. A tender lamb. I know what I should do." Another hag chastises the first, saying, "You've already had your breakfast."

Here's another example for fifth-graders: "'HE'S BEHIND YER!' chorused the children, but the warning came too late. The monster leaped forward and fastening its teeth into his neck, tore off the head. The body fell to the floor. 'More,' cried the children, 'MORE MORE MORE.'" One might be able to imagine this as part of a college curriculum, but this is for *fifth-graders*. As expected, many reports have surfaced about children's subsequent nighttime fears.

In another example, the teacher's manual instructs the teacher to have kids sit in a circle (similar to a witch's coven) and "write and chant a magic spell," to cause objects in the room to levitate. Even if responsible parents had read the child's textbook to know what their child was learning, they wouldn't know what was going on in the classroom because these instructions were in the teacher's manual.

Teachers I have asked about these kinds of outrageous curricula say that they usually "edit" the manual and what they teach, leaving out the objectionable material. At our kids' elementary school, this is the case when most teachers come across this kind of material. This isn't censorship, just good common sense and intelligent selection.

Why in the world would a publisher use graphic and irresponsibly violent themes to teach youths when teen violence has been steadily rising? In this case, the publisher justifies it because they say that these are the kinds of stories kids want to read. The *Friday the 13th* types of TV shows testify to this—*but why cater to it?* The full spectrum of parents and experts, from those with religious beliefs to those without, agree that violent themes and the promotion of magical escapist answers are unacceptable today in our high-risk culture.

Since it's becoming increasingly harder to teach youths, it's predictable that whatever will sustain attention will be given a chance somewhere. The proliferation of graphic occult themes is certain to continue because it's alluring and appealing to hurting youths. But educational materials that use these kinds of occultic escapism and depictions of violence, mirroring unrestrained rage and a desire for a violent release from problems, promote the acceptability of violence and unrealistic escapism.

To counter these disturbing trends, parents must keep abreast of what is being taught in their children's textbooks. Ask questions to find out if the teacher's manual is consistent with what's in the textbook. If necessary, pursue strategies for replacing unacceptable materials with other effective curricula.

Death Education

One of the more bizarre developments in our insecure and violence-driven culture is death classes—designed to assuage a youth's fear of death. In many classes, death is taught as a natural occurrence that shouldn't be feared, because it will eventually happen to all of us.

Death education is now being taught in one out of every ten schools, kindergarten through high school. On the tamest end, grade school children are taken to a funeral home and are encouraged to touch and feel the interior and exterior of coffins. In some high schools, though, students are taken to morgues and mortuaries to examine corpses. The ABC news show *20/20* aired a piece in 1990 on one such class taught at Paint Branch High School, outside Washington, D.C.

Students, who could take this class without parental approval, were taken to a funeral home and shown a cadaver, which had skin and other parts removed to benefit others medically. Later, led by a death education instructor who was not a health care professional, students were encouraged to enter a trance-like state and imagine a person they had lost—a parent, a relative, a friend. Many were overcome by grief and the non-professional use of a therapeutic technique.

These classes are defended, even though some students are needlessly traumatized and no studies have been done to determine the effect of death education on youths. The justification for the classes is that teens are deluged with death through auto accidents, the average 32,000 deaths they will view on television while growing up, and the rising incidence of teen suicide. The rationale by advocates is: maybe if we show youths what death really is, then they will cherish life.

This might be a good tactic with a hardened juvenile or in some isolated situations when taught by those professionally qualified—and with a parent's permission. However, exposing youths to cadavers without a context for absorbing the starkness of the experience is irresponsible. It might actually backfire and desensitize youths to death, cause nightmarish images to linger, or even make death appear more inviting for at-risk students who have contemplated suicide.

The *20/20* report explored one such case in which a young woman considered taking her life because she said that her death education class made death look appealing. She said that her teacher told her that when she died she would get to have all of God's knowledge. Death was not to be feared, but something to be invited. Did death education cause her to contemplate suicide? Probably not. Painful problems drive kids to end their lives—but making death look seductively appealing is certainly no deterrent.

Dr. William Coulson, an expert in psychotherapy techniques, has said of death education:

> These interventions aren't powerful enough, they're not therapeutic enough to keep the troubled kids out of trouble, but they are powerful enough drive the untroubled kids into becoming troubled.
>
> What makes us think that American education is going to do a good job teaching death education? We ought to be

trembling about the fact that schools which have failed to teach academics are now presuming to teach matters of life and death.[6]

At the end of the *20/20* broadcast, an elderly death education instructor, with organ music in the background and a partially veiled corpse in front of him, ghoulishly invited, "If you'd like to feel the difference between life and death, you can touch Stanley. Stanley is very cold because there is no blood. You have lots of blood. You feel warm and full of life." After students came forward and touched "Stanley," the instructor added, "Wonderful. It's good to see you alive. And more, Stanley would wish you an awful lot of life. Live it well."

Check with your local school board to find out if death education is taught in your school district. Even outside the context of religious beliefs, for most students there appears to be little redeeming value, and much potential harm, in using the school system to teach graphic lessons about death.

For Christians, teaching about death apart from faith in God and our redemption from the grave is a corruption of the truth. The issue of why we die and what happens after we die is a matter of faith. There is no place for this kind of death education in public schools.

An exception would be when there is a suicide or murder in a school, and counseling is necessary for kids who have been traumatized by it. Then it's acceptable for a school to provide qualified mental health care professionals to deal with the trauma, but not to sermonize about death. Addressing the differences between life and death and what happens after death should be left to a person's family and church.

SUMMARY

Fear, agitation, isolation, and anger are some of the dominant conditions teachers are trying to confront—let alone working to increase test scores. It's a tough go for teachers today. If you think a particular curriculum is unhealthy for students, be polite and tactful when first visiting teachers and educators. Like the principal at the Carrollton elementary school, many educators aren't even aware that certain materials can be harmful. Be calm. Present the facts. Find alternatives. Refrain from threatening those who can help you.

When we attended our sons' open house, their teachers warmly talked to us about their progress, gave them each a hug, and even asked about our older daughter whom they taught several years earlier.

As a father, I have only genuine appreciation for teachers. Our kids' education has been a plus in their lives.

Education is still a force for good in a young person's life. Most teachers and school districts *do* care and *are* trying everything in their power to help kids learn. It's because people care that new approaches are being taken, even though some of them are misguided. Sure, there may be an occasional curriculum developer with hidden agendas, but most are simply trying to find approaches that will work.

This is why it is the parents' responsibility to lay the groundwork for education by providing a stable home environment. This one factor alone would have the greatest positive influence in shaping the American classroom.

A parent's second responsibility is to pay attention to what children are being taught. Take time to ask questions, read curriculum text, and request to see the teacher's manual for material that appears to be questionable. Take time to read with your child, which has been proven to be a dominant factor in increasing verbal and reading skills.

Finally, be certain that your child develops the critical thinking skills taught in the first section of this book. Particularly helpful here are the principles about where to draw the line in fantasy and imagination, and how to distinguish illusion from reality.

SECTION IV
KNOW THE GOOD

Knowing the streets is part of the bigger picture of knowing the good. We don't have to live in fear of unexpected threats and harmful trends. You can teach your kids the skills they need to pick their way across a hazardous landscape with clearheaded thinking and moral resolve.

This final section provides advice for how to keep moving toward the good: a framework for identifying and resolving problems; the role communities can play in thwarting harmful trends; and the need for the spiritual factor in our lives.

CHAPTER NINETEEN

A Framework for Getting Help

◆

For several days our daughter, who was eight at the time, complained of stomach pains. The pains usually came at night. We questioned her carefully about what ailed her. My wife, who is a retired nurse, and I discussed possible causes. Was it food? Did she have a virus? Was it nerves? Was she afraid of something?

A trip to our pediatrician seemed to rule out a medical explanation. She wasn't running a fever and didn't show any signs of an organic ailment. A few days later we were able to rule out dietary problems, such as an allergic reaction to a particular food or food group. We were concerned.

I then called a family friend, who is a psychiatrist, and asked him what he thought. Immediately, he queried, "Have you spent much time with your daughter during the last few weeks?"

"No," I answered. "I've had to do quite a bit of traveling."

"Well, it's common for young girls to experience the kinds of symptoms you described when the father doesn't show them enough attention," my friend explained. "They don't do it deliberately; it just has to do with their sense of security."

I took his advice to spend more time with our daughter, and within a week her stomach pains went away and never returned.

Don't we wish that all problems facing our kids could be resolved this simply? But the types of issues discussed in this book won't go away so easily. However, the underlying process we used to help our daughter can be applied to most youth problems.

The purpose of this chapter is to supply practical advice for helping youths in trouble, by providing parents with a framework for how to tackle difficult situations. Parents are often overwhelmed when confronted by something that is affecting their child. They may lack an understanding of the problem or of the nature of their child's experience with it. That's why a generic framework for approaching a problem can be helpful. It offers a basic response, with details to be filled in according to individual situations, that can be tailored to the many kinds of trends discussed in this book.

The framework that follows has been successfully used in real-life circumstances and is the result of interviews and dialogue with scores of mental health care experts, juvenile officers, teachers, and other authorities who work with youth.

A BASIC FRAMEWORK

Here are the steps we used to help our daughter find relief for her puzzling stomach ailment. They provide the backbone of a strategy for helping youths in trouble.

Establish effective communication. We were in touch with our daughter and could communicate.

Investigate the facts. We investigated the facts of what she told us. We asked questions and listened.

Use a system of checks and balances. My wife and I discussed with each other the possible reasons for the cause of her pain. This dialogue provided checks and balances on our individual personal opinions, which could have been inaccurate.

Seek help. When no relief was in sight, we sought professional help without alarming our daughter. When one form of professional advice didn't seem to apply, we sought other help.

Develop a preliminary strategy for resolving the problem. Based on our friend's advice, I made plans to change my schedule and spend more time with my daughter.

Implement and refine the strategy, and accept personal accountability. For the next several weeks I reduced my workload and took additional time for my daughter. I did my part. As her stomach pains went away, my friend advised me that spending as much concentrated time wasn't necessary, but also that I should not neglect to give her the time she needed.

Employ proper follow-up. We continued to watch our daughter to be certain she was okay and that her condition and the "cure" had not been misdiagnosed or improperly applied. To this day, I keep a careful watch on all three of our kids as well as my wife, and I'm very sensitive about not letting my work get in the way of family priorities for prolonged periods of time.

Whether you're trying to help your own child with a problem or another youth, these steps can help you frame an appropriate strategy. Ideally, parents should develop the strategy according to these steps, but it's unrealistic to think that this can be done in all situations. Sometimes, for example, the reason for a youth's dilemma is that he or she doesn't have open and clear communication with a parent—in which case the first step might initially have to be postponed.

In the most difficult situations, parents are sometimes not equipped to formulate a resolution because of emotional involvement, lack of knowledge about the specific issue, or other impediments. In such situations, Dr. Margaret Singer recommends that parents select someone who can function as a *strategist.*

SELECTING A STRATEGIST

Dr. Singer, who has many years of experience counseling cult victims, says that a common mistake made by parents of youths involved in cultic activity is to rush a youth into a treatment center or to a therapist without having any particular strategy in mind. She says that at first glance, counseling may seem to be the right course of action. Many presuppose that because mental health professionals treat a person's mind and emotions, such people are ideally the first resource to contact when helping someone exiting from a cult. Thus, this first course of action appears to be a good match.

Instead, what's often most needed at the very beginning, maintains Dr. Singer, is a good *strategist*—someone a parent can consult, who will help identify the "who, what, why, where, and when" questions, followed by some ideas of how to approach the troubled youth. Then a tentative course of action can be mapped out. This course of action may or may not include therapy for the youth, the parents, or both, depending on the situation.

The option of using a strategist can be applied to any of the trends discussed in this book. The strategist role may also be filled by a couple of people working together whose combined strengths can get the job done.

Key Characteristics of a Good Strategist

Regardless of the type of problem a youth is facing, the ideal characteristics that a strategist should possess are:

◆ Good common sense and the ability to develop a short-term plan of action.
◆ Calm under pressure—not given to hysteria.
◆ Some understanding of the particular issue(s) affecting the youth.
◆ Ability to relate to youths and to establish trust between kids and their parents.

These qualifications provide the best criteria for selecting a good strategist, rather than any hard and fast rules about professional training or vocation.

Possibilities for a strategist are: a friend, relative, teacher, juvenile officer, experienced psychologist, minister, or a person who works with an organization that addresses the specific issue. The strategist must be able to survey the situation calmly, which is why emotionally involved parents are sometimes not suited for the task. The strategist, or someone the strategist selects, must be able to forge a dialogue with both youth and parent(s), and then suggest a likely course of action.

When a youth is affected by a trend that is spreading in a school, neighborhood, or community, getting help may involve consultation or coordination with institutions or authorities that work with youths. Therefore, it's important that strategists maintain a balanced perspective and communicate a sense of urgency without hysteria—otherwise, they could be dismissed as extremists. This might prevent valuable information and assistance from being made available to help the youth involved.

For example, when contacting a police officer, you wouldn't want to start by saying, "We're terrified! There are scores of drug dealers in our child's school. You have to *do* something!" A more appropriate approach would be, "Officer, as you probably already know, we have a problem in our school with an increase in drug dealers. My child has been affected. Would you mind if we met to talk about the situation?"

People will often be more cooperative if they don't think they're going to become embroiled in hysteria. Additionally, a reasonable and calm manner can help prevent hysteria when there's a chronic problem. If a strategist is qualified to give good advice but isn't suitable for interacting with community organizations, another person should be selected for making that contact.

In many cases, a parent can function as the strategist. In one situation I observed, a mother was able to do this for her daughter. The daughter, angry about her parents' divorce, had become involved with a destructive group of students. She trusted her mother, however, and her key need was to reaffirm a bond of love between herself and at least one of her parents. Her mother recognized this need, and since the trauma the girl experienced was minimal, the mother was suited for the task. Therapy was never needed.

Deciding When to Seek a Strategist's Help

How do you know whether you should seek help from an outside strategist? Ask yourself these important questions, and answer them as honestly as you can:

1. Can I communicate with my child?
2. Is my emotional involvement free from clouding my ability to make good decisions?
3. Can I evaluate the specifics of who or what is affecting my child and develop an effective plan of action?

If you're in doubt about any of the above, it may be advisable to appoint a strategist. For married couples in which only one parent can answer yes to these three questions, one must consider if the family dynamics will allow that parent to act in the strategic role. If that option is questionable, an outside strategist should be considered.

WHEN PARENTAL DENIAL GETS IN THE WAY

Sometimes it's too painful for parents to admit that they might have contributed to their child's dilemma or that they weren't paying attention and failed to notice the change in their child's behavior. The pain of seeing their youngster victimized, coupled with the sense that they somehow failed their child, can be overwhelming. A strategist can help overcome these common yet traumatic obstacles by becoming the interface between parent(s) and youth.

One parent, who overcame denial, later commented, "When the psychologist said that I should have noticed that something was wrong, I was angry. I refused to accept what he told me. Now, a year later, I can see that in the beginning I was an obstacle to my son's recovery. And as much as I hated to admit it, he didn't start to get better until I faced the problem honestly." Although this parent's spouse didn't join in the process, the impact he made by becoming honestly involved changed the immediate course of his son's life. The strategist in this case was a psychologist, who acted as a buffer between the parent's self-denial and his son's anger.

Detective Gladys Alarcon, of the Hillsborough County Sheriff's Department in Florida, makes this observation of parental denial:

> Parents will say that they think their child is just going through a phase and will grow out of it. What I have found is that after they [can no longer deny that there is a problem], then they will get desperate and ask, "Okay, what do I do?"

She adds that in most cases before anything can be done to effect a long-term solution "the parents have to decide that they have a problem."[1]

HOW TO DEVELOP A PRELIMINARY STRATEGY

Once the strategist is established, whether that person is a parent or someone outside the family, developing a preliminary strategy is critical to getting the resolution process underway.

Establish Effective Communication
Developing an effective strategy requires identifying accurate facts about what is harming or threatening a youth. One of the best sources for this information is the youth affected. That's why it's critical to establish effective communication as soon as possible.

If a parent is unable to communicate, it's crucial to involve someone who can. This is no time for parental denial to get in the way. A youth in trouble needs help, and whoever can best relate to that youth initially will be of the greatest aid.

In many situations, it's the parent who initially attempts to be the strategist. Only after the failure of repeated attempts does the parent usually turn to someone else for help. This is a normal response for a parent who wants to protect the child from harm. However, because of possible problems and friction at home, often the parent isn't suitable to be the strategist.

This scenario doesn't cancel the benefits of the parent's attempts, however initially unsuccessful they may be. When a parent makes a genuine and balanced attempt to help, it sends a message to the youth that at least in that situation the parent cares. Kids may not immediately respond, but later they'll recall, "Yeah, Dad did try. He was concerned."

Regardless of whether the parent or a strategist outside the home initiates the first dialogue, it's important to express personal concern to the youth first, before trying to get to the facts. Here are some examples of helpful approaches:

"I'm really afraid for you. I know that I may not have shown it, but I do care. Please help me so that I can help you."

"You look like you're really in pain. Please let me help, or at least let us find someone who can help you."

"Look, I can't let you go sneaking out anymore. It's not only wrong, but I'm afraid you are going to get hurt."

These expressions of genuine concern are much more likely to open up dialogue than a statement such as, "You're just trying to hurt me by hurting yourself." That approach will accomplish little. It sounds like—and sometimes is—an attempt to make the youth feel guilty.

Investigate the Facts
Once a youth is willing to talk, it's possible to unearth facts that can be very helpful in guiding the direction of the strategy for resolution.

If a youth has been severely traumatized, it's not uncommon for his or her account of a specific situation to be disjointed. For some, this is a function of age or personality; for others, it's a function of fear.

If an opening dialogue is possible, the preliminary strategy takes shape through gathering facts, assessing the harm experienced, and evaluating potential threats to the youth. Sources for this information include the affected youth, friends, other parents, teachers, or other people involved in the surrounding circumstances.

Which questions need to be answered will of course depend on the situation. This is why it's often helpful in the beginning to find an expert who can provide parents with the questions that need to be answered.

Each situation has its own set of unique issues that need addressing. Here are some preparatory questions that will help a strategist form a preliminary plan of action prior to talking to a youth:

- ◆ Are one or more of the parents willing to help? If not, who is close to the youth who can be a support?
- ◆ What are the known facts?
- ◆ Is the youth currently approachable? Who should talk to him or her? Where is the best location to talk to the youth?
- ◆ Is there a current threat to the youth so that law enforcement must be contacted or precautions taken?
- ◆ Is the situation so complex that a professional with experience should establish the opening dialogue with the youth? (This might be necessary, for example, in the case of rape or extreme forms of terror.)
- ◆ Is addiction, rape, or physical or sexual abuse a factor, thus requiring the involvement of a mental health care expert?
- ◆ Have any crimes been committed, requiring contact with law enforcement or the retention of an attorney?
- ◆ For suspected occult, cult, or gang involvement: Considering the reasons why youths exit from a cult (in chapter 15, see the section "Why Youths Disengage from Gang Activity," and in chapter 16, the section "Understanding Kids' Involvement in Cults and the Occult"), which are the most likely reasons that the youth in question will cease his or her involvement? What is the best tack to take to encourage the youth to disengage? Was the youth tricked into the group, or did he or she become involved voluntarily? Who are the available resource persons in the community experienced in dealing with this activity or specific group?

After the known facts have been evaluated, a preliminary strategy should be developed that will (1) reduce the danger to a youth if there is a threat factor, and (2) find a way to disengage the youth from the activity.

To fulfill both of these objectives requires gathering reliable information and discovering what will motivate the youth to cease his or her involvement, if the youth hasn't already done so. The parent or strategist needs to match one or more of the reasons why youths in general withdraw from involvement in this activity with the particular youth in question. If the strategist is not qualified to do this, then a professional should be sought to assist.

One reason why it's important for a parent or strategist to be able to think quickly and improvise is because of the unpredictable nature of adolescent behavior under great stress. It will be necessary to shape, flex, and modify the preliminary strategy as contact is made with the youth and more facts and information are made available.

Use Checks and Balances and Seek Help

Even when a professional isn't directly required, it's still helpful to have someone else to bounce ideas off as the strategy takes shape. A form of checks and balances such as this can help tailor the strategy appropriately. A spouse, a wise friend, a relative, or a juvenile officer are all possibilities here. Sometimes, though, the circumstances warrant direct intervention by mental health care professionals.

Twenty years ago, counseling was rare and carried a stigma with it. Today, so many kids are in counseling that it doesn't have the implications it once did. Most alienated youths already know a friend who is in counseling, which can help allay their reticence.

No absolute methods exist for finding the right qualified professional counselor or therapist for a youth or family. You can start by asking for referrals from a family doctor, a school counselor, or someone who has had a good experience. Don't be surprised if a law enforcement officer refuses to make a recommendation, since most are restricted from recommending medical or legal assistance.

Care must be taken when selecting a mental health care professional, because some states do not require licensing or accreditation to go into business. Check with your state licensing boards if you're uncertain of a particular professional's track record. Also, be careful not to make a selection based solely on the reputation of a clinic, hospital, or treatment center, or on the fact that you have a friend who runs a clinic or hospital. Inquire into who *specifically* will be interacting with your child. I've watched even wealthy families end up with a bad match—or even worse, a therapist with severe emotional problems.

When funds aren't available for counseling, you may be able to obtain treatment or financial assistance from local, county, state, or federal agencies. Since these agencies experience frequent fluctuations in their funding, which influences the services they can render, you will need to inquire about each specifically.

Finally, these professionals, along with teachers and school counselors, are usually the first ones to spot negative youth trends because of the many kids they see one on one. Often they can provide insight into what kids are doing and be a valuable source of information. Sometimes kids will speak more openly with a therapist than with a police officer, especially if there is drug or criminal activity. This is because youths perceive that the therapist is there to help heal the internal problems, while they perceive that the officer is there to charge suspected offenders and uphold the law. While many police departments focus on crime prevention, this is not what some youths, who have been truant or who resent authority, believe is an officer's intent.

HOW TO IMPLEMENT AND REFINE
A LONG-TERM STRATEGY

A long-term strategy for helping youths in trouble should seek to achieve the following universal goals:

1. Removal of the threat of harm to the youth.
2. Identification of the underlying causes for the youth's vulnerability, and addressing those root problems.
3. Strengthening of healthy family relationships.
4. Provide positive alternatives—activities, friends, church, etc.
5. Effective discipline when necessary.
6. Direction that will help a youth in the long-term future.

Remember Fred Crowell's advice about teaching youths? (See chapter 8.) Most parents want to jump over teaching by example and go straight to disciplining a child. The same kind of advice can be applied to helping youths in trouble. Discipline may be appropriate, but parental examples and clear communication of expectations are powerful forces over the long haul.

It's important to recognize that disengaging youths from harmful activity doesn't mean that their susceptibility to being deceived or harmed again has been erased. Only when kids understand *why* they were deceived can they take measures to protect themselves and reduce their vulnerability.

A youth who stops listening to destructive music may continue to live with a hole in his life that is susceptible to being filled with some other negative substitute. Kids should know *why* they were deceived, *what* in their life set them up for being deceived, and finally *what good things* they can claim as their own that will not only reduce their vulnerability, but actually turn the liability into an asset—a personal strength.

Once a plan of action has been determined, then each person must do his or her part. This might sound obvious—but it needs emphasizing, because some parents remove the source of the threat to their child but never spend time to correct the family difficulty that was the real source of the problem.

A Note of Caution to Parents

Of course, we can't trace all bad choices that kids make to family dysfunction. Some youths are simply overtly rebellious; others are testing the waters. However, when a child has been invaded by something harmful, a natural feeling of anger and even jealousy may permeate a parent's behavior; one's child has been invaded and so, too, has the family fabric. Faced with this pain, some parents will make every effort to assist their child and restore the family fabric. This effort to save their child, and sometimes also the family, by giving the situation first priority, is healthy and good.

Other parents unconsciously take on the project to "rescue" their child in order to occupy their thoughts and minimize and deflect their own pain. By focusing on their child's condition and pain, parents can delay having to deal with their own pain or with their own possible contribution to the troubled situation.

In the short term, this rescue orientation can have a positive benefit. As the child receives their support, parents have time to gradually accept the reality of the situation without triggering emotional overload. For some parents, this avoids complete denial and walking away from the situation and their responsibility. For parents who have harmed a child, their efforts can represent to the child and to themselves a small bridging act of atonement.

Some parents, however, have more negative responses, particularly when family difficulties are the root source of the problem. For these parents, the realization that one or both of them is responsible for the family breakdown—knowingly or unknowingly—is unbearable. In this case, common responses include: denial that the child is in trouble; denial of responsibility for the child's lack of emotional well-being; accepting the reality of the situation while being unwilling to help the child because the pain is overwhelming. At the extreme end are those parents who just don't care, and spurn the opportunity to be a part of the solution.

Other parents fall in the middle and adopt what might be called a "crusader complex." For them, the project to save their child becomes obsessive, often resulting in an all-out effort to save other youths as well. Although there is the outward, positive benefit of attempting to help their child and others, beneath the surface problems are left unaddressed. Parents on an obsessive crusade tend to hide root problems behind the front of saving their child and other youths. These neglected problems fester, and neither the child nor the family ever experiences complete healing.

Each parent has a different capacity for absorbing and healing from pain. Some parents can help their child while simultaneously addressing the root problem; others can't. Whatever the parents' capacity, it is critical that in one way or another a strategy is implemented for addressing root problems and seeking counseling, in whatever time frame is possible. Only by successfully addressing root causes can a long-term cure result.

SUMMARY

There are many ways to guide kids away from harmful trends. Some parents will discover that their authority, teaching, and love are enough to help their kids disengage from something harmful. Other parents will need to get outside help as suggested by the full range of options in this book.

I hope you will never have to use the framework in this chapter because a child of yours is in trouble. But if you do, the hallmark of caring parents is acceptance of the truth, no matter how painful, then doing all within your power that is necessary to help a troubled youth.

CHAPTER TWENTY

Community Action Can Make a Difference

◆————

Most people today are acutely aware that federal, state, and local governments can't solve all the problems facing youths. Individual responsibility must be the corrective for most of these dilemmas, starting with the family and followed by those who will step forward to help young people when there isn't a stable family.

However, when there *are* people who will give their time unselfishly, then government—especially local government—can do much to help create a better environment for youths.

Local government can usually be more responsive than state or federal organizations to the needs of the individual community, since it doesn't have to follow dictates from even well-meaning but far-removed bureaucrats who have no firsthand knowledge of specific community needs. For this reason, one of the biggest needs voiced by local government officials is not for huge budgets, but rather for a collective sensitivity in both the private and public sector to make the needs of youths a priority in their community.

Local government can also function as a meeting ground where groups with various, and sometimes opposing, interests can set aside their turf battles for a higher cause.

This might sound like campaign rhetoric, but I've seen one community government that has put this concept into practice: the city of Farmers Branch, a suburb of Dallas with a population of about twenty-four thousand, of which six thousand are youths. Farmers Branch is a diverse community, comprising middle- and upper-middle-class neighborhoods as well as an influx of lower-income families.

Most common problems afflicting youths today can be found in Farmers Branch, and rising gang activity is one of them. What makes this community different from most is that there is a significantly different attitude toward problem solving in city government.

What follows is how this city overcame its fears and successfully addressed its growing but not yet pervasive gang problem. More important than the specific problem and the recommendations enacted by Farmers Branch are the thought process and attitude adopted when tackling its youth issues. While specific solutions for each community will vary, the attitude toward solving youth issues can be transferred to other organizations, from local governments and private agencies to businesses and churches.

AN HONEST APPRAISAL

Richard Escalonte became city manager of Farmers Branch in 1987. A tall, robust, and feisty Chicago native of Hispanic descent, Escalonte comes from a family of steelworkers. He cares about kids and has two teenagers of his own.

We met at a local civic club luncheon, where I was speaking on area youth involvement in gangs and destructive occult activities. Afterward, Richard excitedly described that the solutions to the problems I had outlined were now being implemented as the result of a task force he had assembled. I thought to myself, *With all the negative stuff I have to wade through, if this is true then this good news should be trumpeted.*

When I asked what made the difference, Escalonte said the reasons were complex, but the underlying cause was that *people were willing to look honestly at the problems and then do what was necessary to bring relief.* He was quick to point out that Farmers Branch is not a Utopia, but that there is a perceivable difference when compared to surrounding communities with a similar makeup.

He pointed out that a neighboring community, Carrollton, indicated in a state-wide law enforcement survey that it didn't have a gang problem. From cops I had talked to and from the scores of calls I had received during the last few years about gang activity in the North Dallas suburbs, it was apparent that Carrollton had a *bigger* gang problem than Farmers Branch. Yet Farmers Branch had indicated in that same survey that it *did* have a problem, while Carrollton had not acknowledged what was happening.

My experience is that many local governments fear that if they acknowledge such problems they'll drive away new businesses, which can lead to lower property values, which in turn reduces the community's tax base. Then taxes have to be raised to maintain the same level of services. Although it's not excusable, it's understandable why local governments are reluctant to admit to problems that can threaten the overall quality of community life.

What follows is the thought process that allowed Farmers Branch to overcome its fears and address its growing gang problem.

EARLY IDENTIFICATION OF PROBLEMS

In 1988, Farmers Branch followed the national trends of youth problems: increased crime and acts of violence, drug abuse, teen pregnancy, and so on. Because it wasn't an inner-city environment, these problems were addressed primarily by private agencies and churches. Escalonte and others noted, however, that a number of specific problems were becoming common in urban areas. Some of these were:

- ◆ The beginning of gang activity centered among troubled youths from middle-class and upper-income families, as well as from areas in which apartment dwellings were deteriorating.
- ◆ Lack of summer programs for all youths.
- ◆ Increased number of "latchkey" kids.
- ◆ Insufficient after-school childcare for working single parents.

Additionally, a denial factor was at work by affected institutions. Many school officials, for example, resisted acknowledging their inability to address the growing gang problem. To do so would be an admission of defeat by city professionals. The exception was the new school superintendent, Buddy Davis, whom Escalonte believed was freed up to attack the problem because he was new to the district and had not yet developed close allegiances.

Escalonte also discovered that one directly affected city department, the parks board, didn't identify the growing problems because it didn't perceive itself as having the responsibility to respond. The board considered this the job of the police, schools, and social agencies. Therefore, it was not initiating any studies to determine if all segments of the community were participating in available youth programs. Escalonte believed that this kind of myopic approach needed to change because of the complexity of the problems, and so he organized a task force.

THE FORMATION OF THE TASK FORCE

This task force was unique in that it was *not* formed due to community pressure; rather, it was preemptively initiated by government officials who saw a number of growing problems that would only become worse in the future. To foresee these negative scenarios, all they had to do was look at Dallas with its seemingly out-of-control gang problems.

Farmers Branch had traditionally assumed such issues as gangs in schools, drug abuse, and latchkey kids to be the responsibility of schools or social services, not the city. But this view changed when latchkey kids started committing crimes; it became apparent that in order to solve this problem the city had to consider implementing after-school programs for kids whose single parents worked.

To take effective action, city hall had to change its problem-solving philosophy from "problem-oriented policing" to "community-oriented policing." Problem-oriented policing centers around assigning a particular problem to a specific department or agency. Gang activity, for example, would be handled by law enforcement. In contrast, community-oriented policing views a problem with all its complexities and asks that any department or agency that can contribute to a solution do so, avoiding the typical turf wars that can render competing city government and private agencies ineffective.

The community-oriented approach might sound naive, but many communities have made it work, and the idea is catching on at city manager regional and national conferences. Simply put, the realization is taking hold that to make things better, everyone must contribute unselfishly to get the job done.

With this change of philosophy, the task force was composed of Escalonte, the chief of police, the chief librarian, the parks and recreation department head, and the head of community services—which included everything from building inspection to housing to city codes. Although many communities form such blue-ribbon panels from the private sector, Escalonte felt that he would have a better shot of implementing programs that actually worked if those who were compiling the recommendations were the same people who would later carry them out.

IDENTIFYING NEEDS AND STRATEGIES

The questions that Escalonte wanted the task force to answer were:

- ◆ What are the needs of today's youth?
- ◆ Who, if anyone, is attempting to meet those needs?
- ◆ What should be the city's future role in meeting those needs?

"A key component," Escalonte reflected, "was that the evaluations were *not* to be department based, which can cause people to become defensive. We weren't interested in blaming anyone. We simply wanted to identify the problems and then ask who in the public and private sector was meeting or could meet those needs. By approaching the issue in this way, we avoided turf battles and placing blame.

"The most important factor that we found driving the problems we identified was the disintegration of the nuclear family: a family in which there is a breadwinner, two parents, someone home raising the children, and a family dinner at home on most nights."

After two-and-a-half months, the task force made its presentation for recommendations to the city council. One hundred percent of the recommendations were accepted. Follow-up community and civic group forums helped ensure community participation and backing. The recommendations implemented included:

- ◆ Work with existing inventory of facilities, both public and private, instead of rushing into a building program.
- ◆ Expand from half-day to all-day the ten-week Summer Sunshine Program for two hundred students. Scholarship funds were to be provided for about one-third of the families who couldn't afford the program. No segment of the city was to be excluded.
- ◆ Increase the number of workers in all departments where needed.

◆ Employ additional youth officers, whose sole responsibility was to walk the halls, eat lunch with the kids, work with the teachers, and pay visits to families with youths who were at risk for becoming involved in a gang. These officers were not to work cases, so that they could befriend kids and be seen regularly, like the cop on the beat in former generations. The idea was to build a one-on-one trust between officers and students.

◆ Establish an after-school program for four hundred kids whose parents worked. This would serve as an academic growth and activities-oriented program, not as a daycare program.

◆ Waive some fees for kids at swimming pools and other public recreational areas, and encourage city baseball and football programs to provide scholarships when needed.

◆ Initiate parenting classes for up to three hundred families, particularly in the Hispanic community. In addition to parenting skills, other practical skills would also be taught: study skills, purchasing insurance, managing a budget, etc. During classes, they offered child care, and youth officers met regularly with the kids to build trust.

◆ Conduct weekly ride-throughs by maintenance and building code inspectors to upgrade safety in lower-income apartment complexes.

Note that the way this community chose to head off an encroaching gang problem was to develop programs centered around helping kids find positive outlets, and to assist families in counteracting the effects of deteriorating family conditions. Escalonte hammered home the point that *kids need help all year long* on a multitude of levels.

ASSESSING THE GAINS

While Escalonte concedes that government cannot "fix" all the ills wrought by family decline, he points out that his city has made some marginal gains related to its gang problem. Some of these were:

Within a year, wearing gang colors was no longer "cool" or fashionable.

Not one parent of children who were more likely to participate in a gang complained of visits by youth officers telling them that their child might be a potential gang member.

Unlike similar communities, Farmers Branch experienced only one gang-related shooting from 1989 through the spring of 1992 (when the writing of this story was finalized), and there were no acts of gang violence in the schools. Additionally, the number of other acts of gang violence, such as assaults and intimidation, was dramatically down. (Crimes against property committed by gang and non-gang members, however, were up, as is the case in most communities. Police believed that gang members, many of whom were criminally active before they joined a gang, acted without the direction of the gang hierarchy, and their actions simply reflect the overall trend.)

Scout troops were formed for the first time in lower-income apartment dwellings.

Churches increased their outreach efforts to affected youths.

A local psychiatric hospital offered free first-offender counseling for sixty-two kids the first year.

The cost for the total package of programs was $200,000. No new taxes were required the first year, said Escalonte, "just a refocusing of priorities." The second year, additional tax funds were sought because of declining property values due to over-speculation in the 1980s. But, Escalonte added, "when we had to ask for additional revenue to fund the youth programs because of the drop in overall revenues, no one said, 'Kill the youth programs.'"

Escalonte believes that there were four basic reasons why they were successful in heading off an expanding gang problem:

1. They avoided turf battles and pointing blame.
2. They adopted a community-oriented policing philosophy.
3. They took a businesslike approach. "We presented the facts, the solution, and the resources to do it. It had to make financial sense to the business community. We also keyed off timely news accounts."
4. They realized that the mechanisms for solving social problems were not the same as those for solving city problems, such as street repair. They realized they needed a broader approach.

Escalonte recommends three foundational goals for cities that want to develop the perspective necessary for tackling specific youth problems:

◆ Develop an understanding of the overall community itself: diversity of neighborhoods, types of businesses, source of tax revenues, etc.

◆ Without the expectation of a quick fix, ask what the problems are, and then which structures, combined with what resources, can respond.

◆ Recruit department heads who will adopt a comprehensive view in order to avoid political infighting.

Escalonte says he is under no illusion that his city's action has solved all the youth problems. Juvenile crime, for example, is still up as of the spring of 1992, and three officers were fired for allegedly having sexual relations with a sixteen-year-old, but action by city hall did help to minimize the gang problem.

"City government can't do everything, nor should it try," says Escalonte. "Churches, scout troops, private business, and agencies can all do a better job in specific areas than we can."

Like most of those whom I've interviewed for this book, Escalonte said that the individual commitment to restoring the basic family unit is the most important underlying component to solving youth problems. This statement may not do much to win votes with local electorates, since it places accountability squarely on the voters. But it's the truth.

A STRATEGY FOR TAKING ACTION

Not every problem can be headed off or even alleviated by government involvement. From 1971 to 1981, for example, the federal government spent over $2 billion on family planning, yet the teen pregnancy rate jumped 48.3 percent, followed by a 133 percent increase in teen abortions. Clearly, more direct involvement is needed in the lives of young people: family, church, schools, and private organizations. Before going to your city government with a problem, consider whether it's the institution that can do the best job.

When circumstances necessitate involvement from city government, yet that government refuses to assess its role or accept responsibility for tackling a specific problem, community pressure may be needed to bring about change.

The following outline suggests a strategy for fostering responsible community action to address particular problems. This outline is intended only as a guideline, and will have to be modified for each specific situation.[1]

1. Identify the problem(s).
   a. Detail how it relates to your community.
   b. Answer the "who, what, why, where, and when" questions.
2. Know your community.
   a. Understand how your local government works.
   b. Chart the diversity of neighborhoods.
   c. Identify public or private groups or agencies that are already working on the problem or can be recruited.
   d. Identify sympathetic, local, qualified experts who can assist.
3. Decide on what can be done to solve the problem(s).
   a. Seek expert advice.
   b. Prepare a written proposal appropriate for the audience to whom it will be presented.
   c. Go to the library and perform a computer database search of news and journal articles indicating how other communities have successfully taken positive action.
   d. Compile a list of resources necessary to address the problem—financial, agencies, departments, etc.
4. Identify who can implement the program, or assemble a task force or committee, to enact and/or revise your solutions.
5. Recruit community support for your proposal.
   a. Identify groups or blocks of individuals who have an interest.
   b. Direct public opinion back to key decision-makers.
6. Make appointments to present your case.
7. Work with the media.
   a. Send out press releases announcing your efforts.
   b. Take reporters to actual stories.
   c. Do talk show interviews.
   d. Avoid the appearance of fanaticism—let local stories poignantly tell the story to avoid hysteria.
8. Continually sharpen your strategy.
9. If community action is taken, follow through.
   a. Monitor action.
   b. Find ways to encourage city officials who have taken action.
10. If community action is not taken, respond accordingly.
    a. Work to elect or appoint sympathetic officials.
    b. Continue public relations efforts.

c. Stay abreast of new developments, statistics, etc.
d. Be alert for other communities that have successfully addressed the issue and forward letters, articles, or other pertinent information to appropriate persons.

SUMMARY

Local government can minimize and help prevent the damaging consequences of youth problems, but it cannot correct the root source of most negative youth issues. This can be done only in the family, with support from affected organizations and institutions. Still, community governments are good clearinghouses for monitoring problems, finding community-wide solutions, and enacting programs that can help all segments of a community.

CHAPTER TWENTY-ONE

The Spiritual Factor

◆

"**S**trong ties to churches, more than the presence of parents in the home, region, or urban density, appear to influence students to say no to drugs."

This conclusion was reached by Dr. Jerald Bachman, a social psychologist who is one of the authors of a landmark study of high school seniors conducted by the Institute for Social Research at the University of Michigan. Released in February 1991, this study surveyed 70,000 students from 135 high schools during 1985 to 1989.[1]

As already cited, study results showed that substance abuse was lower among blacks than among whites. Bachman attributes this to the fact that 80 percent of the black students surveyed indicated that spiritual values played an important part in their lives, in contrast to only 50 percent of white students. These findings indicate that *religious commitment is an even greater deterrent to drug abuse than close family ties.* (It should also be noted that a host of other studies also reveal that spiritual values are a deterrent to harmful trends.)

John Wallace, a sociologist and coauthor of the study, points out another significant finding: "For *both* African-American and white youths, those who are *least* likely to use drugs are those who attend churches that have more fundamentalist beliefs."[2] Since this is an important factor, it is crucial to understand clearly what is meant by the term *fundamentalist* and to distinguish *fundamentalism* from *legalism*.

A fundamentalist view of Christianity bases doctrine and interpretation on the literal truth of the Bible. Legalism insists on strict adherence to a set of laws and practices, which may or may not be mentioned in the Bible—such as women being forbidden to wear pants, or men having to keep their hair trimmed above the ear.

When I told one associate pastor that a five-year study concluded that the importance youths placed on spiritual values drove down drug abuse, he said, "That must be because of a change in the students' peer group." That could be one explanation.

Some have speculated that kids who regularly attend church are more likely to adopt a strong Judeo-Christian moral outlook on life because of a combination of teaching and the support of the church community for their stand.

However, youths who abuse drugs usually come from troubled homes. Because this is often the underlying cause, it would seem that if family relationships are restored, then substance abuse—a mask, distraction, or illusive empowering device over one's pain—should drop.

Yet spiritual values, not the family, seem to be the dominant factor. Why?

After working for several years with hundreds of at-risk kids of all backgrounds and races, I believe the answer is due to the fact that there really is a God who works in peoples' lives for good and that the teachings in the Bible have a power of their own.

THE EVIDENCE OF CHANGED LIVES

At our church, I work with kids in what's called the "bus ministry." Every Sunday, ten school buses travel about three miles from our parking lot to apartment complexes that are just north of Interstate 635, the northern loop around Dallas. The residential neighborhoods north of the loop are middle-class to upper-middle class. Interestingly, within this area are low-income apartments where kids live who participate in our bus ministry.

These apartments, located just a mile-and-a-half from the high-tech employer Texas Instruments, were originally built for singles. Over the last ten years, however, many low-income families began to move in, hoping for a chance to give their kids a better education by taking advantage of the excellent schools. We bring about 350 kids—first through twelfth grade—to our church for Sunday school and worship because there isn't a church in their immediate area.

Over the last four years since I began helping out, over 400 different kids have attended. Many of these students' parents don't come to church because they face cultural barriers, they're embarrassed about not having a "Sunday" suit of clothes, or they simply don't want to attend. (Our church's next challenge is to establish a mission church close to the apartments.)

About 50 percent of the kids are black, 25 percent Hispanic, and 25 percent white. But color, race, and heritage are irrelevant to how we treat each child in our class. Many of these kids come from seriously dysfunctional homes, and about one-third have seen acts of violence in their neighborhood—one of the higher crime rate areas in Dallas.

As stated earlier, incredibly, not one youth to our knowledge has ever joined a gang. This in a city noted for its gang activity. Is this success story due to a sophisticated curriculum and campaign? The answer is no, because none exists.

During the first hour, the kids attend Sunday school with the other kids from our church. Although economically disadvantaged, they're certainly at no mental disadvantage. Many are the top performers when memorizing Bible verses.

During the second hour, we have uniquely tailored worship services for these students, dividing them by age groups. I work with about 120 fourth through sixth graders. Our aim is to relate the worship hour to their various cultural backgrounds and maturity levels. For example, one Sunday we explained and then sang the three different kinds of Negro spirituals originating with slaves in colonial America. On another Sunday we asked a woman in our church who was born in mainland China to explain how she came to embrace the Christian faith, even though she was raised in a militantly atheistic country.

In this simple context we have seen many kids' lives changed.

In 1990, two girls who were cousins visited our class in the middle of the school year. Having interviewed a number of sexually abused children and adults, I suspected that the girls—ages eleven and twelve—had been sexually molested. The younger girl, Lisa, had no relationship with her parents, who had abandoned her. Lisa lived with her older cousin, Becky. I asked one of the female teachers to give them some extra time and befriend them.

Three weeks later, they confided that their uncle had molested them, and that they had to testify in court. It was a difficult time. Neither girl ever smiled, and both were perceptibly afraid when around any male adults.

After their uncle's conviction, one of the couples who helped during the worship hour, Ron and Claudia Giancolo, bought each girl a dress for Christmas. Within a few weeks, even though the girls' sparse living conditions hadn't changed, smiles came more easily; and by the end of the year, their fear of adult males was greatly reduced.

Another story involves a nine-year-old boy. Short and thin, Alex could never sit still. He had been physically abused a year before by his father, who was no longer living at home. Each Sunday I made it a point to ask him about his school work and whether he was making friends at school. I looked for opportunities to pay him a compliment. For the first three months he resisted. He wouldn't even "give me five" or respond when I showed him a magic trick.

But by the end of the year, with continued teaching from the Bible, persistently letting him know that I loved him—even when he would have to be disciplined and sent out of the room for disturbing those around him—eventually Alex was indistinguishable from kids who came from healthy homes.

Showing Lisa, Becky, and Alex that we loved them with words of encouragement and our actions contributed to the positive changes in their lives, such as increased self-esteem and the emergence of joy. But I think the real reason for the long-term changes in these kids' lives transcends teachers who give of themselves. The verses of Scripture these kids soak in every Sunday reach deep into their hearts and minds, starting a healing process that a human being alone cannot effect. Added to this is the growing knowledge that God does love them, and that there really is a source of good and truth that will not harm them.

By stating this I am not discounting the value of excellent professional counseling or a Sunday school teacher's personal one-on-one influence; however, history is clear: God's living Word is alive and can permanently change a young person's life.

Aleksandr Solzhenitsyn, the Russian dissident who suffered many years in the *gulag,* a desolate Soviet prison camp, wrote that in desperate situations, those who are brutalized don't cling to human writings, such as the Bill of Rights, for hope. In the gulag, he observed one man who would steal away to read Scriptures that he had carefully written out by hand and concealed from the guards. These Scriptures, Solzhenitsyn believed, were what gave this man an extraordinary spark of light— apparent to his fellow prisoners—even in the face of an agonizing death.

At the extreme, I have seen people's lives changed even when they attended a church led by a corrupt pastor. One pastor in particular, who taught with clarity the teachings of Jesus, succumbed to a number of adulterous affairs. Yet I witnessed many people whose lives were changed through the Scriptures, which were the foundation for his teachings.

In another example, I interviewed a woman whose father, a minister, tortured and raped her when she was young, all the while quoting Scriptures to her to justify his behavior. She said that as a young girl, she was bewildered when trying to reconcile the verses with her father's demented acts. One might assume that this woman would grow up hating the Bible and the Christian faith because of her father. However, she said that it was clinging to the thoughts of goodness expressed through the verses her father quoted that actually gave her hope that the assaults and torture would one day stop. Today, she says that her love for God's Word is a significant force in enabling her to confront the pain of her childhood honestly.

If people can be positively affected by Scriptures communicated by a deceiver, imagine the impact a loving Sunday school teacher or pastor can have on the lives of young people. That love can make the truth of the Bible even more appealing, inspiring youths to be more diligent in all their thoughts, words, and actions.

This is not a mystical observation. There *is* something about God's words that transcends all that humans are or can even aspire to become on their own. This is why one of the finest influences on children is involvement in a local church that really does care about kids and teaches them in a way that they can intimately comprehend.

Yes, there are corrupt church leaders and churches, but most people can usually find at least one church, even in a small town, that is honestly faithful—not perfect, just faithful. Becoming and remaining a committed member of a local church requires discernment, but a trustworthy church can have an immeasurable impact on a child's life.

THE CALL TO TEACH

If so much good can come from spending time with youths, teaching them to live as Jesus did, then why is one of the biggest problems in our church—and many churches around the United States—a shortage of adults volunteering to teach children's Sunday school classes?

Our staff members and teachers regularly point out that we have to ask *fifty* or more people to teach before we enlist even *one* volunteer. Even if you eliminate those folks who feel inadequate to hold a youngster's attention, new Christians who need to be in their own class to learn about the faith, and the elderly—whose hearing prohibits them from being around increased noise levels—there should still be enough adults who are willing to serve. But it's often not the case. Why?

As in politics, kids have the smallest voice, and their needs are often not given priority. When congressmen are lobbied about two bills, one that is related to kids and another that isn't, it's a sure bet that the one that *isn't* will get first attention. As our culture has become increasingly hostile to kids, this indifference in politics has only grown.

The same is often true in a church: Ask for teachers for an adult class, and you'll probably see many hands go up. But ask for teachers for a children's class, and hands are kept close at their sides. People have become more selfish about giving time to nurture kids. This destructive trend must be reversed, and each of us must do our part.

Years ago, most Sunday school classes were taught by mothers who didn't work outside the home, and it was easy to find teachers. Over half of the women in the United States, however, have entered the workplace, and many feel they are too busy to teach. Yet considering the numbers of kids from troubled homes, the need for teachers is more acute now than ever before. To their shame, capable men have never been exempt, but traditionally the ones who volunteer are in the minority. This indifference in men must be reversed.

The spiritual pulse of a church can often be monitored by how it treats its weakest members. Kids can't lobby, wield power, or make large contributions. Teaching and giving time to them is a selfless act. When a church begins to turn its back on children, it's an indication that it's headed for decline, deteriorating into a self-absorbed institution that responds to power plays rather than to the needs of its members or community.

Let's encourage each other to give unselfishly to our kids as well as other kids outside our home. Ron and Claudia Giancolo, the couple I mentioned earlier who demonstrated the love of God to the two young abused girls, are a sterling example. What I didn't tell you was that Ron was diagnosed with a malignant brain tumor two years before they helped Lisa and Becky. A year later, they quietly retired from service because he was concerned that his physical appearance, which was expected to change due to radiation therapy, might frighten the kids. But even in the midst of their personal pain, they couldn't keep from coming by.

One Sunday in the fall of 1991, I was shorthanded. Adult volunteers failed to show as promised. Eighty-seven kids were present. Ron, whose appearance (I'm thankful) hadn't visibly deteriorated, checked on the class, saw the situation, and he and Claudia volunteered to help. I never even asked them. They chose to volunteer because they love kids.

When Ron taught, was he an eloquent speaker? Not at all. In fact, his memory started to slide a year before he had to stop teaching, but the kids didn't care. Sure, it was more difficult for him to relate to them and hold their attention, but God's grace is far more powerful than Ron's condition. As his ability to relate slipped, there was barely a discernible difference in the kids' attentiveness.

You may not think that you can be used to make a difference in a child's life—but that's the point of the gospel. You don't have to be a child psychologist, a gifted speaker, or a brilliant theologian to teach children. You just have to love kids, explain the lessons and Scriptures as clearly as you can, and be there every week. I believe that if more people—however busy their schedules—took the time to cherish this simple and honorable task, coupled with parents learning to live with one another as Christ taught, it would unleash the greatest possible long-term force for good in our country.

OUR FAMILY'S EXPERIENCE

Up until the third or fourth grade, our kids' teachers passed out simple surveys for them to fill out to get a better understanding of their students. The surveys had questions such as, "Do you have a hobby?" and "How long have you lived in your current neighborhood?"

One question usually went something like this: "What do you like best about your mom and dad?" In the first grade, one of our kids answered, "My mom and dad love God." All of our kids invariably wrote something like this, either in a paper or one of these surveys. As they became older, one wrote, "That my parents are both Christians. My dad is fun to play with, and Mom is a great cook."

While writing this book, I asked my daughter, now fifteen, what she thought was the best thing we did in raising her. She answered, "That you and Mom both raised us in a Christian home—that you are

Christians." Notice that she didn't say we were perfect! Just that we instilled Christian values in her.

Both my sons, nine and eleven, voiced similar sentiments. In fact, two years ago they asked if they could get up with me at 6:15 a.m. for Bible study before school. I didn't initiate this; each came to me separately. The younger one asked first, and so we studied Scriptures and prayed together every school morning. Then about three months later, his older brother asked if he could join us. This takes place every day before school. When I tuck the boys in at night, they often say, "Don't forget—6:15."

My daughter is also self-motivated and does her own Bible study with her *NIV Student Bible* translation. I'm not trying to make it sound like we never quarrel, are never insensitive to each other, and are always kind to each other. If this were true, it would have to be an illusion! We're just like any other family. The difference is that our kids cling to what they know is good, because they genuinely love God and they know that the streets are tough. It's not uncommon for them to share their faith—spontaneously, without prompting from us—with their friends, who have many times responded. In addition, their teachers at school and at church consistently report that they are all well-adapted and sensitive to the needs of others.

I'm sharing this not to boast, but rather to encourage you to *take time to share God's love with your kids.* Through your friends and caring Sunday school teachers, expose them to other Christians who cling to God's teaching without hypocrisy. This positive exposure has been one of the most significant factors in our kids' lives and in the hundreds of at-risk kids I have taught. Take the initiative to share God's Word regularly with your kids. A couple of times a year we even stay home from church and have an all-morning time of Bible study, worshiping, and praying together.

Does this mean that our family has been and always will be insulated from harm, or that not one of us will make horrible mistakes? No. Does this guarantee that none of our kids will go the way of the prodigal son, as did Billy Graham's son, Franklin, who eventually turned back to embrace the faith? No. But this I can say, with the conviction of having watched many who have strayed: Those who turn away nearly always make an arduous journey back to what they remember and experienced as being good when they were young. Solomon was right when he wrote: *Train a child in the way he should go, and when he is old he will not turn from it* (Proverbs 22:6).

SUMMARY

Statistically, youths who believe and cling to what the Bible says is true are least at risk for being negatively influenced by surrounding threats. In part, this is because of following a moral code, an honorable path for one's life. On another level, the Bible makes a young person wide awake to what is true and what isn't, giving them peace even when they can't change their environment and are surrounded by chaos.

It's not a point of weakness to state proudly that we had a mother or father who nurtured us. Neither is it a display of weakness to state that there is a God who made us and cares for us. Declaring our faith, and, more importantly, quietly living out the teachings of Christ, frees us up from lying illusions and whims of the moment.

In the midst of our personal weakness, this honest Christian way of life allows us to live from a point of strength, expressed through our love for God in the lives of others. If kids don't learn this from their parents or concerned adults, who will they learn it from? Who will teach them to develop a love for the truth, modeling that love as it expresses itself in giving to others unselfishly? If we truly love kids, each of us must do his or her own part.

A Final Note

◆

Saturday morning, May 2, 1992.

I began this book by telling you about some threats in our own neighborhood that have surfaced in most communities. We then looked at how to take positive action and preventive measures regarding what can harm our kids and how to point them to the good.

This week, what my family and our nation have experienced is reflective of much of what I have written.

As I'm sure you are aware, riots broke out in Los Angeles, causing over fifty deaths and 500 million to nearly one billion dollars in property damage, igniting over 4,000 fires. Similar riots spread to cities across the United States. Yet with the nearly 100 hours of combined network coverage, one never heard a single person state that the utter destruction of the family— which is far more devastating than economic conditions—must be reversed in those neighborhoods.

The day before the rioting began, a single father, two doors down from us, fled the state with his kids under suspicious circumstances. He had withdrawn them from school that morning. The kids had no forewarning, and they looked scared. He then frantically packed a U-Haul, and by night they were gone. The next day, after informing the police, I took off from work and tried to track down where the kids were going to be certain they were safe. My attempts were unsuccessful.

In contrast, a young Hispanic high school sophomore from our church's inner-city ministry, who lives with his single mother, came over to our house during the first night of rioting to bone-up on his study habits. Even though he has ability, he had been making poor grades. We talked about acquiring head knowledge and we talked about loving the truth more than we fear our pain. It was good to know that I could help someone in need.

The next night, Sandy and I attended our son's annual spring play. As I panned my home video camera across the stage, these kids, which were of all races, stood in stark contrast to the young looters rampaging through the city streets of Los Angeles, Atlanta, and Seattle. As I chatted with my son's principal, he said, "I can't tell you how proud I am of the involvement of the parents of our kids. There is no question that it is the most important factor in what you see here."

The whole week continually seemed to contrast kids who were in trouble and those who weren't—those who wanted to help kids, and those who didn't.

Even though the inner-city ministry at church can only be viewed as an extraordinary and successful shot in the arm for youths, for months various staff and lay leaders have sought for selfish reasons to reduce the number of kids that come on the buses from 400 to 200. Some even wanted the ministry dismantled permanently. Fortunately, there have been more concerned people who have resisted this effort. In fact, we are sending over seventy-five students to the inner-city camp, K-5 (to whom this book is dedicated), this summer. That's nearly double the number we sent last year.

Parents and others who can affect kids lives have more resources to help our own kids and those at risk to resist deceptive trends than at any time in history; but paradoxically, there is also a growing resistance to helping kids in the United States and abroad. We must be vigilant and do our part.

You are your child's greatest asset in developing the discernment that will help protect him or her from the threats of the streets. If you're aware of how to think about deception, knowledgeable about deceptive trends, and can communicate this information appropriately to your kids, they will become streetwise and nearly foolproof. In the next few years, kids will need these skills, and their parents, like never before.

The two negative youth trends most likely to intensify in the future are violence and escapism. If adult anger and frustration increase, fueled by family and economic discontent, violent behavior by youths is likely to follow—but at a more intense level. Like the music they listen to, kids act out their feelings at a higher energy level than their parents. If this occurs, violent behavior is likely to manifest itself with a greater intensity in many of the trends covered in this book: gangs, cults, occult, physical assaults, and so on. Additionally, escape or empowering mechanisms will continue to be sought through radical forms of music, sex, and other channels.

After former neo-Nazi David Duke (who briefly ran in the 1992 presidential campaign) made an unsuccessful 1991 bid for the Louisiana governor's office, one columnist noted:

The country is suffering from the social diseases that are the historic breeding grounds of bigotry and Fascism—unemployment, corruption, cynicism, racial and religious clashes.[1]

What the columnist did not identify are the conditions in the American family that ultimately cause many of these social ills in the first place. Our hope must be that as concerned parents become aware of these conditions, we will see a dramatic change of priorities.

On the positive side, a 1991 study revealed that 84 percent of adults strongly believe that the "family is the place where most basic values are instilled," an increase of 24 percent since 1989. And not surprisingly, the importance of "having nice things"—materialism—dropped from 36 to 26 percent. Even respect for one's parents as a cherished value jumped from 38 to 47 percent.[2]

But the main reason for my positive expectations for individual American families is that I have seen, firsthand, many take the initiative to change for the good. And watching their kids become street-smart has been just one of the benefits.

In its 1991 report, The National Commission on Children wrote,

It is a tragic irony that the most prosperous nation on earth is failing so many of its children. As a society, we have lacked the vision and political will necessary to address these problems head on.

In September 1990, the United Nations held the World Summit for Children, attended by the largest gathering of heads of state in history.

While these leaders acknowledged—if only by a token appearance—government's role in helping kids, former Prime Minister Margaret Thatcher focused on the need for good parenting by denouncing "absent fathers who don't take responsibility for their children."[3]

Parents can't afford to wait for government to solve their family problems and protect their kids from harmful trends. The only way a long-term change will take place is when bedrock values and discernment are taught in the home and reinforced in churches and schools. Then government and other institutions can follow, since they are most effective when following those at the grassroots.

Our hope should be that the family will resume its once cherished position and that Judeo-Christian values will be unashamedly embraced. Even if this occurs, it will still take many years for the damage to be reversed; and so the threat to kids remains. But we *can* live without our thoughts being dominated by fear. *We can love the truth more than we fear our pain.*

As the major studies and common sense tell us, for such a change to take place, families will need to cling to biblical principles and truths. For without embracing the God who created us, to whom we are ultimately responsible, there is no permanent and enduring reason to consistently stay the course. May we each be diligent to this end.

Streetwise Resources

♦

Christian Faith Materials (Reinforcing Why It Is True)

Anders, Max. *Thirty Days to Understanding the Bible*; *Thirty Days to Understanding the Christian Life*; *Thirty Days to Understanding Christian History*. Brentwood, TN: Wolgemuth & Hyatt, 1988, 1991, 1991.

Stewart, Don. *Ten Reasons Why You Should Trust the Bible* (out of print; check libraries for availability).

Stewart, Don. *You Be the Judge: Is Christianity True?* San Bernardino, CA: Here's Life, 1983.

Community Action Resources

International City Management Association, Washington, DC, can provide guidance on the latest and most effective ideas used by city governments in addressing many of the issues in this book (202-289-4282).

Cults and Cult Prevention Materials and Resources

Answers in Action, P. O. Box 2067, Costa Mesa, CA 92628 (714-646-9042).

Cult Awareness Network (national offices), 2421 West Pratt Boulevard,

Suite 1173, Chicago, IL 60645 (312-267-7777).

Hassan, Steven. *Combatting Cult Mind Control.* Rochester, VT: Park Street Press, 1988.

Spiritual Counterfeits Project, P. O. Box 4308, Berkeley, CA 94704 (415-540-0300).

Drug Information Agencies

Drugs and Crime Data Center & Clearinghouse (800-666-3332) can provide many resources, including the *State Drug Resources: A National Directory* and *Drugs of Abuse* (1989), published by the Drug Enforcement Administration.

National Clearing House for Alcohol and Drug Information is another source for printed materials (800-729-6686).

Office for Substance Abuse Prevention (5600 Fishers Lane, Rockville, MD 20857) can provide the *Citizen's Alcohol and Other Drug Prevention Directory: Resources for Getting Involved.* This excellent directory provides both national and state drug prevention agencies and organizations.

Partnership for a Drug Free America offers excellent educational materials (212-922-1560).

Gangs

Although not available at the time of the release of this book, Dan Korem is preparing a detailed treatise for law enforcement officials that will expand on the information in this chapter. Please write to the address provided on page 324 for additional information.

Music Trends

Gore, Tipper. *Raising PG Kids in an X-Rated World.* Nashville, TN: Abingdon, 1987. This book also provides helpful information on the entertainment media.

The Parents' Music Resource Center, 1500 Arlington Boulevard, Arlington, VA 22209 (703-527-9466).

The News: Learn More About It

CNN (Cable News Network) is a recommended news broadcast for most kids. The *McNeil-Lehrer Report* on PBS and *Nightline* on ABC are usually good sources for in-depth reporting for teens.

From the *Kid Tricks* series, the video *Check It Out!* features how a newsroom works and is excellent for ages five to twelve (see the list of materials on page 324).

Occultism Information

For preteens: Part 4 of *Kid Tricks* video series, *Tricks or Powers?* For information about this series, see description on page 324.

For teens: *Psychic Confession* video exposé of psychic James Hydrick. For more information about this forty-seven-minute video, see description on page 323.

Powers: Testing the Psychic and Supernatural, by Dan Korem. For more information, see page 324.

Sexual Trends Resources

Focus on the Family Ministries, 420 North Cascade, Colorado Springs, CO 80905 (719-531-3400).

Notes

---◆---

Chapter One—The Challenge to Meet Unexpected Threats
1. Jane Brody, "Why Many Efforts Fail to Change Habits," *New York Times,* 28 April 1987.

Chapter Three—Secrets, Lies, and the Truth
1. Interview with Dr. Maria Kopp, Semmelweis Medical University Office, Budapest, Hungary, 2 February 1992.

Chapter Five—Fantasy and Imagination: Where to Draw the Line
1. "Video Game in Europe Uses Nazi Camps as Theme," *New York Times*, 1 May 1991.

Chapter Seven—Family: The First Line of Defense
1. Willard Cates, Jr., M.D., M.P.H., "The Epidemology and Control of Sexually Transmitted Diseases in Adolescents," *Adolescent Medicine*, vol. 1, no. 3, October 1990.
2. U.S. Census Bureau.
3. Telephone interview with Dr. Paul Amato, 31 August 1990. Dr. Amato's figures were culled from various sources, but the

breakdown for the 31.7 percent estimate is as follow: 8.3 percent of adults came from homes where parents were divorced; 20.7 percent of adults have been divorced in their own marriage; 2.7 percent have experienced both. It must be understood that just because the current ratio of marriages to divorces per year is now running at two-to-one doesn't mean that half of all marriages end up in divorce. Couples married thirty years ago, for example, are not divorcing at this rate. However, if the current trend continues for another thirty years, there could be a fifty-fifty percentage rate of marriages that end up in divorce. Additionally, 50 percent of all divorces involve children, according to a 1989 U.S. Census Bureau report.

4. Judith Wallerstein and Sandra Blakeslee, *Second Chances: Men, Women and Children a Decade After Divorce* (New York: Ticknor and Fields, affiliates of Houghton Mifflin, 1989).
5. Quoted in Barbara S. Cain, "Older Children and Divorce," *New York Times Magazine,* 18 February 1990, page 26.
6. Diane Medved, Ph.D., *The Case Against Divorce* (New York: Donald Fine, 1989).
7. Julie Stacey, "Missing Mom More," *USA Today,* 10 May 1991.
8. From a 1990 University of Pennsylvania study cited by Tamar Lewin in "Father's Vanishing Act Called Common," *New York Times,* 4 June 1990.
9. From a 1989 study by the Institute of Medicine.
10. From a telephone interview with Lee Dogoloff, October 1991.
11. Dr. Ray Guarendi, *Back to the Family* (New York: Villard Books, 1990).
12. The competition for selection as Teacher of the Year is invigoratingly rigorous. During the screening process, for example, one candidate compiled a seventy-five page scrapbook of her teaching experiences, starting with her first job. She then had to undergo a series of extensive interviews in the state capital.
13. Guarendi.
14. Guarendi.
15. Guarendi.
16. Guarendi.
17. Guarendi.
18. Daniel Goleman, "Therapists See Religion as an Aid, Not an Illusion," *New York Times,* 10 September 1991.

Chapter Nine—A Streetwise Approach to the Entertainment Media

1. Quoted in Aljean Harmetz, "Hollywood Pays Court to the Young Adults," *New York Times,* 13 May 1990. Richard Zanuck spent four years raising money for the award-winning movie *Driving Miss Daisy,* which has no sexual or violent scenes.
2. Quoted in *New York Times,* 31 December 1989.
3. Quoted during an interview on the *ABC World News Tonight* broadcast, 2 November 1990.
4. Camille Paglia, *New York Times,* 14 December 1990.
5. Quoted in *Dallas Morning News,* 27 December 1990.
6. Quoted in *Dallas Morning News,* 17 August 1990.
7. Bob Greene, "Madonna's TV Concert Isn't as Shocking as Our Reaction," *Dallas Morning News* (from the Tribune Media Services), 19 August 1990.
8. Ed Bark, *Dallas Morning News,* 6 December 1990.
9. John J. O'Connor, "On Teen-Age Virginity, or Its Loss, on Television," *New York Times,* 25 September 1991.
10. As quoted in *Southwest Airlines Magazine,* July 1981.
11. Telephone interview with Nelson Flannigan, 5 June 1991.
12. Michael Medved, in an address at Hillsdale College, Hillsdale, Michigan, March 1989.
13. Medved.
14. Medved.

Chapter Eleven—Music Trends You Should Know About

1. *Dallas Morning News,* 19 September 1990.
2. From wire reports appearing in the *Dallas Morning News,* 8 July 1990.
3. Ted Nugent, "Violent Love," from the album *Scream Dream* (Epic, FE36404). Written by Nugent.
4. Mötley Crüe, "Tonight (We Need a Lover)," from the album *Theater of Pain* (Elektra/Asylum, 60418-1-E). Lyrics by Nikki Sixx.
5. Mötley Crüe, "Ten Seconds to Love," from the album *Shout at the Devil* (Elektra/Asylum, 60289-1). Lyrics by Nikki Sixx and Vince Neil.
6. Judas Priest, "Eat Me Alive," from the album *Defenders of the Faith* (Columbia Records, FC39219). Written by Glenn Tipton, Rob Halford, and K.K. Downing.
7. Carnivore, "Predator," from the album *Carnivore* (Roadracer

Records, GWD90534). Written by Peter Steele.

8. Elizabeth F. Brown, M.D., and William R. Hendee, Ph.D., "Adolescents and Their Music," *Journal of the American Medical Association*, vol. 262, no. 12, September 1989, pages 22, 29.

9. Telephone interview, 16 May 1990.

10. Telephone interview, 16 May 1990.

11. Tipper Gore, *Raising PG Kids in an X-Rated World* (Nashville, TN: Abingdon Press, 1987).

12. Patricia McCormack, "High-Achieving Teen-Agers Tell of Considering Suicide," *Washington Post,* 14 September 1986, section A, page 7.

13. Ozzy Osbourne, "Suicide Solution," from the album *Blizzard of Oz* (Jet, JZ36812). Words and music by Ozzy Osbourne, Bob Daisley, and Randy Rhoads.

14. Suicidal Tendencies, "Suicidal Failure," from the album *Suicidal Tendencies* (Frontier, FLP1011).

15. Jane Gross, "Surge of Rock Fans; Then Death, Grief and Anger," *New York Times,* 25 January 1991.

16. Quoted in Gross.

17. Bob Greene, "'Festival Seating' Is So Dangerous It Should Be Illegal," *Dallas Morning News,* 3 February 1991.

18. Slayer, "Necrophiliac," from the album *Hell Awaits* (Combat/Metal Blade, MX 8020). Lyrics and music by Hanneman and King.

19. Venom, "Sacrifice," from the album *Here Lies Venom* (Combat Records, MX8062). Written by Dunn, Bray, and Lant.

20. Venom, *Welcome to Hell* (Neat Records, 1-002).

21. Richard Corliss, "X Rated," *Time,* 7 May 1990, page 92.

22. Quoted in James LeMoyne, "For Rap Singer, Rags to Riches Through Music," *New York Times,* 13 June 1990.

23. Jon Pareles, "There's a New Sound in Pop Music: Bigotry," *New York Times,* 10 September 1989.

24. Jon Pareles, "A Rap Group's Lyrics Venture to the Edge of Obscenity," *New York Times,* 14 June 1990.

25. "Rock 'n' Raunch," *Dallas Morning News,* 19 May 1990.

26. John N. Rosenthal, "Modern Comics Misuse Humor's Power," *Dallas Morning News,* 2 July 1990.

27. Michael Bloodgood, "Out of the Darkness," © 1989 Broken Songs. Used by permission. All rights reserved.

28. Venom, "In League with the Devil" (Neat Records, 1-002).

29. John R. Vokey and J. Don Read, "Subliminal Messages," *American Psychologist*, vol. 40, no. 11, November 1985.
30. Christian Death, "Stairs," from the album *The Scriptures* (Normal).
31. Michael Walker, "A Bit of Girl Trouble," *New York Times*, 8 May 1991.
32. Edna Gundersen, "This 'Dare' Is Never Dull," *USA Today*, 10 May 1991.
33. Gundersen.
34. Ben H. Bagdikian (professor of journalism, University of California), letter to the editor, *New York Times*, 19 June 1990.
35. Advertisement in *New York Times*, 28 April 1992.

Chapter Twelve—Sex and Teens, Part One:
A Threatening Firestorm

1. The Alan Guttmacher Institute, 1990.
2. Dave Anderson, "Sorry, But Magic Johnson Isn't a Hero," *New York Times*, 14 November 1991.
3. Anderson.
4. The Alan Guttmacher Institute, 1990.
5. Survey by the Centers for Disease Control, 1991.
6. Ed Bark, "Doogie Faces Sexual Rite of Passage," *Dallas Morning News*, 24 September 1990.
7. John J. O'Connor, "On Teen-Age Virginity, or Its Loss, on Television," *New York Times*, 25 September 1991.
8. Bark.
9. Center for Disease Control, 1990.
10. The Alan Guttmacher Institute, 1990.
11. Randall Rothenberg, "Drive to Aid Children Has New Twist," *New York Times*, 3 April 1990.
12. The Alan Guttmacher Institute, 1990.
13. The Alan Guttmacher Institute, 1990.
14. As reported by *ABC News* from various studies, 26 June 1989.
15. Willard Cates, Jr., M.D., "The Epidemiology and Control of Sexually Transmitted Diseases in Adolescents," *Adolescent Medicine*, vol. 1, no. 3, October 1990.
16. Timothy C. Brock and Laura A. Brannon, "Sex Partner Numbers," *New York Times*, 23 November 1991, letter to the editor.
17. Catalina Camia, "Teen AIDS Increasing," *Dallas Morning News*, 20 August 1990.

18. Dimitri N. Shalin, "Glasnost and Sex," *New York Times,* 23 January 1990, quoting statistics in the now defunct *Komsomolskain, Pravada,* the Communist Youth League newspaper.
19. Appearing in *New York Times,* 15 December 1989.
20. Rothenberg.
21. As reported in the *New York Times*, 24 April 1992.
22. Daniel Goleman, "When the Rapist Is Not a Stranger," *New York Times,* 24 August 1989.
23. Quoted in Goleman.
24. Goleman.
25. Goleman.
26. Chris O'Sullivan, "Campus Rape Is Usually Fraternity-Related," *New York Times,* 5 December 1990.
27. O'Sullivan.
28. Quoted in Goleman.
29. Letter to the editor, *New York Times,* 7 August 1990.

Chapter Thirteen—Sex and Teens, Part Two:
Joyfully Preparing the Way

1. Cal Thomas, "Magic Is Trying to Deliver the Wrong Message on AIDS" (distributed by the *Los Angeles Times* Syndicate), *Dallas Morning News,* 12 November 1991.
2. Adapted from Tim Stafford, "Teaching Teens to Say 'No'," *Worldwide Challenge,* June 1987.
3. Cited in Felicity Barringer, "Doubt on 'Trial Marriage' Raised by Divorce Rates," *New York Times,* 13 June 1989.

Chapter Fourteen—The Drug Menace

1. Sandra Blakeslee, "Crack's Toll Among Babies: A Joyless View of Even Toys," *New York Times,* 17 September 1989.
2. Knight-Ridder wire service, "Illicit Drug Use Estimated," as reported in *Dallas Morning News,* 20 June 1991.
3. U.S. Department of Justice, "1989 Drug Use Forecasting Annual Report," NCJ-123941 (Washington, DC: U.S. Department of Justice, June 1990).
4. From a telephone interview with Lee Dogoloff, October 1991.
5. Figures in table 14.1 are adapted from Gina Kolata, "Experts Finding New Hope on Treating Crack Addicts," *New York Times,* 24 August 1989.
6. According to a 1990 study by the Institute for Social Research,

University of Michigan, as reported in *New York Times,* 23 June 1991.

7. Table 14.2 is adapted from *American Journal of Public Health,* vol. 81, no. 3, March 1991, page 373. Data reflects annual prevalence of thirteen types of drugs during 1985–1989.

8. Cited in Steve McGonigle, "Cocaine Use Understated, Report Says," *Dallas Morning News,* 11 May 1990.

9. Cited in "Drugs and Crime," study by National Institute of Justice, August 1991.

10. "Drugs and Crime."

11. Cited in Ralph Blumenthal, "For Children of Detectives, Torment Over Drugs," *New York Times,* 19 September 1989.

Chapter Fifteen—Gangs: From the Inner City to the Suburbs

1. Barri Flowers, *The Adolescent Criminal—An Examination of Today's Juvenile Offender* (Jefferson, NC: McFarland & Co., 1990), page 108.

2. Flowers, page 108.

3. Flowers, page 108.

4. Seth Mydans, "Not Just the Inner-City: Well-to-Do Join Gangs," *New York Times,* 10 April 1990.

5. Mydans.

6. Mydans.

7. Terry Box, "Widening Turfs," *Dallas Morning News,* 20 May 1990.

8. Curtis Howell, "330 Youths Likely Gang Members," *Dallas Morning News,* 21 December 1991.

9. David Binder, "Violence by Skinheads Startling East Germans," *New York Times,* 21 August 1990.

10. Associated Press, 1 May 1990.

11. Jason DeParle, "1989 Surge in Anti-Semitic Acts Is Reported by B'nai B'rith," *New York Times,* 20 January 1990.

12. "Tough Love" (editorial), *Dallas Morning News,* 26 May 1990.

Chapter Sixteen—Cults and the Occult, Part One:
A Parent's Primer

1. Per telephone interview with David Bezilla, Director of the Gallup Youth Survey, 9 January 1992.

2. Richard Delgado, "Religious Totalism," *Southern California Law Review,* November 1977.

3. Quoted in L. C. Wynne, S. H. McDaniel, and T. T. Weber, *Systems Consultation: A New Perspective for Family Therapy* (New York: Guilford Press, 1986).
4. *Webster's Encyclopedic Unabridged Dictionary of the English Language* (New York: Portland House, 1989).

Chapter Eighteen—Public Schools: Trends that Need Monitoring
1. Karen De Witt, "Eighth Graders' Math Survey Shows No State Is 'Cutting It,'" *New York Times,* 7 June 1991.
2. Karen De Witt, "Low Test Scores Renew Debate on TV," *New York Times,* 28 August 1991.
3. Karen De Witt, "Verbal Scores Hit New Low in Scholastic Aptitude Test," *New York Times,* 27 August 1991.
4. Jill Anderson, *Pumsy in Pursuit of Excellence* (Eugene, OR: Timberline Press, Inc., 1987).
5. John Leo, "The Trouble with Self-Esteem," *U.S. News and World Report,* 2 April 1990.
6. Interview on the television show *20/20,* 21 September 1990.

Chapter Nineteen—A Framework for Getting Help
1. Telephone interview with Detective Gladys Alarcon, 8 May 1990.

Chapter Twenty—Community Action Can Make a Difference
1. Parts of this outline have been adapted from the book *Healthy Sex Education in Your Schools,* by Anne Newman and Dinah Richard, Ph.D. (Colorado Springs, CO: Focus on the Family, 1990).

Chapter Twenty-One—The Spiritual Factor
1. "Black Churches Deter Drug Use, Study Says," *Detroit Free Press,* 25 February 1991 (released by KRTN Newswire).
2. Telephone interview with John Wallace, 23 September 1991.

A Final Note
1. A. M. Rosenthal, "The Louisiana Lesson," *New York Times,* 19 November 1991.
2. Survey by Mellman and Lazarus, Inc., commissioned by Mutual Life Insurance Company; reported by the Associated Press, 18 November 1991.
3. Allesandra Stanley, "For Each Leader There Was a Child and a Chance to Savor New York," *New York Times,* 1 October 1990.

OTHER MATERIALS
Also By Dan Korem

◆

The following materials for youths and adults are helpful when addressing deception, cults, and occultism.

PSYCHIC CONFESSION

Forty-eight-minute videotape presentation in which the psychic demonstrations of James Hydrick are exposed as trickery, and he gives history's first recorded confession of a leading psychic. This excellent program, critically acclaimed by the *Los Angeles Times*, is suitable for both adults and youths. ($25.50 postage paid)

KID TRICKS VIDEO SERIES

Four different thirty-minute videotapes for ages five to twelve that teach about deception and discernment. Dan Korem uses footage he has shot from real-life situations coupled with stories he tells and tricks he performs and teaches to clearly illustrate the theme of each video. The lessons taught are invaluable for any youngster, and a clear Christian perspective concludes each video. (Each videotape is $20.00 postage paid; $60.00 for the entire series.) Here is a snapshot of each:

When a Trick Is Not a Trick
Teaches why anyone can be fooled; the difference between good and bad tricks; when it's okay to trick someone, and when it isn't.

It's a Secret
Explains the difference between good secrets that we're supposed to keep and bad secrets that we're not supposed to keep. Emphasizes never to keep bad secrets because of embarrassment or fear. This is an excellent lesson for the prevention of abuse.

Check It Out!
Teaches the difference between illusion and reality; how to watch the news; how to check facts.

Tricks or Powers?
Teaches kids how they can be tricked by people claiming to have powers and warns about games that promote these false powers. Emphasizes the positive alternative of good games kids *can* play safely.

POWERS: TESTING THE PSYCHIC AND SUPERNATURAL

This 232-page book details: (1) How psychics can apparently read minds. This is the first comprehensive explanation available to the public and goes beyond the obvious, such as reading body language; (2) how psychics apparently help solve crimes; (3) the story of psychic James Hydrick as mentioned earlier in video; (4) Old and New Testament perspectives on sorcerers, magicians, seers, etc.; (5) Korem examines the resurrection of Jesus Christ as if examining a modern-day case and explains why he believes it actually occurred. ($10.00 postage paid)

TEENS AND SATANISM

A text on the issue of teenage involvement in satanism will be available early in 1993.

To obtain any of these materials, write:

> Korem Productions
> P. O. Box 1587
> Richardson, TX 75083

Author

---◆---

Dan Korem, the president of Korem Productions, is a critically acclaimed investigative journalist and speaker. The author of several books, he also independently produces investigative television specials and educational videos.

Prior to 1981, Dan earned his livelihood as a world-class magician. He invented numerous professional effects. Incorporating his sleight-of-hand skills, he speaks to university, corporate, and professional groups worldwide on such topics as deception, ethics, gangs, hate groups, profiling techniques, and youth issues.

A portion of the proceeds from this book will be donated to Kanakuk #5 (K-5), a Christian sports camp for inner-city and mentally handicapped youths. The camp is run by Kanakuk-Kanakomo Kamp in Branson, Missouri, which has four other campsites that attract 5,000 youths ages eight to eighteen from forty-four states and eleven foreign countries.

As noted in a December 15, 1990 *Los Angeles Times* article, fourteen-year-old Jamie White started the White Sands Clothing Company to raise money for K-5. In the first year (1989), she grossed over $200,000 in sales on her line of clothes for teenage girls. Sales the following year were even higher. Jamie donates all her profits to K-5, which will eventually accommodate 2,000 inner-city and handicapped youths. During the past two years, over 4,000 such youths have been sponsored by Kanakuk-Kanakomo Kamp—formerly owned and run by Jamie's grandfather, Spike White, and now by her father, Joe.

Jamie's entire family—parents Joe and Debbie Jo, sister Courtney, and brothers Brady and Cooper—are all enthusiastically involved.

If you would like to obtain more information about this wonderful project, please write:

> Kanakuk-Kanakomo Kamp
> Box K
> Branson, MO 65616